BUSINESS STUDIES

FOR A2 | REVISION GUIDE

Edited by
Ian Marcousé

Andrew Hammond
Ian Swift

PO120

Acknowledgements

The advice provided here comes from the experiences of the authors with their students at John Ruskin College, Cardinal Newman College, Darrick Wood School and Lambeth College. Many thanks to past and present students, especially all those who asked 'why?' or 'what do you mean?'

Our other source of expertise is from marking horrendous numbers of exam papers every January and June. Writing comes at the short-term cost of family life, so love – and apologies – to the Hammond, Swift and Marcousé families.

Andrew Hammond, Ian Swift and Ian Marcousé

Orders: please contact Bookpoint Ltd, 130 Milton Park, Abingdon, Oxon OX14 4SB. Telephone: (44) 01235 827720. Fax: (44) 01235 400454. Lines are open from 9.00–6.00, Monday to Saturday, with a 24-hour message answering service. You can also order through our website www.hoddereducation.co.uk.

If you have any comments to make about this, or any of our other titles, please send them to educationenquiries@hodder.co.uk

British Library Cataloguing in Publication Data
A catalogue record for this title is available from the British Library

ISBN-10: 0 340 81107 2
ISBN-13: 978 0 340 81107 8

First Published 2005

Impression number   10 9 8 7 6 5 4 3 2 1
Year   2010 2009 2008 2007 2006 2005

Hodder Headline's policy is to use papers that are natural, renewable and recyclable products and made from wood grown in sustainable forests. The logging and manufacturing processes are expected to conform to the environmental regulations of the country of origin.

Typeset by Phoenix Photosetting, Chatham, Kent.
Printed in Spain for Hodder Arnold, an imprint of Hodder Education, a member of the Hodder Headline Group, 338 Euston Road, London NW1 3BH.

CONTENTS

iii

Objectives and strategy

Exam skills and technique

Answers

Index

iv

INTRODUCTION

This revision book is written to help push every reader's A2 results up by at least one grade. It does this by focusing the subject content on the exam skills sought by examiners. The writing style is analytic, but applied to the context of real businesses, just as the examiners want. Every chapter points out key evaluative themes within the syllabus. As knowledge of the syllabus counts for only one-fifth of the marks at A2 level, revision must do more than re-hash facts and definitions. This Revision Guide teaches the reader to develop all the exam skills needed for success, but with a particular focus on application.

Each unit within the book covers a different section of the A2 specification. All the key concepts are explained, with the more difficult ones getting longer, fuller explanations. The content is full of references to real firms, and application is further enhanced by dedicated sections in the units. There are also questions to test yourself in every unit. The answers are set out at the back of the book, to provide immediate feedback on how your revision is going.

There are three other features to help build grades:

- At the end of each section (Marketing, Finance and so on) is a final unit containing many questions, including exam-style papers; again, answers are at the back to help you study for yourself.

- Towards the end of the book are four articles providing advice on exam technique; you should read these with care.

- Also at the back are revision checklists to prompt you to consider carefully whether you know everything you should.

The authors

Ian Marcousé has devised the format of the book and edited all the text and questions. Ian was the AS/A2 Chief Examiner for AQA Business Studies until 2004 and is a leading author. He is also the founding editor of *Business Review* magazine and teaches at Lambeth College, London.

Andrew Hammond is an experienced author, a regular contributor to *Business Review*, and a Senior Examiner for a major exam board. He is also Head of Business Studies at Darrick Wood School, Bromley.

Ian Swift is an experienced author and a Senior Examiner for A2 papers for a major exam board. He is Head of Business Studies at Cardinal Newman College, Preston.

KEY AS ISSUES IN MARKETING

The AQA specification for A2 Marketing states:

Candidates are expected to gain an understanding of marketing in an integrated context within the organisation and the wider environment, drawing from the whole of the AS subject content. The material set out below should build on key concepts from the Marketing section of AS Module 1 such as objectives, strategy and the need for data upon which to base decisions. Candidates should analyse and evaluate the potential of different marketing strategies, tactics and techniques for enabling businesses to identify and adapt to changing market opportunities and achieve their objectives.

The key issues raised at AS on which to build A2 marketing knowledge are outlined below.

Objectives, Strategy and Tactics

AS introduced the differing concepts of objectives, strategy and tactics. At A2 an understanding of the relationship between these marketing concepts is crucial. Whereas much of AS marketing was focused on tactical decisions such as price changes or promotional offers, the emphasis at A2 shifts to the bigger picture. The focus is on a broad-based strategic approach to marketing and an assessment of how marketing decisions are made.

Questions on marketing strategy form the basis of many A2 questions. These necessarily require an understanding of marketing objectives, and lead on to marketing plans. The decision-making process is carried out through the marketing model. This, too, hinges on marketing objectives. Therefore AS material on marketing objectives and strategy is exceptionally important.

The key to marketing objectives is that they are more ambitious than just 'increase sales'. They are usually based on a longer term ambition such as survival (the reason *The Independent* newspaper switched from a broadsheet to a tabloid format in 2004, thereby distinguishing itself from *The Telegraph* and *The Guardian*). Other ambitions include product differentiation (Versace or BMW) or to become Number 1 (L'Oreal or Tesco).

Research and market analysis

A significant grounding in gathering and analysing marketing data is included at AS. This helps to prepare for the section to be covered at A2 on scientific marketing decision making. Benefits can be gained from analysing the state of the markets in which a firm is operating or planning to operate, considering factors such as market growth, market size and market share. This allows a clear assessment of the attractiveness of that market, suggesting entry or not, or even departure from an increasingly unattractive existing market. Good A2 marketing answers will be based on awareness of how well a firm understands its market. This, in turn, will depend on the accuracy of market research – and how well the findings have been interpreted.

Product differentiation and price elasticity

It could be argued that all marketing activity centres on attempts to differentiate a product from those of its rivals. Certainly product differentiation is a key concept at both AS and A2 levels. The critical benefit of successful differentiation is the flexibility to raise prices without demand falling too much. In other words, a highly differentiated product tends to have a relatively low price elasticity. Inelastic demand means that a firm facing rising costs will be able to pass on those increases to customers through higher prices, thus protecting their profit margins. Alternatively, a firm that is generating insufficient profit would be able to increase price on a price inelastic product and generate higher profit margins as a result. Given the strategic importance of this topic, careful revision of AS notes is necessary.

When revising elasticity of demand, take care to revise income elasticity as well as price. Make sure to keep them quite separate. Elasticities do not have to be the same, as is shown by the table. Note how a sports car such as a Porsche 911 can be price inelastic, yet highly income elastic.

Estimated elasticities of demand for different products

	Estimated price elasticity	Estimated income elasticity
Porsche 911 sports car	−0.2	+3.0
Esso brand petrol	−5.0	+0.1
Tesco Value Orange Juice	−4.0	−0.2

Choosing a marketing strategy – niche versus mass

At AS the two broad choices regarding marketing strategy were niche or mass marketing. These concepts work well as an indicator of the A2 issue of marketing strategy. Strategy decisions relate to the big picture of marketing; it is the role of the marketing plan to detail the actual marketing actions to be taken. When bringing this AS topic into A2 answers, it is important to show understanding of wider issues such as the impact of a switch from niche to mass marketing on the operations and personnel departments.

Portfolio management and product life cycles

AS marketing introduced the concepts of the product life cycle and product portfolio management. The Boston Matrix is a strategic management tool and will therefore be useful when making strategic marketing decisions at A2 level. Firms such as Cadbury's use this type of analysis to decide not only which brands to concentrate on, but also broader decisions such as whether to move more aggressively into the market for mint sweets or chewing gum. Decisions such as these are fundamental to A2 work.

E Exam insight

It is unwise to structure an answer to any marketing question on the four Ps, tackled one by one in separate paragraphs. In order to demonstrate effective analysis and evaluation, the key is to understand the need to integrate the marketing mix for any product.

T Test yourself (60 marks)

1. Explain one benefit and one drawback of launching a product into a market that is growing rapidly. (4 marks)
2. State the formula for calculating market share. (2 marks)
3. State two methods of measuring market size. (2 marks)
4. Briefly explain why a firm may benefit from segmenting its market. (4 marks)
5. a) Distinguish between quantitative and qualitative market research. (3 marks)
   b) Which would be more appropriate when assessing:
      i) what price to charge for a new product;
      ii) why people prefer a rival product's packaging. (2 marks)
6. Outline three possible causes of unreliable quantitative research results. (6 marks)
7. Distinguish between strategy and tactics. (3 marks)
8. Identify two potential variables that may feature in marketing objectives. (2 marks)
9. Briefly explain two benefits of niche marketing. (4 marks)
10. Briefly explain two benefits of mass marketing. (4 marks)
11. Identify four possible routes to adding value. (4 marks)
12. Outline how product differentiation reduces a product's price elasticity. (3 marks)
13. State the formula for calculating price elasticity. (2 marks)
14. State the formula for calculating income elasticity. (2 marks)
15. Briefly explain what is happening to net cash flows during the different stages of the product life cycle. (3 marks)
16. Distinguish between pricing strategies, methods and tactics. (5 marks)
17. What is meant by the term distribution targets? (3 marks)
18. What are the two variables measured by the Boston Matrix? (2 marks)

ASSET-LED VERSUS MARKET-ORIENTATED MARKETING

These are two differing approaches to thinking about how a firm markets its products.

Market orientation

A market-orientated approach puts customer tastes at the heart of the marketing process. Market orientated firms will base their marketing decisions on what needs and gaps are identified in the market, and what competitors are doing within the market. These opportunities and threats will then be dealt with by developing an appropriate strategy to suit their external environment. It can be summed up in the cliché 'The Customer is King'.

Pros

- The identification of unfilled needs or gaps in the market should ensure that demand for the products offered actually exists.
- Heavy investment and focus on market analysis and research should enhance the firm's ability to forecast likely changes in the market, thus allowing them to gain a first mover advantage in spotting unfilled gaps before other rivals.

Cons

This approach is frequently criticised for failing to deliver genuine innovations. The giant leaps forward that create new markets usually come from product innovation rather than 'what the customer wants'. Market research often finds that people play safe rather than express any desire for change. To be really market oriented a firm needs to guess what people will want in the future, but that can be hard to see. Innovations such as the iPod and the 3G mobile phone were based upon more than just customer opinions – they were rooted in the technical strengths of firms such as Apple and Nokia.

Required strengths

If market research is key, the firm is likely to have its own in-house research specialists. A substantial budget for research should ensure that the research department can conduct the necessary ongoing research. Meanwhile the department must also be experienced in analysing the markets in which the firm operates, and be able to spot and deduce the implications of changes within the external environment.

Implications for marketing strategy

As suggested, new products are likely to be developments of existing products, or copies of competitors' products. Pricing is therefore likely to be competitive, with the firm unable to differentiate its products significantly. Promotional activity will centre on persuading customers to choose one product over similar alternatives on the market. Nevertheless there are many markets in which the ability to cater to customers' needs is all-important. Good examples include the local restaurant that provides quick service and low prices at lunch, but a more relaxed, enjoyable meal in the evening. Or a business such as Asda that keeps offering the low prices its customers want.

Asset-led marketing

Asset-led marketing puts the firm's existing strengths at the heart of its marketing strategy. That is not to say that the market is ignored, just that the firm's first question will be 'are we good at this?' before deciding whether to pursue an idea. Strengths come in many forms, including:

- strong brand image;
- excellent distribution network;
- reputation for quality;
- reputation for innovation linked to strong R&D;
- excellent customer service;
- detailed customer database.

Asset-led firms will still conduct thorough market analysis, but will only explore any opportunities identified if they can build on an existing strength.

Business application

Many thought that BMW was mad to purchase then develop the traditional British Mini. The car had never made money for its British owners, and BMW had never made a small car. BMW saw that its production and marketing strengths would enable it to produce a trendy, sporty small car to meet a worldwide market niche. This was asset-led marketing – and looks very successful so far, with sales exceeding BMW's expectations.

Pros

- Basing a strategy on existing strengths suggests that the firm will be working in areas where it has existing, proven expertise.
- Without a blinkered focus on what the market wants, asset-led firms may be more likely to come up with genuine innovations; by shifting focus internally, asset-led firms that can count R&D or 'out of the box' thinking as a strength may be willing to let technical staff dream up what may seem strange ideas in order to generate whole new markets.

Cons

A struggling firm may find it hard to pick out particular strengths on which it can base its marketing. At the time of writing, Sainsbury's was in that position. Meanwhile the real world can be a harsh place, where the firm's strengths do not match the major opportunities within the current marketplace. In such situations, asset-led firms may be forced into considering strategies that allow them to 'mark time' for a while, limiting growth opportunities, or they may be forced into abandoning their reliance on existing strengths.

Implications for strategy

Asset-led marketing strategies are likely to start with a full internal audit identifying the firm's key strengths. The list of strengths will then be viewed alongside market research information in order to check for any matches between opportunities within the research data and existing strengths. Once a match is found the firm will develop the right product or plan to hit that gap in the market through the use of an identifiable strength.

Application – the brand as asset

Two great examples of firms that use their brand image and its recognition as a tool for marketing new products and services are Virgin Group and Easy Group. Both firms have incredibly distinctive brands, which are powerful enough to bring the values associated with their existing products to any new markets that the firms decide to try entering.

E **Exam Insight**

In your initial reading of the case study it is sensible to try to identify which approach to marketing is used by the firm in the case. Do try to identify the firm's strengths, not only as a way of assessing the extent to which it uses an asset-led approach, but also to gain a clearer picture of the firm's overall position. This may help in answering other questions.

S **Student howler**

'A firm that pursues an asset-led approach to marketing bases its marketing strategy on its fixed assets.'

T **Test yourself (24 marks)**

1. Outline two reasons why a firm might benefit from pure market orientation, rather than taking into account its assets. (4 marks)
2. Analyse how an asset-led firm might benefit from using well-established distribution networks to launch a new range of products. (7 marks)
3. To what extent are market-orientated firms condemned to pursue a low-cost strategy based on copying competitors' successes? (8 marks)
4. Outline how asset-led marketing matches business competencies with market opportunities. (5 marks)

MARKETING DECISION MAKING

The marketing model

What is it?
The marketing model sets out how to make marketing decisions logically. It is decision making based on scientific methods rather than hunch.

Fig. 1.3A: Marketing model diagram

How does it work?

1. *Set objectives*: As with all functional areas, the role of marketing is to work towards the achievement of corporate objectives. Therefore, the company's overall objectives should be the starting point for any marketing decision making. Marketing objectives are then set that will enable the firm to achieve its corporate goals. For example, if the company sets a growth objective, the marketing department will need to set objectives relating to increasing sales volumes.

2. *Gather data*: Gathering data will be necessary before the company can make any effective decisions as to how best to achieve the stated marketing objectives. The data can come from internal sources, such as sales figures and distribution levels, or external, such as primary and secondary market research. These data should include information on market size, share and growth, on market segmentation and product differentiation.

3. *Form an hypothesis*: With all the data ready to hand, the marketing department can now identify the possible options that would enable the objectives to be met. If, for example, the objective is to increase sales by 10% within the next 12 months, the hypothesis may be that there are three viable options:

i) launch the two new products the firm has already developed for two different but growing market niches;

ii) increase by 25% the advertising support behind the company's rising star brand;

iii) cut the prices on the firm's problem-child brands in order to build a market share in sectors where the firm's sales are weak.

Decisions relating to the marketing mix will be made and alternative draft marketing plans can be constructed. This will enable managers to estimate the costs of each of the alternatives.

4. *Test the options*: Once the short-listed options are agreed, they should be tested as fully as possible given the constraints of time and money. The ideal would be full test marketing. Testing real products in real shops with real people is great; however, it not only takes time, but also ensures that competitors can see exactly what you are up to.

   Due to the disadvantages of test marketing, much testing of the plan will use primary research to gauge consumers' reactions to the proposals put forward. Once the results are gathered, the firm should be ready and confident in implementing their chosen marketing plan.

5. *Control and review*: The marketing plan will include budgeted figures – targets that the firm hopes to achieve, relating to variables such as sales, market share, distribution levels or share of advertising expenditure within the market. The control and review stage of the model allows decision makers to analyse variances between actual results and budgeted figures. If targets are missed, changes to the plan will be needed; if targets are exceeded, the firm will attempt to identify the key reasons for this success in order to maintain these successful actions.

The process should be an ongoing cycle, with the model being worked through regularly, to ensure that monitoring and adjustment is taking place frequently.

Scientific decision making

The model focuses decisions on the results of carefully controlled experiments. The results of the experiments are analysed in order to identify any possible improvements before action is taken. The role of data is paramount here. Without data available to measure success or failure, marketing decisions will be little more than guesswork. Market research, in many guises, will form the backbone of the scientific approach to making marketing decisions – providing the quantitative data necessary to measure the results of marketing experiments.

Benefits
- Market research will never eliminate the risk of making poor decisions, but it will reduce that risk. Firms that use the marketing model are less likely to suffer marketing disasters such as Coca-Cola's 2004 bottled water embarrassment.
- A methodical approach to marketing decisions should ensure that all the options available have been considered. Since the model requires the consideration of the strategic options available to the firm, the strategy selected to be tested is more likely to be a success.

However
- Rigid use of the marketing model and an over-reliance on research before decisions are made can slow down the marketing decision-making process. The consequences of this may be severe, since faster moving competitors may be able to use the extra time to gain a competitive edge.
- It is also important to remember that even the best-planned marketing strategies can go wrong. Sainsbury's 2001–2004 advertising strategy of using Jamie Oliver came across very well in market research, but the supermarket's market share kept slipping.

Hunches

Not all great marketing decisions are backed up by research. Some firms are willing to press ahead with a marketing strategy without conducting research, while others have ignored research results because they felt they were right anyway. The marketing process does require a spark of genius, and often marketing successes are the result of doing something that has never been tried before. Research has a tendency to give poor results for genuine innovations, since respondents find it hard to see how a totally new product will be of use to them. There is a place for hunch in marketing, yet an over-reliance on educated guesses may well lead to a string of disasters.

Application – The iPod hunch

The Apple iPod was originally the idea of Tony Fadell, who tried but failed to sell the idea to a number of consumer electronics firms. Eventually Apple hired Fadell to develop the idea of a combined MP3 player and 'Napster'-style system for downloading songs. Apple boss Steve Jobs became fully involved and influenced the project in many ways. He insisted that he should be able to download and play any tune within three button presses. He also insisted on a redesign of the appearance, to make it look more special. And the iPod has the potential to play music exceptionally loudly because Steve Jobs is partially deaf! None of these features of the iPod was researched. Neither

was the idea itself. It was kept so secret that very few people within Apple knew about the development before its launch in 2001. Nor was everyone on the project team convinced it would succeed. One senior figure in the iPod launch was Ben Knauss, who quit just before the launch because he thought it would flop.

Is marketing an art or a science?
Once in a while a truly creative spark may be pursued and lead to massive success, even though research suggested it would not work. This is the artistic side of marketing, where creative genius can lead to a stunning advertising campaign or a hugely innovative product idea. However, these sparks of genius come infrequently and the day-to-day process of making marketing decisions should rely on research, given its ability to reduce the risk of failure.

E Exam Insight

Your case study should give enough hints for you to be able to work out whether the key decision makers within the firm are risk takers – more likely to allow decisions to be made on the basis of hunch or guesswork. Alternatively, other firms will be characterised by a risk-averse culture, where no major decision is made until careful research has been conducted. Once you have assessed what type of business you are dealing with in the case, you should be able to apply the possible benefits of an alternative approach to any questions about future marketing decision making.

S Student howler

'The marketing model consists of the four Ps.'

T Test yourself (25 marks)

1. Why might you expect the marketing model to help produce better marketing decisions? (3 marks)
2. Why may small firms make little use of techniques such as the marketing model? (3 marks)
3. Analyse the benefits of using the marketing model to make marketing decisions in a high fashion retailer. (5 marks)
4. To what extent does a scientific approach to marketing decision making reduce the likelihood of technological breakthroughs? (9 marks)
5. Explain the likely dangers of basing all marketing decisions on hunch or guesswork. (5 marks)

NUMERICAL MARKET ANALYSIS

In analysing the market in which they are operating, or markets they may wish to enter, a range of numerate techniques are available to enable firms to draw greater insight from market data. The two techniques covered here are extrapolation and correlation.

Extrapolation

Extrapolation means forecasting future events by assuming that past trends will continue into the future. In fact analysing these past trends can offer significant insight into factors affecting sales. In order to use extrapolation to make future forecasts, it is necessary to identify long-term trends in past data.

Time series data
This term refers to any series of data that covers a run of consecutive time periods. Time series data may be presented in year-by-year, month-by-month or even week-by-week figures. Assuming that enough data are available, it is useful to establish the underlying trend in the data.

Identifying a long-term trend
Identifying the long-term trend in the data means ironing out fluctuations caused by short-term factors such as seasons or advertising campaigns. Identifying the underlying trend in time series data involves the calculation of moving totals and moving averages. It is these moving averages that represent the long-term trend data.

Calculating the long-term trend can allow a manager to analyse why actual sales may have been particularly good or bad during any time period. In periods where actual sales were well above the trend, investigation might enable a manager to judge the success of an advertising campaign or promotional offer. However, good or bad sales might well be due to more than one particular factor. Conclusions based on this type of analysis need to be treated carefully unless there is clear evidence that no other factors were in play.

Numerically extrapolating
Extrapolation means extending a trend into the future as a means of predicting future events. Extrapolation can be carried out once the long-term trend has been identified using moving averages.

Numerical extrapolation involves calculating the average change between consecutive time periods in the moving averages. Once the average change has been calculated, this can be added to the final moving average figure as many times as is necessary to reach the required forecasting period. In other words, if forecasting eight quarters in advance of the final trend figure, add eight times the average change to the final moving average.

Graphically extrapolating
This means extending the trend line on a graph. It is as straightforward as it sounds – the key equipment required being a ruler. Neither method of extrapolation is likely to give accurate results, but does indicate the likely direction of sales from the long-term trend.

Seasonal adjustments
For firms with sales that follow a predictable seasonal pattern, extrapolated trends can be adjusted to allow for these variations. By calculating the average amount by which actual sales have varied from moving averages in the past, an average seasonal adjustment factor can be calculated for each month or quarter. This can be applied to the forecast trend data to make an actual sales forecast.

Correlation

The term correlation refers to the relationship between two variables. A scattergraph is a diagram to show the correlation (Fig 1.4A). Plotting the two variables on the graph will produce a collection of different points.

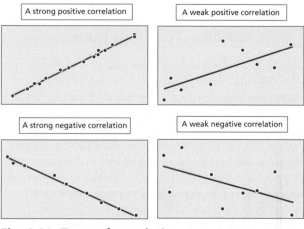

Fig. 1.4A: Types of correlation

Once points have been plotted, a 'best fit line' is drawn. If all the points on the graph are close to the line the correlation is strong. A weaker correlation is shown when the points lie further away from the line. The direction of the best fit line will indicate whether the correlation is positive or negative. A positive correlation shows that as one variable increases the other moves in the same direction, for example temperature and sales of soft drinks (the hotter it is, the more we buy). A negative correlation occurs when one variable increases as the other decreases. The best example of this is price and sales. As prices are pushed up, sales go down.

Correlation and causality

The skill in using correlation lies with the assessment of causality. Cause and effect need to be judged by the analyst. Sometimes it is clear – hotter weather increases sales of ice creams. At other times the cause and the effect may not be as clear cut – do higher distribution levels lead to higher sales or do higher sales encourage more retailers to stock the product? Indeed, although a correlation may appear to exist, sometimes there is no causal relationship between the variables. Just because perfume producers advertise in December does not mean that their jumps in sales in December are *caused* by the advertising. The real cause of the extra sales and the extra advertising is Christmas.

The fundamental evaluative theme for any sales forecasting technique must be to question the validity of the method used. Standard phrases such as 'any forecast may be inaccurate' demonstrate weak judgement. More sophisticated evaluations will offer a careful consideration of just how reliable these specific forecasts seem to be, probably accepting the possibility of inaccuracy but recognising the need to forecast in order to plan effectively for the future.

Good judgement in assessing correlation will depend on an ability to be realistic about the likelihood of a cause and effect relationship existing. Don't jump to conclusions just because a graph shows a nice clear best fit line. Think carefully about what is cause and what is effect.

E Exam Insight

If you are given data in your case study it will almost certainly be useful and relevant. It is up to you to interpret what the data are saying in the case. This could involve asking whether two variables show a correlation and, if so, whether it is strong or weak and therefore reliable or perhaps less so. Extrapolation should be treated with care – always be careful to consider the reliability of the trend data and how far into the future the extrapolation is done. The further into the future a forecast goes, the less reliable it becomes because there are more chances for variables to change.

S Student howler

'There is a clear correlation between advertising expenditure and sales. This means that extra sales lead to more advertising.'

T Test yourself (25 marks)

1. What is meant by the term 'extrapolation'? (2 marks)
2. Explain the meaning of the phrase 'strong positive correlation'. (3 marks)
3. Study the graph in Figure 1.4B. Decide whether it shows a correlation between temperature and sales. State what type of correlation it shows. Suggest what the product might be. (7 marks)
4. Using the data in the table below, plot a graph showing sales and the long-term trend in sales. Identify three years where sales varied most significantly from the trend. (6 marks)

Year	Sales (m units)	5 Year moving total	5 Year moving average
1989	2		
1990	2.2		
1991	2.1		2.2
1992	2.5		2.26
1993	2.2	11	2.28
1994	2.3	11.3	2.44
1995	2.3	11.4	2.38
1996	2.9	12.2	2.4
1997	2.2	11.9	2.42
1998	2.3	12	2.34
1999	2.4	12.1	2.24
2000	1.9	11.7	2.3
2001	2.4	11.2	2.36
2002	2.5	11.5	2.4
2003	2.6	11.8	2.56
2004	2.6	12	
2005	2.7	12.8	

5. Analyse the possible problems with basing decisions on extrapolated data. (7 marks)

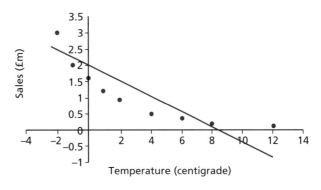

Fig. 1.4B: Scattergraph of weekly sales and average weekly temperature

SALES FORECASTING

Why do firms need to do it?

All business decisions relate to the future. Even if you are correcting past mistakes, you are doing so to affect the firm's future performance. Therefore the ability to forecast sales is crucial. Ideally, a firm wants to be able to forecast:

- What sales will be if things carry on as they are;
- What sales will be if changes are made;
- What the sales will be of a new product.

As a result, the firm can ensure stock and production levels are set correctly, that pricing decisions can be made more effectively and that the HR department can devise an effective strategy based on workforce planning.

How to do it for existing products

Sales forecasts for existing products are likely to be based on the use of backdata (previous sales figures). By the use of moving averages (see Unit 1.4), a long-term trend in past sales can be identified. This trend can then be extended into the future. This process is called extrapolation. Once the long term trend has been extrapolated, an actual sales figure can be forecast for a particular month or week, by applying a seasonal adjustment factor. This is a measure of how far above or below the long-term trend sales tend to be in that particular period.

Application

How to get it McWrong

To celebrate 25 years in the UK, McDonalds decided to run a 'buy one, get one free' offer on Big Macs in the late 1990s. On the first day of the offer, restaurants were provided with double the number of Big Macs they usually sold, to allow for the effect of the offer on the number of burgers sold. Someone had failed to make an effective forecast, however, as they failed to allow for any increase in the number of customers.

Use of sales forecast	Explanation	Possible problems caused by inaccurate forecast
Planning production levels	Production planning needs data on expected sales for accurate ordering of materials and components. They will also be checked to ensure that production capacity can cope with the expected level of demand	Underestimating sales in the forecast may result in the firm being unable to satisfy demand. This may lead customers to switch to other suppliers. Overestimating sales may lead to stockpiling of materials or finished goods. This ties up space and working capital. Stock may perish or become obsolete
Financial forecasting	In order to set budgets, forecast cash flows and appraise and raise funds for investments, financial forecasts need to be made. These will all be based on sales forecasts	Unrealistic budget targets may demotivate staff or lead to excessive spending. Inaccurate cash flow forecasts may lead to liquidity problems. Inaccurate forecasts within investment appraisals may cause poor decision making, costing the firm substantially in terms of the opportunity cost of the investment selected
HR planning	Workforce planning involves ensuring that the right numbers of staff with the right skills are available when needed. Sales forecasts are likely to determine how many staff are needed in each functional area	If forecasts are too low, understaffing may lead to quality or customer service levels being poor. This happened to British Airways in August 2004, when flights were cancelled due to lack of staff

Many restaurants had run out of Big Macs by 11 a.m. of the first day.

How to do it for new products

With no previous sales figures on which to base forecasts, predicting sales for new products is a much harder job. The most common basis for forecasting sales of new products is quantitative, primary market research. This is because the results of the research will need to be statistically significant to provide the basis for a statistical estimate of future sales. Yet there are often surprises, even for firms with experience of previous product launches. In 2003, Mars was taken by surprise by the huge sales success of White Maltesers. It had to withdraw the product from the market while building the production capacity to relaunch the brand in 2004. Yet as many as six in seven new products flop in the marketplace, implying that firms are often forecasting higher sales than proves true in reality.

Test marketing

For products that are ready to go into production, test marketing may be used to make a sales forecast. Test marketing involves launching and marketing a product in a small geographical area in order to gauge customer reaction. The sales achieved can be used as a basis for forecasting sales once the product undergoes a full-scale launch. This method, though expensive, can provide very reliable forecasts.

Factors influencing sales forecasts

Forecasting is difficult because sales can be affected by a wide range of different factors. Internal factors are probably easiest to build into a forecast. The effects of running a particular promotion may be easy to factor into a forecast, especially if the promotion has run before. The effects of changes in price can be forecast using knowledge of a firm's price elasticity.

Effects of external factors are harder to predict. Some can be foreseen, such as the effect of different seasons on sales of seasonal products such as lawnmowers. Economic forecasts can be used, in conjunction with knowledge of income elasticity, to allow sales forecasts to reflect changes in the phase of the trade cycle.

Other external factors may be totally unforeseen, or their effects may be impossible to accurately forecast.

E | Exam Insight

If asked to make a sales forecast it is vital that you do actually give one. Marks will be available for quoting the figure that you believe the firm will achieve in the period asked for. The bulk of the marks for questions like these will, however, come from showing a logical method of arriving at the forecast. Even if your method is logical guesswork, you must ensure that you provide enough justification for the examiner to understand the rationale behind your forecast.

It's just a forecast

If asked to judge the accuracy of a forecast, do remember that a forecast will rarely claim to be entirely accurate. Frequently a forecast will be accepted as being accurate even if it is out by, say, 5%. Don't be too quick to condemn the skills of a forecaster if they are wrong by an insignificant amount.

But businesses need them

For the reasons shown at the start of this unit, businesses need to attempt to forecast sales. Indeed, forecasting techniques can be very sophisticated and give reliable forecast data. Do not assume that all forecasts are wholly unreliable.

T | Test yourself (30 marks)

1. Explain how test marketing differs from market research. (3 marks)
2. State two ways in which Top Shop might benefit from forecasting sales turnover for the coming Christmas. (2 marks)
3. Assess the effect on sales forecasts of operating in a fashion market. (8 marks)
4. Analyse the importance of sales forecasting to a company's marketing planning. (7 marks)
5. Using the data in the table below and possibly some graph paper, extrapolate the data to forecast the trend level of sales for Quarter 3 next year. (10 marks)

Year	Quarter	Sales (000 units)	Quarterly moving average trend
3 years ago	4	120	
2 years ago	1	100	
	2	100	108.75
	3	110	111.25
	4	130	112.5
Last year	1	110	112.5
	2	100	113.75
	3	110	116.25
	4	140	120
This year	1	120	125
	2	120	
	3	130	
	4		
Next year	1		
	2		
	3		

MARKETING PLANS AND BUDGETS

A marketing plan is a detailed explanation of the rationale behind the marketing strategy, plus the costs and activities involved in implementing the strategy.

Contents of a marketing plan

Section	Contains
Introduction	A brief summary of the plan and the logic behind it
Objectives	Both corporate and specific marketing objectives
Strategy	An overview of the strategic approach that the firm will take
Action plans	Clear lists of all the marketing activities that will take place in order to implement the strategy. This will include details of all promotional activity, pricing methods and distribution methods
Budgets	Detailed expenditure budgets will be included, covering each aspect of marketing activities
Control mechanisms	The ways in which budgets will be monitored will be explained

Though creating a marketing strategy may require vision and imagination, the detailed work within the marketing department consists of deciding how to put the strategy into action. Individual action plans are needed for each aspect of marketing activity. They will include deciding precisely what market research will be done and how, planning which media will be used and with what frequency, and which distribution channels will be used.

The overall marketing budget will be split up between the different functions, and systems for monitoring the effectiveness of each section will be put in place. Without an effective monitoring system, there is a danger that the marketing expenditure may be wasted, with money being poured in and no clear picture of its value. A marketing cliché (attributed to Lord Leverhulme) is that 'I know half my advertising spending is wasted, but I don't know which half'. The budgets – and the systems for monitoring the budgets – should ensure that the firm is able to gain a clearer picture of the effects of its marketing activities.

Marketing budgets

Remember that budgets are both limits on spending *and* targets for sales. A marketing budget will therefore include sales targets, drawn from the marketing objectives. For example, if the marketing objective is to raise market share, sales targets will be set, probably month by month, that over the course of a year will enable the objective to be achieved. With the sales targets in place, the way in which marketing spending will be used can be decided.

How are marketing budgets set?

The main methods used by firms to decide on their level of marketing expenditure are briefly explained below:

- *Incremental budgeting*: This involves taking last year's figure and adding a little. Though common, this method is not particularly effective – it does not cope easily with changes required by shifts in the market place.
- *Task-based costing*: The budget is set by deciding exactly what needs to be done to achieve objectives, and then calculating the cost of those activities.
- *Percentage of sales*: Setting marketing expenditure as a percentage of sales will allow firms to benefit from increased marketing budgets at times of growth.
- *Competitor parity spending*: Ensuring that the firm spends as much money on marketing as its rivals should mean that its 'promotional voice' is not drowned out by louder voices in the market.

How is the marketing budget used?

The whole range of activity within the marketing function will be funded from the overall marketing budget. The budget will need to cover the costs of both above and below the line promotional activity. In addition, market research expenditure will be a part of the whole marketing budget. A number of factors will influence how much is allocated to each element of the mix:

- *Product life cycle stage*: Products in the early stages of their life will see a greater amount of promotional spending. This will leave less money available to support more mature products.

- *Position on Boston Matrix*: Cash cows will be milked to allow funds to be diverted towards supporting stars and trying to increase the market share of problem children.
- *Market orientated or asset led*: A market-orientated firm, basing its strategy on the needs and wants of the market, is likely to divert substantial sums to market research. Ongoing detailed research will form the cornerstone of the marketing strategy and therefore needs to be funded.
- *Scientific marketing decision makers*: Will want to spend substantially on research and test marketing in order to provide them with the feedback required by the use of the marketing model.

Application – EasyGroup – where branding is cheap

Part of the EasyGroup philosophy is to slash costs to the bone in order to offer customers the lowest possible price. This philosophy extends to their marketing budgets, which are very low for a business of its size. However, the budget available is used exceptionally well in building brand awareness. Much of this is the result of using cheaper methods of promotion, perhaps most notably PR appearances and stunts by owner Stelios, combined with a brand designed to stand out from the crowd.

Themes for evaluation

Marketing plans – paralysis by analysis
If the marketing plan is too detailed, or takes too long to develop, there is a danger that the firm will miss opportunities in the market. Speed of reaction to market changes can be critical in gaining a competitive edge – if no action can be taken until a detailed plan is developed, the firm may become a ponderous, slow-moving imitator of more agile market leaders. Hence the phrase 'paralysis by analysis'.

Marketing budgets – does size matter?
The initial response to this question must be that it is not the size that matters – it's how you use what you have. Small budget marketing can be effective if targeted correctly. Firms such as Next, Innocent Drinks, Fat Face and Phat Farm have succeeded with very low marketing expenditure.

E | Exam Insight

You may be asked to suggest a marketing budget for next year in a case study question. If this is the case, score analysis marks by using one of the four methods described above. If comparative data for other firms are given you will be able to justify your budget by using *competitor parity spending*. If the case material includes information on previous years' budgets, you could use *incremental budgeting* to justify the figure you suggest.

S | Student howlers

'The marketing budget shows how much the firm is going to spend on advertising its product this year.'
'The marketing budget is a statement of all the money the firm will spend on marketing this year.'

T | Test yourself (24 marks)

1. Would you expect marketing spending to be high, low or zero on a firm's:
   a) problem children;
   b) rising stars;
   c) cash cows;
   d) dogs.   (4 marks)
2. Explain why it is likely that Pepsi uses competitor parity spending as its method for setting its marketing budget.   (4 marks)
3. Analyse the pros and cons of using a task-based costing approach to setting marketing budgets. (6 marks)
4. The need for careful marketing planning is less when operating in a rapidly growing market because sales growth is easier to come by. Comment upon this statement.   (8 marks)
5. Analyse the possible effect on next year's marketing budget of an unsuccessful advertising campaign this year.   (8 marks)

INTEGRATED MARKETING

Innovative marketing

The ability to produce an innovative product can be a huge advantage for any company. An innovative marketing strategy can also bring huge rewards. If marketing strategists can think creatively, they can revolutionise the way in which a product is perceived by customers, thus almost creating a new market. For example Vodafone's 2003 'Beckham phone' introduced picture messaging to the UK mass market. This was especially clever as it prevented phone users from appreciating that the phones supplied by '3' were actually far superior technically. Marketing departments that are able to look beyond what everyone else in the market is doing can gain a type of 'first mover advantage' without necessarily developing a new product.

Firms that fail to understand their market may suffer from 'marketing myopia'. First coined by Theodore Levitt, this is when firms fail to understand the bigger market in which they are operating and therefore miss both threats and opportunities. Levitt blamed the decline of American railway companies in the 1960s on their failure to recognise that they were in the transportation market, rather than the railroad market. They therefore ignored the threat posed by cheap internal air travel.

Integrating marketing with other business functions

Marketing is just one of several functional areas within a business. Therefore any marketing activity must tie in with the way the business manages its operations and human resources, and controls and plans its finances. Some of the links are shown in the table below:

Functional area	Links with marketing
Operations management	The quality of production will be a crucial element in setting the marketing strategy Output levels will need to be linked to sales forecasts produced by the marketing department New product development will be carried out by the R&D section
Human resources	Workforce planning will be based on sales forecasts from the marketing department Will marketing sit as a separate function in the organisation's structure or will each division have its own marketing team if the structure is product based?
Finance	Pricing decisions will need to involve financial staff who are aware of the costs of the product Break-even analysis may be useful in setting prices Budget setting throughout the firm will be based on sales forecasts

When hunches go wrong

Jerry Roberts was the golden boy. Fresh from university, he had joined South West Foods Ltd as a trainee in the marketing department. His rise to New Product Manager had been nothing short of meteoric and it seemed he could do little wrong. Jerry had a knack for knowing just what customers wanted, building a reputation as something of a maverick. He had now successfully overseen the launch of two hugely successful new products, EZee Cheese Snacks and Friendly Freddie's Fish Sticks. Both of these launches had been pushed through by Jerry despite poor results in primary research tests.

He had now been working on Vitalize isotonic yoghurt for 6 months and felt he had the right strategy mapped out to turn this into the product that revolutionised the chilled desserts market. Having conducted very little research on this product in the light of his previous launches, Jerry was, as usual, relying on his instincts. He argued that the new segment in the soft drinks market created by Lucozade Isotonic could be replicated in snack markets. Now the time had come to see if his instincts were right.

Despite reservations from some directors, Jerry had been given the go-ahead to launch, and a £3 million launch budget to enable him to do so. Jerry planned to position the product as a health-enhancing food, priced high to reinforce its quality. It would be distributed through chemists and health food shops to further enhance the brand's healthy credentials. Promotional activity would centre on below the line methods designed to explain clearly the scientific benefits of the product. Much of this activity would take place in retailers, with the provision of extravagant point of sale materials.

Jerry's assistant Zoe was in charge of constructing a sales forecast for the new product. Her forecast of £30 million sales in the first year formed the basis of the decision to pass the requested £3 million launch budget.

Comparative figures from previous chilled dessert launches within the last year

Product	Launch budget (£ms)	First Year sales (£ms)
New flavour Miller Fruit corners	2	40
Mini Miller Rice Pots	3	28
Skate Lo Fat	1.7	12
Fruity Fromage Frais	0.8	10
Yog	2.5	25

Three months after the launch, Jerry's reputation lay in tatters. Sales had failed to reach anything like the levels forecast by Zoe, while the trade press had been scathing in its criticism of the 'ill thought-through launch plan'. Jerry was called before the Board where Chief Executive Arthur MacDonald grilled him over the details of the research used to back up the decisions he had made in constructing his marketing plan. Jerry left the meeting with a moderately attractive redundancy package. Arthur was left with the unenviable task of justifying to the major shareholders how £3m had been wasted on an unsuccessful launch that had damaged the good name of South West Foods within the retail trade.

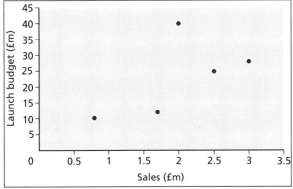

Fig. 1.7A: Graph showing possible correlation between marketing budget and first year sales

KEY AS ISSUES IN FINANCE

The AQA's specification introduces the A2 finance and accounting section with the following quote:

Candidates are expected to gain an understanding of Accounting and Finance in an integrated context within the organisation and the wider environment. The material set out below should be used to revisit concepts covered in the Accounting and Finance section of AS Module 1 such as contribution, profit and cash flow.

Candidates are required to use a range of performance measures critically and to evaluate the appropriateness of different financial techniques in shaping decision making in the context of the wider strategic objectives of business.

Candidates should acquire the ability to see how financial concepts such as cash flow, gearing, liquidity and profit are affected by factors outside the control of individual firms, such as the economy and the degree of competition and how firms' strategies should reflect this.

In essence this takes the focus of financial decision making into more of a real world context, expecting you to be able to make informed financial decisions that take into account the external environment faced by businesses.

Contribution, profit and cash flow

Your AS studies introduced you to the idea that profit is revenue minus costs. This fundamental principle still holds true at A2 level but you will learn of different types of profit, notably when you study profit and loss accounts. You should also have learned that firms classify costs in different ways – not just as variable or fixed, but also as direct and indirect. It is this classification that is used in construction of profit and loss accounts (see Unit 2.5).

Last year should have introduced you to the concept of contribution, initially as a means to calculate a firm's break-even output. This year you will be using contribution in order to help make decisions on whether or not to accept special orders at prices lower than normal. The key to contribution is to remember that it excludes fixed costs. It only measures the surplus of price over the variable cost per unit (or

revenue compared with total variable costs). This strengthens the analysis, because it excludes the costs that are unaffected by changes in output. Many business decisions are taken on the basis of contribution, most obviously the pricing policies of low-cost airlines such as easyJet and Ryanair.

Break-even charts reappear in A2, but in a more complex form. You will be expected to be able to shift lines on the graphs to indicate changes faced by the company in question. Or interpret graphs that show a more complex situation than revenue and costs for a single product. For example, when choosing between two short-listed business locations, it would be helpful to make a comparison on the same graph, with the same axes.

At AS level you studied the difference between profit and cash flow, and how to construct a cash flow forecast. Recalling this work will help you to tackle the A2 material relating to investment appraisal. As at AS, distinguishing clearly between profit and cash flow is vital.

Example of cash flow versus profit

A specialist kitchen supplier receives a £345,000 order from Gordon Ramsey restaurants. A brand new kitchen must be built and equipped within 8 weeks. The contract specifies a 10 week credit period for the customer. The kitchen supplier has worked out that the total costs for the job will be £300,000, giving a £45,000 profit.

That's fine. £45,000 profit for an 8 week job sounds pretty good! But look carefully at the graph. For the first 8 weeks the kitchen supplier is paying out £300,000 on materials, machinery and labour. After completing the work the firm waits 10 weeks to be paid. Then the cheque for £345,000 arrives, transforming the cash flow position from –£300,000 to +£45,000. The profit and the cash flow both end up as +£45,000. But unless the firm had carried out a cash flow forecast it would not have known the severe effect of the order on its cash flow forecast. If the kitchen firm's bank had not been willing to allow a £300,000 overdraft, the order could never have been completed.

So remember:

1. Cash flow and profit are different.

2. Both must be calculated and considered with care before going ahead with a project.

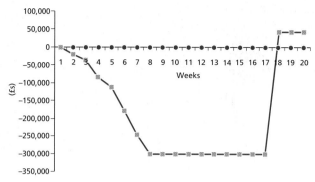

Fig. 2.1A: Cash flows on a £345,000 contract

Sources of finance

Once you begin to look at balance sheets, you will be able to see sources of finance in action. With the balance sheet listing the sources that have been used by a business to gain finance, your understanding of the advantages and disadvantages of different sources should assist you in the interpretation of balance sheets. It is quite possible that you will be presented with a balance sheet and asked to assess the most appropriate source of finance for that firm to use when financing an investment project.

It is important at A2 to be able to distinguish clearly between internal and external sources of finance, and between short- and long-term sources.

Budgeting and cost and profit centres

There is no equivalent development at A2 of the work done at AS on budgeting and cost and profit centres. However, it would be sensible to brush up on this material as you consider the people management aspects of the A2 course since budgets and cost and profit centres are key organisational tools.

T Test yourself (60 marks)

Test yourself on these questions to see whether you know enough AS Finance to provide a sound basis for the A2. Check your answers carefully against the answers at the back of the book. If you suspect that there are quite a few things you have forgotten, refer to the *Business Studies for AS Revision Guide*, edited by Ian Marcousé (Hodder & Stoughton 2003).

1. Define fixed costs. (2 marks)
2. Distinguish between direct and indirect costs. (3 marks)
3. What formula is used to calculate a firm's break-even output? (2 marks)
4. What are the three key lines shown on a break-even chart? (3 marks)
5. Define margin of safety and describe what it would look like on a break-even chart. (4 marks)
6. State two reasons why a firm benefits from forecasting cash flows. (2 marks)
7. How is a firm's net cash flow calculated each month? (2 marks)
8. Explain what is meant by the term overtrading. (3 marks)
9. Outline one advantage and one disadvantage of using an overdraft as a source of finance. (4 marks)
10. What is meant by the term venture capitalist? (2 marks)
11. Explain why profit and cash flow are different. (6 marks)
12. Briefly explain two methods of setting budgets. (4 marks)
13. Explain why delegating budgetary control may help to motivate middle managers. (4 marks)
14. a) Calculate Company X's profit if it makes and sells 2000 units at a selling price of £15 per unit. Variable costs are £7 per unit and fixed costs per month are £10,000. (4 marks)
    b) Calculate Company X's break-even point. (2 marks)
    c) What is Company X's margin of safety? (2 marks)
15. Fill in the gaps on the following cash flow forecast: (11 marks)

	January	February	March	April
Cash in	45	40		40
Cash out	40		36	42
Net cash flow		(3)	8	
Opening balance	15			
Closing balance				

A2 BREAK-EVEN

At AS level, you learned how to construct a simple break-even graph, showing fixed costs, total costs and total revenue lines. This allows a firm's break-even point to be identified, along with the identification of profit or loss at any level of output and the firm's current safety margin. You also learned of the strengths and weaknesses of break-even analysis, as summarised below:

- 'What if' questions can be asked;
- The technique provides a graphical focus of attention for meetings.

But break-even is based on assumptions – two key assumptions being:

- The firm sells every unit it makes;
- Linearity – all the lines on the chart are assumed to be straight.

The major extra skill required with A2 level break-even analysis focuses on the first key advantage. By shifting lines on the graph firms can identify what would happen to profit, break-even and safety margins if their costs or selling prices are changed. The three possible changes are shown and explained below.

Changes to selling price

Increasing or decreasing the selling price of a product will alter a firm's break-even chart. The change will be seen as a change in the gradient of the total revenue line. If the price is increased, the revenue line will rise more steeply, allowing the firm to break-even at a lower level of output (Fig. 2.2A). If the price is cut, break-even will occur later as the total revenue line will swivel downwards (Fig. 2.2B).

Changing fixed costs

Fixed costs are, of course, only fixed in relation to output. This means that fixed costs may well be different next month, or year, if salaries increase or if rent is put up. Therefore, break-even needs to be able to show the effect of a change in fixed costs by moving the fixed cost line. This, in turn, changes the level of the total costs line. An increase in fixed costs will shift the total cost line up, in parallel to the old total cost line. This would increase the firm's break-even point (Fig. 2.2C). The opposite is true if fixed costs are reduced.

It is also possible to represent a situation in which a fixed cost line shows a step at a certain level of output. This may occur if a firm needs to hire extra machinery or equipment to produce more than its former maximum capacity level. The graph can become confusing, since it is now feasible to see two break-even points if the step is large enough. The graph shown in

Figure 2.2D shows a simple scenario where the step does not put the firm back into a loss-making situation.

Changing variable costs

A change in variable cost per unit, perhaps due to a

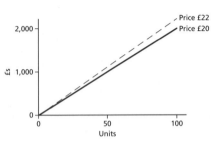

Fig. 2.2A: Price up from £20 to £22

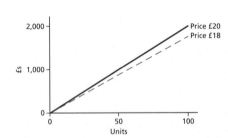

Fig. 2.2B: Price down from £20 to £18

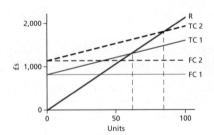

Fig. 2.2C: Increasing fixed costs

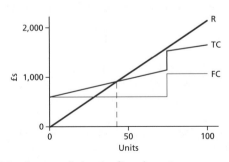

Fig. 2.2D: Stepped rise in fixed costs

supplier raising their prices, would have the effect of making the total cost line rise more steeply.

Application – Ryanair's bid to lower break-even

Ryanair's massive success in the low-cost airline market has been achieved by pursuing a strategy of constantly lowering their break-even point. The capacity utilisation on flights (known as the load factor) is the key measure of break-even. Ryanair's focus has been on reducing both fixed and variable costs in order to lower the proportion of seats needing to be sold to break-even. Not only does Ryanair use break-even analysis on a flight-by-flight basis, but they are also basing a whole business model around continuous efforts to alter the position of their total cost line.

Themes for evaluation

Does the use of complex break-even eradicate the weaknesses of break-even analysis?

No, but changing lines on the graph does show a key strength – the ability to ask 'what if' questions. Once more it is important to remain aware of the limitations of break-even analysis but balance your possible scepticism with a real appreciation of what can be shown using such a clear visual representation. The technique retains its strengths and, as with all decision-making techniques, the right amount of critical interpretation of its accuracy and reliability is needed before assessing the information it gives.

E Exam Insight

When focusing on the maths of break-even, there is a danger that you ignore the reasons *why* variables on a break-even graph have changed. Think through the implications of any change shown, or marked by you, on a break-even chart. Consider the likely effects of the change not just on the firm's break-even point, but on other issues such as the level of sales, the quality of the product being produced, and on the motivation of staff.

T Test yourself (28 marks)

1. For each of the following changes, state the effect on a firm's break-even point:
   a) Increased piece rate payments to production staff;
   b) An increase in selling price;
   c) A reduction in the number of units sold;
   d) Negotiation of cheaper rental for factory. (4 marks)
2. Discuss the usefulness of break-even analysis for a rapidly growing fashion clothing manufacturer. (8 marks)
3. Smithson Ltd manufactures tins of shoe polish. It faces the following situation at present:
   Selling price: £1
   Current sales: 80,000 units per month
   Variable cost per unit: 50p
   Fixed costs: £36,000 per month
   Maximum capacity: 100,000 units per month
   NB: after making any changes, go back to these original figures before going on to next question.
   a) Calculate Smithson's current break-even point and safety margin. (2 marks)
   b) Calculate the new break-even point if fixed costs increase to £40,000 per month. (2 marks)
   c) Calculate the new break-even point and safety margin if variable cost per unit is cut to 40p. (4 marks)
   d) Calculate the new break-even point if Smithson's increase its selling price to £1.20. (2 marks)
   e) Using your answer to part d) and the information that Smithson's shoe polish has a price elasticity of –0.5, calculate the new sales level and safety margin at a selling price of £1.20. (6 marks)

S Student howler

'If the firm increases sales, its break-even point will fall.'

Summary

	Direction of change	Effect on break-even point	Effect on safety margin	But note that...
Price	Increase	Falls	Depends on new sales level	Changes to selling price will affect the amount sold. The rate of change depends on the product's price elasticity
Price	Decrease	Rises	Depends on new sales level	
Fixed costs	Increase	Rises	Decreases	It is important to keep a close check on fixed costs to avoid excessive damage to operating margins
Fixed costs	Decrease	Falls	Increases	Cutting fixed costs has implications – does a cheaper location mean fewer customers or does a delayered hierarchy mean communication problems?
Variable cost per unit	Increase	Rises	Decreases	We may be able to pass on the increased costs to customers via a price rise
Variable cost per unit	Decrease	Falls	Increases	Cutting VC p.u. may lead to lower quality output – possibly damaging reputation and sales

CONTRIBUTION AND SPECIAL ORDER DECISIONS

Contribution refers to the amount contributed to covering fixed costs and profit once variable costs are deducted from a product's selling price. Both contribution per unit (selling price – variable cost per unit) and total contribution (total revenue – total variable costs) are used widely in business decision making.

The major use of contribution at A2 level is to help make what are referred to as special order decisions. These generally relate to an offer to buy a firm's products at a lower selling price than usual.

Frequently, special order questions will include mention of a firm's average cost per unit. This figure is calculated by taking variable cost per unit and adding fixed cost per unit. Therefore, this figure will change if the firm sells more products, since the fixed cost element will shrink. This is because total fixed costs will not increase as output rises and therefore those fixed costs will be spread more thinly over more units. It is therefore quite possible that a special order will be arranged at a selling price that is lower than the firm's existing average cost per unit.

E Exam insight

When answering special order exam questions, the key is to use *variable* cost data, not *average* cost. Usually, the best advice is to ignore average cost information, as it is only there to distract you from the key to success – contribution per unit and therefore the contribution generated by the special order.

Special orders – what to look out for

The fundamental financial principle behind special order decisions is to assess whether the order will generate a positive contribution. If the firm is already past its break-even point, fixed costs have already been covered. The result is that if the special purchase price is higher than the variable cost of each unit, the order will generate extra contribution and extra profit.

Another issue to check is that the firm has the spare capacity to satisfy the order. Should this not be the case the order is unlikely to be accepted.

The following fully explained example should be worked through carefully.

Example

Ferguson's Ltd has a maximum capacity of 2000 units per month. Current sales are 1000 units at a selling price of £10 each. Variable costs are £5 per unit, while the firm's fixed costs are £4000 per month.

The firm's current profit is $1000 \times £5$ (contribution p.u.) = £5,000 (total contribution) – £4,000 (FC) = £1000.

Ferguson's has received an order for 800 units. The customer is offering to pay £7 per unit. Ferguson's boss is not keen to accept, since Ferguson's average costs are running at £9 per unit.

Here we see the 'red herring' of average cost. We can calculate the effect of accepting the order on the firm's profit:

- Extra order brings a contribution per unit of £7 – £5 = £2. This is multiplied by the 800 units to be sold to gain a total contribution of $£2 \times 800 = £1,600$.
- Because fixed costs were already covered by the firm's 'normal' output, all of this extra contribution is pure profit. Therefore, when judging whether to accept the order, we can compare the profit without the order, of £1,000 per month, to the extra profit of £1,600 generated by accepting this order. In other words, profit leaps from £1,000 per month to £2,600.

The order clearly looks attractive on financial grounds.

Other factors to consider when thinking about special orders

No decision should be based on purely quantitative factors, so you need to also consider a number of other issues when considering a special order.

Will it lead to a new regular customer – and what price will they pay?

Orders from potential new customers should be considered carefully. If the new customers are likely to become regulars, this is clearly a positive factor. Of course, if they expect the same low price all the time it would be less attractive.

Will existing customers find out and be annoyed?

Existing customers would argue that if anyone deserves a special price it should be those that have shown loyalty to the firm. If current customers find out that the firm is offering a special low price they may become disenchanted with this supplier and there is a danger that business may be lost.

Do we have spare capacity? Will we still have enough time for routine maintenance?

Of course if a special order requires an increase in capacity, extra fixed costs will be incurred. This is not desirable. However, even if the order can be fulfilled using spare existing capacity, it is worth considering whether there will still be time for routine preventative maintenance to be carried out. Will working too close to maximum capacity have a detrimental effect on the firm's quality or reliability?

Will costs remain unchanged?

We have been working on the assumption that no extra fixed costs are incurred and that variable costs per unit will remain unchanged for any extra output. This may not be realistic, perhaps most notably because the firm may need to pay staff overtime rates to cope with the extra order.

Themes for evaluation

Any decision needs to be based on a careful balance between the quantitative and the qualitative. Special order decision questions expect you to calculate the profit gained from the order. Yet it may be that there are sufficient qualitative factors suggesting that the order should not be accepted for you to justify a negative response, even if the order generates extra profit.

S Student howler

'The firm should not accept the order because the price being offered is less than the current average cost per unit.'

T Test yourself (20 marks)

1. Explain why average unit costs fall at higher levels of output. (3 marks)
2. Identify three reasons why a firm might decide to accept a special order at a reduced price. (3 marks)
3. Identify three reasons why a firm might turn down a profitable special order at a reduced price. (3 marks)
4. Briefly outline the problems of working at full capacity. (3 marks)
5. Calculate the effect on monthly profit of accepting the following special order: (8 marks)

Current position	Special order
Selling price: £20	Price: £14
Variable cost p.u.: £12	Quantity: 800
Fixed costs p.m.: £5,000	The firm does have spare capacity for the order. VC p.u. would remain at £12
Current sales: 1000	

BALANCE SHEETS

A balance sheet is a statement of a firm's assets, liabilities and capital at a particular moment. Assets are items the firm owns. Liabilities are debts owed by the firm. Capital is money invested in the business by its owners.

A balance sheet shows the wealth of a business and enables the analyst to judge various aspects of that wealth. Does the firm have enough cash to be able to cope easily with any opportunities or threats that arise? Toyota, for example, had over £8,000 million in cash in its 2004 balance sheet – enough to buy up half the European motor industry without needing to even talk to its bankers about it. Among the other key issues a balance sheet shows is whether the firm's capital is largely borrowed. If so, this highly geared position places it in a risky position if it hits a period of poor trading. In recent years the poor performance of Marks & Spencer has been cushioned by the huge strength of the company's balance sheet.

Structure of a balance sheet

The skeleton of the balance sheet is shown below – entries that are underlined are followed by an individual item; entries in bold represent totals or subtotals:

- Fixed assets – items a firm owns for the long term (at least a year).
- Current assets – items a firm owns for short-term use (cash or assets that will soon be turned into cash).
- Current liabilities – debts payable within 12 months.
- Net current assets (working capital) – current assets minus current liabilities.
- **Assets employed** – fixed assets plus net current assets.

Financed by:

- Long-term liabilities – debts payable in more than 12 months' time.
- Shareholders' funds – money invested by shareholders consisting of share capital and profits retained within the business (reserves).
- **Capital employed** – shareholders' funds plus long-term liabilities.

What the balance sheet shows

The lower section of the balance sheet (from *Financed by* downwards) shows where the firm got its money from – its long-term sources of finance. The total for this section (the **Capital employed**) will always balance with the upper section of the balance sheet – the **Assets employed**. The latter section shows how the firm has used the money it has received. If any extra finance comes into the business, the bottom section shows where the finance has come from, and the top section shows what assets have been bought with the money.

An outline balance sheet – What to look for

	£000s
Fixed assets	1,000
Current assets	200
Current liabilities	180
Working capital (net current assets)	20
Assets employed	**1,020**
Long-term loans	360
Share capital	400
Reserves	260
Capital employed	**1,020**

The working capital section of the balance sheet shows the firm has just enough current assets to meet its current liabilities. Current assets are items that should be turned into cash within the next month or so, such as stock and stock that has been sold on credit to a customer (debtors). Therefore it is vital that there should be sufficient to pay the bills that are due in the next month or so – the current liabilities.

Long-term loans should be smaller than shareholders' funds, since loans as a long-term source of finance carry the cost of interest payments. The cost of share capital can be thought of as dividends, but the level of dividends is decided by the firm itself, unlike interest payments on loans. Loans are a perfectly acceptable source of finance, but should not account for too large a proportion (usually less than 50%) of a firm's total capital employed.

Expansion

A business pursuing a policy of growth will have a balance sheet worth more than in previous years. Extra money will have come into the business – the source will be seen in the lower section. Growth will tend to involve the purchase of extra fixed assets and this will show up in the top part of the balance sheet.

	This year (£000s)	Last year (£000s)
Fixed assets	1,200	1,000
Current assets	200	200
Current liabilities	180	180
Working capital (net current assets)	20	20
Assets employed	**1,220**	**1,020**
Long-term loans	550	360
Share capital	400	400
Reserves	270	260
Capital employed	**1,220**	**1,020**

This firm has financed its expansion (purchase of new fixed assets) by using the £10,000 of retained profit from last year and borrowing the other £190,000. This means its debt levels are creeping up towards a worrying level.

Squeezing finance from working capital

A possible source of extra finance is the working capital section. If a firm feels it is carrying more stock than is necessary, stock levels can be reduced, effectively freeing up this money for use elsewhere. In addition, firms may seek a reduction in the time their debtors take to pay. This would reduce debtors and turn credit sales into cash much faster. The cash generated by cutting stocks and cutting debtors could then be used for another purpose. Tesco has financed much of its rapid expansion from squeezing its working capital. As with the balance sheet below, Tesco usually operates with negative working capital.

	This year (£000s)	Last year (£000s)
Fixed assets	1,070	1,000
Current assets	150	200
Current liabilities	200	180
Working capital (net current assets)	(50)	20
Assets employed	**1,020**	**1,020**
Long-term loans	360	360
Share capital	400	400
Reserves	260	260
Capital employed	**1,020**	**1,020**

Money has been taken from current assets, with more generated by increasing current liabilities. It has been used to purchase more fixed assets. Notice that the firm's net current assets (working capital) is now a negative figure, suggesting it may struggle to pay its short-term bills.

The most effective evaluative theme when studying a balance sheet is to consider what it doesn't show. A single year's figures with no comparative data will provide little information about a firm, and as we will see in Unit 2.8 they can be 'dressed up' to show a rosier picture than is really the case.

E Exam Insight

Two simple things catch students out in exams:

1. In the hurry to make calculations, they ignore the heading of the balance sheet columns. They then write down an answer saying that, for example, Tesco's annual profit is £2,000, whereas the actual figure is £2,000 million.
2. Students muddle the columns if 2 years' figures are provided. This can mean they talk about fixed assets rising when they have actually fallen. Tradition dictates that this year's figures are in the left column on a balance sheet, with previous years' figures appearing on the right.

S Student howler

'Firms should try to keep as much working capital as possible.'

T Test yourself (25 marks)

1. What is meant by the term 'shareholders' funds'? (2 marks)
2. What balances on a balance sheet? (2 marks)
3. a) How does a balance sheet show the firm's working capital? (2 marks)
   b) How much working capital should a firm aim to have? (2 marks)
4. Analyse the changes shown in this firm's finances. (9 marks)

	This year (£000s)	Last year (£000s)
Fixed assets	1,200	950
Current assets	210	260
Current liabilities	200	200
Working capital	10	60
Assets employed	**1,210**	**1,010**
Long-term liabilities	600	500
Share capital	500	450
Reserves	110	60
Capital employed	**1,210**	**1,010**

5. To what extent does a balance sheet tell the whole story of a firm's financial position? (8 marks)

PROFIT AND LOSS ACCOUNTS

All but the smallest limited companies are required, by law, to publish a profit and loss account each year. This shows their revenues, costs and uses of profit over a 12-month period.

Structure of the profit and loss account

The basic structure of the profit and loss account is relatively straightforward. Starting with sales revenue at the top, direct and indirect costs are deducted, the uses to which profit has been put are shown, ending up with the profit retained within the business. The following section shows the full detail of profit and loss accounts, though in exams a simplified version is used.

Profit and loss account for XYZ Ltd. for the year ended 31/12/05

The title will indicate the year to which the profit and loss account is referring. You may be given 2 years' figures in one account. In this case the most recent information is usually in the left hand column.

- Sales turnover: The total value of sales made in the period – a sale is recorded when items change hands – there is no need to wait for cash to be received. Sales turnover means the same as sales revenue.
- *Minus* cost of sales: This figure represents the direct costs of the business. Largely these are variable costs. For a retailer, cost of sales would include stock purchases, the cost of stock wastage and the cost of extras such as carrier bags or delivery. The cost of sales is deducted from the revenue to give the gross profit.
- = Gross profit: Not a particularly meaningful figure unless other years' or other firms' figures are available for comparison, because no allowance has yet been made for the overhead costs.
- *Minus* overheads: The indirect costs of running the business, such as salaries, advertising and office rents and expenses. This will include depreciation (see Unit 2.6). In accounts used in exams, interest charges are also included in the overheads total.
- = Operating profit: This is the indicator of the ongoing profit for the firm generated by its normal trading activities.

- + or − One-off items (extraordinary items): These one-off items are not likely to occur again and should therefore be regarded as 'low quality'. For example, if British Airways made £80 million profit on foreign exchange transactions in 1 year, it would be a one-off (the following year they might lose a comparable amount). Extraordinary items should be excluded from most financial analysis.
- = Profit before tax (pre-tax profit).
- *Minus* tax: The corporation tax payable by the business on this year's profit. This is set as a percentage of profit, so the higher the profit the higher the percentage. In 2005 large companies in the UK will pay a corporation tax rate of 30%.
- = Profit after tax: This figure is sometimes called earnings – referring to the amount earned by the firm for its shareholders.
- *Minus* dividends: The total amount that will be paid this year to shareholders as dividends – their share of the company's profit. The amount paid in dividends is decided by the company directors.
- = Retained profit: The amount of profit kept within the business. This can be used for any purpose, whether to boost fixed or current assets or to reduce current or long-term liabilities.

And now with some numbers…

	Year ended 31/03/05 (£000s)	Year ended 31/03/04 (£000s)
Sales turnover	150	140
Cost of sales	100	100
Gross profit	50	40
Overheads	35	30
Operating profit	15	10
Extraordinary item	(5)	–
Profit before tax	10	10
Tax	3	3
Profit after tax	7	7
Dividends	4	5
Retained profit	3	2

S | Student howler

'You can't trust the figures in profit and loss accounts because they can be window dressed.'

Key issues to look for on a profit and loss account

Controlling direct or indirect costs

Comparing profit and loss accounts from previous years indicates how well a firm is controlling its costs. Generally the cost of sales can be expected to rise or fall proportionately with any increase or decrease in sales. Although overheads can be expected to rise as a firm grows, many of these may be fixed costs which ought not to change unless capacity is increased. Are costs kept under control or do they seem to be escalating at a faster rate than sales or for no obvious reason?

One-off items

These can have a significant effect on a firm's profit after tax – a figure widely quoted in financial circles. High profit figures that are the result of one-off items, such as selling fixed assets at a profit, will not be repeated – these profits are therefore considered to be of a poor quality. Good quality profit comes from the firm's normal trading activities, since these profits are likely to be repeated year after year by a successful business.

Application – A good year for one-offs at Old Trafford

In the year that they sold Beckham, Stam and Veron, Manchester United's profit figures benefited significantly from the addition of one-off profits. So despite generating an operating profit of £3 million less than 2004, 2003's profit after tax was £10 million higher. This was not, however, an indication that the business was operated any better in 2003 than 2004. It is not every year that Manchester United offloads so many big name players.

Look for dividend policy

Check to see what proportion of a firm's profit after tax has been paid out to shareholders and how much has been retained for future investment. Retained profits are the best long-term source of finance for a business. Therefore firms investing in their own future are likely to retain fairly high levels of profit, on average some 50%. Firms with a greater focus on keeping shareholders or the stock market happy in the short-term will pay out a far greater proportion of their profit after tax in dividends. Indeed, some firms will actually pay out dividends that exceed their profit after tax. This will leave them with a retained loss.

Application – MISYS PLC

MISYS, one of the UK's oldest information technology software companies announced a retained loss in 2004 of £10 million. This came despite generating a profit after tax of some £24 million and was the result of a decision to pay dividends of £34 million, leaving a retained loss despite an operating profit. This represented an increase in dividend paid per share on the previous year and was in keeping with the directors' commitment to maintain growth in dividend per share year on year. This is a policy that is clearly designed to keep shareholders happy, preventing a rush to sell shares.

As is the case with balance sheets, a profit and loss account simply forms part of a larger picture of a firm's evolving financial position. Do not rush to judge on the basis of one year's figures. You should also carefully consider the reliability of the information provided (see Unit 2.8). When doing so, make sure to use evidence from the case. If there is deliberate discussion among managers of how a change in the depreciation provisions 'could boost profit', be willing to suggest that this seems like deliberate window dressing.

E Exam Insight

Be alert to the issue of quality in relation to profit and to dividend pay-outs. Examiners love to slip in a hint that everything is not what it seems. Rising profit may be down to one-off (low quality) factors. Or rising dividends may be a sign of desperation rather than confidence in the firm's future.

T Test yourself (25 marks)

1. What is meant by the term 'profit quality'? (2 marks)
2. Why might a PLC choose to increase the annual dividends to shareholders even though its profits are falling? (3 marks)
3. Rearrange the following jumble of figures to construct a profit and loss account for Whittakers PLC for the year ended 31/12/04. (6 marks)

	£000s
Cost of sales	650
Tax	15
Dividends	15
Sales	1,200
Expenses	350
Interest	40
One-off expense	140

4. a) Fill in the gaps on the following profit and loss account: (6 marks)

	Year ended	
	31/03/05 (£000s)	31/03/04 (£000s)
Sales	240	
Cost of sales	140	150
Gross profit	100	100
Overheads	75	65
Operating profit		35
Extraordinary item	–	
Profit before tax	25	20
Tax		
Profit after tax	15	13
Dividends	10	8
Retained profit	5	

b) Analyse the changes shown in the firm's financial performance. (8 marks)

REVENUE AND CAPITAL SPENDING

What?

Accountants distinguish between these two types of spending for accounting purposes. Capital expenditure is money spent buying assets that a firm will keep to use over and over again, such as machinery or vehicles. Revenue expenditure is money spent on items that are used once and then gone, such as materials or monthly bills. Revenue expenditure appears on the profit and loss account; items of capital expenditure are accounted for on the balance sheet.

Application of definitions

It is important to recognise that some items will represent revenue expenditure for some firms and capital expenditure for others. A computer bought by a computer retailer is an item of stock and is treated as revenue expenditure, whereas the same computer bought by a plumber to do his accounts will represent an item of capital expenditure.

Why distinguish between capital and revenue spending?

The distinction is necessary to ensure that accounts show a fair view of a firm's financial position. The wages of a shop assistant should be charged in full against the revenue generated in the year s/he was working for the company. Therefore wages are categorized as revenue expenditure. Yet if a firm buys a £1 million piece of machinery planned to last for 10 years, it would be absurd to charge the cost in full against the first year's accounts. Far better to show the cost of this machine spread over those 10 years of useful life. Machinery is a form of capital (investment) expenditure.

Distinguishing between capital and revenue expenditure ensures that firms are not put off investing in assets of long-term value to the business. Spending £1 million on machinery this year requires £1 million of cash, but that sum will not be charged against the profit and loss account. The only charge will come from the estimated loss in the value of the asset over time, i.e. the depreciation. If this is calculated on the basis of 10 year straight line depreciation, the charge will be £100,000 in year one instead of £1,000,000.

Depreciation is the way that accountants show the fall in value of an asset over time. Only capital spending is depreciated. This means that a portion of the value of the asset bought is deducted on the firm's profit and loss account each year. The value of the asset is reduced on the balance sheet by the same amount to present a true view of its worth.

How is depreciation calculated?

The annual depreciation expense on an item of capital expenditure can be calculated using the straight-line method. The amount of value to be deducted each year is worked out as follows:

$$\frac{\text{Original cost} - \text{residual value}}{\text{Years of useful life}}$$

The original cost is a matter of fact – how much was paid for the asset. The residual value is the amount that the firm believes it will be able to gain from selling the asset when it has finished using it. Some assets will have no residual value. The useful life is the number of years that the firm expects the asset will last.

Example

A firm buys a van for £24,000. The van is expected to last for 5 years and have a re-sale value of £4,000 after 5 years. The annual depreciation expense can be calculated using the formula shown above:

$$\frac{£24,000 - £4,000}{5 \text{ years}} = £4,000 \text{ per year}$$

The van's balance sheet value will fall by £4,000 per year, as shown in Figure 2.6A. The graph indicates that with a set fall in value each year, the value of the asset falls in a straight line over its life. After 3 years the

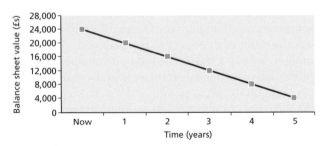

Fig. 2.6A: Fall in value of a fixed asset over time

balance sheet value is £12,000. Over the 5-year life of the asset the accumulated depreciation is £20,000.

Depreciation in the final accounts

The depreciation figure is needed to draw up both the balance sheet and the profit and loss account. The profit and loss account must include the depreciation expense for the year on each asset. This is deducted as an expense before calculating operating profit. The balance sheet shows the value of all fixed assets as their original cost minus all accumulated depreciation on that asset.

What is the effect of depreciation?

It may be appropriate to consider the effects of differing depreciation assumptions on a firm's annual profit. A low depreciation figure will lead to a higher profit for the year. This may impose pressure on accountants to make unrealistic assumptions on the useful life of an asset in order to reduce the depreciation expense and seemingly boost a company's profits. Prudent firms will make pessimistic assumptions on useful life and residual values.

Application – spot the troubled firm

Firms that are in deep trouble or have a less careful approach to accounting may be more willing to make risky depreciation assumptions in order to boost profit figures. Careful reading of a case study can indicate whether a firm is likely to consider using techniques like this to try to make their accounts look a little healthier.

Themes for evaluation

Question the reliability of company accounts by pointing out that two of the three variables used to calculate depreciation may be guesses. How can anyone know how long an asset will be useful for? Or how much it will be worth in 5 or so years' time? The residual value and useful life are often uncertain and the firm will need to make assumptions about these to calculate depreciation. This calls into question the true accuracy of a company's profit and asset figures. It is true that independent auditors check these accounts for reliability, yet even audited accounts sometimes show a false picture of a firm's finances – as with the collapse of Enron.

K **Key term**

Depreciation – the tool used by accountants to spread the cost of a fixed asset over its expected useful lifetime.

E **Exam Insight**

Many exam answers can be strengthened by explaining that depreciation is based upon assumptions, not facts. Therefore both the balance sheet and the profit and loss account are theoretical, not factual.

S **Student howler**

'If depreciation is too high, the firm will have cash flow problems.'

T **Test yourself (25 marks)**

1. What is the purpose behind treating capital expenditure differently from revenue expenditure? (3 marks)
2. How do firms value the assets they put down in their balance sheets? (2 marks)
3. a) Calculate the annual depreciation on a £100,000 coach with a useful life of 5 years and an expected residual value of £20,000. (2 marks)
   b) What would be the effect on the firm's annual operating profit of a change in the assumptions so that the expected useful life becomes 10 years and the residual value £30,000? (4 marks)
4. Outline two reasons why a finance director might decide to allocate no residual value to an asset that may have re-sale value at the end of its useful life. (6 marks)
5. Analyse the effect of depreciation calculations on the reliability of published accounts. (8 marks)

RATIO ANALYSIS

If Michael Owen scored 10 goals last season and Thierry Henry scored 30, which is the better striker?

Based on the data given, you would have to answer Thierry Henry. However, if Henry played 60 games and Owen played just 10 games, you may wish to reassess your response. This is because, perhaps without realising, you have calculated the ratio of goals per game for each player.

Financial ratios are based on the same principle – absolute figures have little meaning – only when data on profit or sales are compared with other information can meaningful conclusions be drawn.

You are required to assess three main areas of a firm's financial position using financial ratios:

- Profitability;
- Financial health;
- Financial (or operating) efficiency.

To analyse a firm's performance in each of these three categories, you would rarely need to use more than two ratios. It is your job, though, to decide which ones are appropriate to answer the question set. Use the following summary:

- Profitability ratios: *gross profit margin; operating (net) profit margin; return on capital* (ROC) employed. Generally the most useful of these are ROC and operating margins.
- Financial health: *acid test* measures short-term health (liquidity); *gearing* measures long-term health (level of indebtedness) and *return on capital* shows whether the operating position of the business is profitable.
- Financial (or operating) efficiency: *debtor days* shows how quickly customers pay up; *stock turnover* shows how quickly stock is sold out and replaced; *asset turnover* shows the level of sales revenue generated from the money invested in assets.

In addition, you may be required to know the value to shareholders of the dividend yield ratio.

In total you will need to know the formulae for nine ratios. These ratios, along with their formulae, ideal values and meanings and other useful information are shown in the following table:

Ratio (type)	Formula	Ideal value?	What it measures?	Factors that improve it	Factors that may worsen it
Gross profit margin (Profitability)	$\dfrac{\text{Gross profit}}{\text{Sales turnover}} \times 100$	Higher is better	The proportion of profit left after direct costs have been deducted from sales. A raw measure of profitability	Push up your prices or reduce your direct costs, perhaps by finding a cheaper supplier	Raw material price increases may push up direct costs, e.g. plastics. Manufacturers will find gross margins hit by an increase in oil prices, unless they are able to push their prices up proportionately
Operating profit margin (Profitability)	$\dfrac{\text{Operating profit}}{\text{Sales turnover}} \times 100$	Higher is better, but needs comparison with rival firms	What percentage of sales is profit – the commonest measure of profit	Reduce overheads – this could be achieved by delayering or reducing marketing or training budgets	Inefficiencies may lead to higher overheads proportionate to sales. It may be evidence of diseconomies of scale hitting a growing firm

Ratio (type)	Formula	Ideal value?	What it measures?	Factors that improve it	Factors that may worsen it
Return on capital (Profitability)	$\dfrac{\text{Operating profit}}{\text{Capital employed}} \times 100$	Higher is better – should definitely be higher than rate of interest	The return (profit) on money invested in the business (capital). Often called the primary efficiency ratio	Either increase profit levels using the same capital employed or generate the same level of profit while paying off loans or returning money to shareholders	Difficult economic conditions tend to cause ROCs to fall throughout the economy. This is the result of falling profit, generally down to lower sales
Stock turnover (Efficiency)	$\dfrac{\text{Cost of sales}}{\text{Stock}}$	High is good, but beware too high a figure since stocks may run out	The number of times a firm sells out its average level of stock in a year	Reducing stock levels, perhaps by investing in more efficient stock control techniques. A switch to JIT would increase a firm's stock turnover, but cannot be done overnight	Buying items that fall out of fashion may make it harder to shift stocks, so firms must be careful to avoid heavy stockpiling of such items
Debtor days (Efficiency)	$\dfrac{\text{Debtors}}{\text{Average daily sales}}$	The lower it is, the more quickly the firm is receiving cash that it can use elsewhere in the business	The average amount of time taken to pay by customers sold goods on credit	Hiring a credit controller to send out reminders and chase late-payers. Cutting the credit period offered to customers should help reduce the debtor days figure	Attempts to boost sales by offering generous credit terms will worsen the ratio, but so will an inefficient credit control section
Asset turnover (Efficiency)	$\dfrac{\text{Sales turnover}}{\text{Assets employed}}$	High is good (on average, firms' asset turnover tends to be about 2)	How hard your assets are working at generating sales	Close down underperforming branches or factories. This allows assets to be transferred to areas that generate more sales. The higher a firm's capacity utilisation the stronger will be its asset turnover	A downturn in trade will damage a firm's asset turnover. Anything that will cause the firm's capacity utilisation to fall will have a detrimental effect on this ratio, e.g. excessively rapid expansion
Gearing (Financial health – long term)	$\dfrac{\text{Long-term loans}}{\text{Capital employed}} \times 100$	Start to worry if it gets above 50%, which is highly geared. The closer to 100% the more risky the firm's position	The reliance of a company on long-term liabilities as a source of finance	Reducing debt levels by paying back loans is obvious, but using alternative sources of finance to straightforward loan capital may also reduce the gearing ratio	Excessive borrowing (often used to finance grand expansion plans) may push company gearing levels to remarkable heights

JIT, just in time.

Ratio (type)	Formula	Ideal value?	What it measures?	Factors that improve it	Factors that may worsen it
Acid test (Financial health – short term)	$\dfrac{\text{Total current assets} - \text{stock}}{\text{Current liabilities}}$	Around 1	The ability of a firm to meet its short-term debts	Increase the amount of assets held in liquid form, by cutting stock levels or by selling underused fixed assets. It is also possible to lower the level of current liabilities by relying less on trade credit	Growth places a severe burden on a firm's cash flow and acid test levels may drop during a period of sustained rapid growth. Too few profitable investment options may cause a firm to operate with too much cash – causing the ratio to be too high
Dividend yield (Shareholders)	$\dfrac{\text{Dividend per share}}{\text{Current share price}} \times 100$	A higher % than the interest rates offered by banks to savers	A measure of the return received on an investment in shares.	Higher dividends would lead to an increased dividend yield – making shareholders happier	An increase in share price reduces the dividend yield – as does a decision by directors to cut the annual dividend

JIT, just in time.

Application – Britain's biggest retailer on the brink of insolvency?

Tesco is Britain's biggest retailer, lauded for its exceptional performance over the last 10 years in building a clear lead in the UK grocery market. However, Tesco regularly operates with an acid test ratio of around 0.3. This does not mean it is about to be driven out of business by angry creditors. Tesco sells stock so rapidly that generating cash is not a problem for the firm. This is an example of a situation where the acid test should be viewed in relation to stock turnover. Companies with a high stock turnover are likely to be able to trade on acid test values well below 1 since they are likely to find it easy to generate cash. To find out Tesco's latest acid test and stock turnover figures, go to www.tesco.com, then look for 'investor relations' in the 'About Us' section.

Comparisons

Ratios do provide more insight than simply looking through a profit and loss account and balance sheet. However, their real analytical power shows itself when they are used to make comparisons. Comparing ratios to previous years' results will show clearly trends in a firm's financial position, while inter-firm comparisons allow far better judgements to be made than simply studying the figures in isolation.

A useful comparison can be made by pitting Tesco against Sainsburys. Sainsburys latest accounts are at www.sainsburys.co.uk; click 'Our company' and click again on 'corporate information'.

Do not expect ratios to provide answers by themselves. Ratios are designed to trigger further investigation of particular areas of a firm's finances. A strange looking figure may well be the trigger to investigate a firm's stock-holding policies further. Or perhaps a falling asset turnover ratio suggests that the firm needs to reassess the way in which it is using its property. A sensible judgement based on the calculation of ratios is unlikely to suggest that the answer is clear, simply that the ratio analysis has highlighted certain areas for further investigation.

E Exam Insight

Do not be afraid to calculate ratios. However, be sure to know why you are calculating them. It is crucial that you are aware of what each ratio is measuring. Too often in previous exams, students have been asked to assess a firm's financial efficiency and have failed to calculate one of the efficiency ratios. Meanwhile, a quick calculation of gearing and acid test can help you to add insight to most financial questions, even if the question itself does not ask for the calculation of these ratios.

S Student howler

'With an acid test of 0.98 which is less than the ideal figure of 1, this firm is heading for disaster.'

T Test yourself (28 marks)

1. Using the following profit and loss account and balance sheet, calculate the ratios listed below for both this year and last year:

Profit and loss account for Michaelis Metals PLC for year ended 31/03/05

	Year ended 31/03/05 (£m)	Year ended 31/03/04 (£m)
Sales	240	220
Cost of sales	180	150
Gross profit	60	70
Overheads	45	55
Operating profit	15	15
Tax	5	5
Profit after tax	10	10
Dividends	7	5
Retained profit	3	5

Balance sheet for Michaelis Metals PLC as at 31/03/05

	As at 31/03/05 (£m)	As at 31/03/04 (£m)
Fixed assets	105	128
Stock	12	15
Debtors	9	6
Cash	4	3
Current liabilities	10	12
Net current assets (working capital)	15	12
Assets employed	**120**	**140**
Long-term loans	40	80
Share capital	47	32
Reserves	33	28
Capital employed	**120**	**140**

NB. The firm had issued 32 million shares by 31/03/04. A further 15 million were issued by 31/03/05. Market share price as at 31/03/05 was 210 pence; market share price as at 31/03/04 was 290 pence.

a) Acid test.   (2 marks)
b) Gearing.   (2 marks)
c) Gross profit margin.   (2 marks)
d) Operating profit margin.   (2 marks)
e) Return on capital.   (2 marks)
f) Asset turnover.   (2 marks)
g) Debtor days.   (2 marks)
h) Stock turnover.   (2 marks)
i) Dividend yield.   (2 marks)

2. Comment on the firm's:
a) Profitability.   (5 marks)
b) Financial health.   (5 marks)
c) Efficiency.   (5 marks)
d) Ability to please shareholders.   (5 marks)

RELIABILITY OF PUBLISHED ACCOUNTS

The auditing process

Accounting documents that are published by public limited companies must be audited. The process of auditing involves an independent accountant checking the information contained in the accounts to ensure that they present a true and fair view of the firm's financial performance. Auditors should also check to ensure that accounting regulations have been adhered to.

Application – Independent auditors?

Although auditors are independent of the firm whose accounts they are auditing, this does not mean they have no link to the company. A number of worrying situations have been brought to light recently where a firm employed to audit the accounts of a PLC has also been acting as a consultant to the same firm. The accusation is that auditors may sign off a set of accounts that include some inconsistencies in order to ensure that their company still retains the consultancy business with the firm whose accounts are being checked.

Technical problems

There are a number of areas within a firm's finances that present problems to accountants. These generally revolve around the difficulty of attaching a realistic monetary value to items that should appear in the firm's accounts.

Valuing stock

Stock can increase or decrease in value once it has been bought and possibly worked on by a business. Therefore it can be hard to determine an accurate value for a firm's stocks to be shown on the balance sheet. The rule is that stocks should be valued at the lower of cost or net realisable value. This ensures that accounts take a conservative view of stock valuation. Cost refers to how much was originally paid for the stock, and any money that has been spent on processing the stock since it entered the business. This is the more common valuation, but for stock whose value has fallen since it was purchased, perhaps the result of a change in fashion or technology, these items should be valued at their net realisable value – what the firm could get for it now.

Valuing fixed assets

Valuing buildings, machinery and equipment accurately can also be difficult. As we saw in Unit 2.6 which dealt with depreciation, fixed assets such as machinery are valued by deducting accumulated depreciation from their original cost. Although this makes sense, it is important to remember that depreciation calculations involve two assumptions – the asset's useful life, and its residual value. The result is that fixed asset valuations cannot be considered to be 100% accurate given the guesswork involved in their calculation. Buildings, land and property tend to be nudged up in value as time goes by to reflect their market value. Firms wishing to add to the value of their fixed assets may be able to do so, simply by carefully choosing when to revalue their property.

Application – A rare high profile fraud – Parmalat

Italian food giant Parmalat was hit by an accounting scandal in 2003. Investigations by the firm's auditors revealed a huge hole in the firm's accounts. A bank account reported to contain €3.95 billion actually did not exist, and was only there as a result of a forged document by certain Parmalat staff. This over-inflation of the company's assets and sales had helped to hide losses made within the business over several years. Those found to have been involved in the fraud faced criminal charges. The company is fighting desperately for survival, and is taking the auditors to court, claiming that they should have spotted the fraud earlier.

Window dressing

This is the general term used to describe deliberate attempts to make a firm's published accounts look more attractive to the reader. Many techniques do not, as such, infringe accounting regulations or the law; however, they may still adjust the look of a firm's published financial documents.

Major areas for window dressing

Improving liquidity

Since liquidity is the indicator of short-term financial health, a business that is trying to prove its short-term stability will try to ensure that it has a relatively healthy acid test ratio, or at least has an acceptably large pile of cash. A Finance Director who sees that the balance sheet data will show a weak liquidity position might hide it by arranging a sale and leaseback deal on fixed assets. This would show as a reduction in fixed assets, but might be less of a worry to investors than evidence of falling liquidity.

Boosting sales figures

It should be clear when a sale has been made and therefore when that sale should be counted as revenue. The basic principle here is that revenue can be recorded when goods have changed hands or services have been provided. There is no need to wait until cash has been received to enter revenue into the accounts. Yet firms pursuing ambitious profit targets have been known to boost this year's sales figure by including revenues that should have come into the following year. In effect, with a financial year ending on December 31st, they anticipate January's sales as well as December's, therefore bringing 13 months' sales into the current year. This boosts sales and profits for this year – but of course leaves only 11 months' sales for the following year! (Such activities seem absurd, yet large companies such as Wickes have been caught doing this in the past.)

Boosting asset valuations

Depreciation provides tempting opportunities for window dressing. If a firm switches from depreciating assets over 3 years to depreciating over 5 years, the charge to the profit and loss account is reduced, which boosts the profit. At the same time assets lose value more slowly, so the balance sheet looks stronger. When analysing accounts, always look out for changes to depreciation periods.

Application – Shell's annual report misleads, but you can't blame the auditors

Senior management resignations, a tumbling share price and various internal investigations were the result of the discovery in late 2003 that Shell had overstated the amount of oil and gas that it owned but had not yet extracted. This does not seem to have been the result of a deliberate attempt to mislead external users, rather the result of internal pressures for managers to show good results for their area of the business. Oil companies are required to publish estimates of their 'undeveloped reserves', yet these are not audited since they are impossible to measure accurately. They do, however, appear in the firm's annual report, alongside their audited accounts. Meanwhile the amount of oil reserves is clearly a critical figure for investors trying to assess the future profitability and wealth of the business. Investors are unable to make effective decisions without reliable information from businesses. In fact, the restatement of Shell's reserves shifted the market's perception of the company from one that had been profitable while maintaining its excellent record of exploration, to a firm that had spent 10 years protecting profitability by cutting back on the exploration costs that could protect its long-term future.

Evaluation – Can published accounts be trusted?

Sophisticated judgements about the reliability of accounting documents will help in scoring good marks on A2 exams. An ability to question the reliability of financial statements is little more than knowledge. To score high marks you must carefully check the case study for signs of 'creative accounting' techniques while considering whether the firm is under particular pressure to publish attractive financial statements. You must also be sure to avoid getting carried away, since for every Enron there are thousands of reliable sets of accounts – accounts must be checked by auditors and in the vast majority of cases they do a sound job of confirming that a 'true and fair view' is reported.

Other evaluative themes

What don't accounts value?

Accounting documents can only value items that can be measured in monetary terms. Assets such as machinery and property can be shown, but what of firms whose major asset is the knowledge and experience of their staff? People are not valued within a firm's accounts, yet on many occasions people are the most important asset of the business.

Social costs

A firm's activities can have a number of detrimental effects on society – external costs – which do not appear on their profit and loss account. These might include environmental damage, damage to customers' health (fatty fast foods) or the damaging effect on society of unemployment caused by redundancies. Attempts to see a clearer picture of a firm's impact on society are dealt with in Unit 5.8 which covers social auditing.

E | Exam Insight

Beware of generalising about accounts. Most are reliable; however, some get out of date quickly, and a few are window dressed deliberately. Your job is to judge the reliability for the specific business in the exam case study.

S | Student howlers

'Accounting scandals such as Enron prove that accounts cannot be trusted.'
'Since depreciation expenses have been carefully calculated to give an exact value, these figures are accurate.'

T | Test yourself (20 marks)

1. Outline how the need to account for the depreciation of fixed assets causes problems in producing accurate accounting data. (6 marks)
2. Analyse the effect on a firm's profit and loss account and balance sheet of selling and leasing back a fixed asset for more than its previously stated balance sheet valuation. (6 marks)
3. Discuss the extent to which investors can rely on the accuracy of audited published accounts. (8 marks)

INVESTMENT APPRAISAL

What is it?

Investment appraisal is the process of making decisions about possible future investment projects using quantitative and qualitative information.

How is it done?

The usual process is to make a quantitative assessment of the alternatives facing a business, then balance these against other, qualitative considerations such as the effect on the firm's corporate image.

There are three main quantitative investment appraisal techniques – all three techniques rely on forecasting the future cash flows resulting from an investment project. In other words the firm must estimate all the cash outflows and all the cash inflows to be expected over the lifetime of the investment. These future cash flows are often summarised in the format:

Year	Net cash flow (£s)
0	(50,000)
1	10,000
2	20,000
3	30,000
4	40,000

These figures will be used in each worked example.

Payback

- *What it means*: The payback period for a project is the length of time taken to recover the initial investment.
- *How to calculate it*: Count up the number of full years taken to recover the initial investment. When you only need part of one year's net cash flow, apply the following formula to calculate the number of months through that year before payback occurs:

$$\frac{\text{Amount still needed for payback}}{\text{Total net cash flow for that year}} \times 12$$

Example:

£50,000 must be recovered. Year 1 brings £10,000; by the end of year 2 we have an extra £20,000,

bringing the total amount recovered to £30,000. Year 3 brings more than the £20,000 still needed, so payback will be 2 years and:

$$\frac{£20,000}{£30,000} \times 12 = 8 \text{ months}$$

- *How to use the answer*: Shorter payback periods mean less risk is involved in a project. A short payback means that the project will begin to generate a profit for the company more quickly. If comparing two projects, short is preferable, but if only one project is being appraised look for clues as to the specific company's circumstances. For instance, if there is a hint in the case that the firm is struggling with its cash flow, a quick payback would be especially important.

Average rate of return

- *What it means*: The percentage calculated represents the percentage profit generated on the investment per year, averaged across the project's lifetime. It is the average annual profit as a percentage of the sum invested.
- *How to calculate it*: Remember the three simple steps:
  — Step 1: add all the project's net cash flows (including the initial investment) to calculate the total lifetime profit;
  — Step 2: divide by the number of years that the project lasts to get the average annual profit;
  — Step 3: express the average annual profit as a percentage of the initial investment – this is the ARR:

$$\frac{\text{Average annual profit}}{\text{Initial investment}} \times 100$$

Example:

Step 1: £100,000 − £50,000 = £50,000 lifetime profit

Step 2: £50,000/4 years = £12,500 profit per year

Step 3: $\dfrac{£12,500}{£50,000} \times 100 = 25\%$

- *How to use the answer*: A project's ARR should be compared with other projects' ARRs – the higher the better. However, the ARR should also be compared with alternative uses of capital. If the money were invested in the bank, what return would be generated? The ARR allows a direct comparison with prevailing interest rates. The amount by which a project's ARR exceeds the current interest rate may be referred to as the reward for risk (Fig. 2.9A). Alternatively, the ARR could be compared with the firm's return on capital. ARR on future prospects would be expected to exceed the firm's current or forecast ROC.

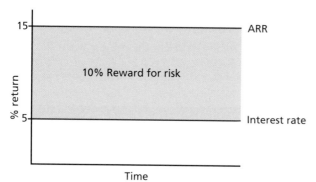

Fig. 2.9A: Reward for risk

Net present value (discounted cash flow)

- *What it means*: The net present value tells you the value of the whole project in today's terms. It allows for the fact that money received in the future is not worth what it seems, since had you received it today it could have been earning interest. For this reason, the net present value requires the calculation of discounted cash flows – reducing future cash flows to allow for their reducing value the further into the future they are received.
- *How to calculate it*: Select a set of discount factors (these will be given to you) that most closely reflects the expected interest rate over the project's lifetime. Multiply each year's net cash flow by the corresponding discount factor. Then add the discounted cash flows, remembering to include the initial investment, which will not be discounted, and you have the net present value.

Example:

Year	Net cash flow (£s)	× Discount factor	Discounted cash flow (£s)
0	(50,000)	1	(50,000)
1	10,000	0.91	9,100
2	20,000	0.83	16,600
3	30,000	0.75	22,500
4	40,000	0.68	27,200
Net present value			+25,400

These discount factors allow for a 10% cost of capital, and therefore a 10% discount factor.

- *How to use the answer*: If the net present value is positive, the project is more profitable than placing the money in a bank. Net present value is generally used as a comparative figure, allowing judgements to be made as to the relative financial merits of two or more projects, especially where cash flows arrive at different times during those projects.

Other factors to consider in any investment decision

Reliability of cash flow forecasts

As stated earlier, the financial investment appraisal techniques rely on forecasts of future cash flows. Future cash flows, as with any forecast, may be inaccurate – especially those that are in the more distant future. Questions must be asked when assessing these figures as to how they were arrived at. Did the person doing the forecast have a particular interest in providing especially attractive figures?

Objectives of the business

Any investment should only be undertaken if it fits in with the firm's objectives. A new investment is likely to form a key part of an overall strategic plan, therefore an attractive investment must complement the rest of the firm's activities. If a new direction breaks away from the firm's existing strategic plan, that investment may well lead to a loss of focus within the firm that could spell trouble for overall performance.

Can they afford it?

The source of finance will need careful consideration. To gather the initial investment required may place a huge financial strain on a firm's balance sheet. If the initial investment will force the firm into a dangerous financial situation it may be that it is an opportunity best left alone.

E Exam Insight

Expect to be asked about the merits of the quantitative techniques described in this unit. Payback doesn't consider profit, ARR doesn't take into account how soon inflows arrive, while NPV is based on another forecast – the basis of the decision over which discount factors to use. When written questions follow a calculation, make sure to apply your answer to the case, using the data and results you have just been working on.

When asked to suggest which choice a firm should make be sure to give full consideration to qualitative factors – perhaps half your answer. Be certain to write a conclusion in which you spell out (and justify) your recommendations clearly, to score high marks for evaluation.

Application to different management teams

- *Risk takers*: These management teams will be less concerned with payback than with ARR and NPV – measures of profitability. A management team that has a record of success in previous risky ventures may well be happy to invest on the basis of minimal quantitative appraisal or fairly speculative cash flow forecasts. They will be happy to accept the strength of argument on a qualitative basis.
- *Risk averse*: Management teams that avoid risk if at all possible will have a particular concern for payback periods. Just as lower break-even points are safer, since positive losses are avoided earlier, so a quick payback means that the firm will only be 'out of pocket' for the shortest time possible. Of course these managers may tend towards choosing smaller projects – thereby tying up less money in investments that could fail.
- *Centralised decision makers*: Many directors tell staff the minimum criteria they demand for any investment to get approved. These criteria are purely quantitative. At Topshop, for instance, new store proposals are only approved if the payback period is estimated at a maximum of 12 months. This is known as a *criterion level*. Other firms might set an ARR criterion level of +20% or an NPV criterion of at least +10% of the investment outlay.

No project will be assessed on purely quantitative grounds. This is sensible since all quantitative data will be based on uncertain forecasts. It is critical to understand that businesses need to see the big picture behind investments. In many cases the financial appraisal is simply a prompt for discussion of the far broader range of factors that may be important to a Board of Directors trying to take a strategic view of a firm's future plans.

S Student howler

'Firms should always select the project with the shortest payback.'

T Test yourself (20 marks)

1. Calculate payback and ARR for the following project: (4 marks)

Year	Net cash flow (£000s)
0	(100,000)
1	25,000
2	50,000
3	30,000
4	20,000

2. Explain why a firm may choose to ignore a highly profitable investment opportunity. (8 marks)
3. Identify two reasons why the results of a quantitative investment appraisal may prove unreliable. (2 marks)
4. Calculate the NPV for the following projects using the 6% discount factors provided: (6 marks)

Project A		Project B		Discount factors at 6%
Year	NCF (£m)	Year	NCF (£m)	
0	5	0	5	1
1	4	1	0	0.94
2	2	2	1	0.89
3	1	3	2	0.84
4	1	4	6	0.79

INTEGRATED FINANCE

Results of calculations

Once financial calculations have been done, the results are unlikely to answer many questions by themselves. Financial ratios raise questions and areas for further investigation, rather than providing clear answers. Knowing that a firm has a gearing ratio of 48% tells us little without understanding its current profitability, liquidity, the interest rates payable on their loans and forecasts of all this information for the future. Although the calculations may seem like the hard part, *using* the results is the part that generates the most marks.

Qualitative factors

Decision making should not be based purely on financial factors. Although some firms may consider the most profitable course the only option, there remains the issue of whether short- or long-term profit is more attractive. A high-achieving business student should be able to see the bigger picture when making a decision. This will involve considering the marketing, people and operational issues involved, even though the financial factors must also be considered. Some of the issues covered above, such as the source of data, can be classed as qualitative factors although they are related to the financial aspects of decision making.

Decision making

A2 exams often expect you to make some kind of decision. A business decision must consider financial factors carefully, even though other issues may well be factored into the process. Do not hesitate to make a decision; far too many students are indecisive. They write 'The firm should do some more research before deciding' when in fact there is plenty of evidence already.

E Exam Insight

Check the trigger word of any financial question carefully. Only if the trigger word is 'calculate' will you be required to write no words. Many questions will expect a calculation followed by an interpretation of the meaning of the results.

Is profit the only measure of success?
Traditionally, and from an accounting perspective especially, profit has been viewed as the key measure of the overall success of a business. However, many modern managers look for other ways to measure a business's performance in other functional areas, such as market share, productivity or cash flow. Try to take an equally broad view.

T Test yourself (60 marks)

1. Distinguish between capital and revenue expenditure. (4 marks)
2. Briefly explain two ways in which depreciation calculations may introduce inaccuracy into accounting statements. (4 marks)
3. Outline what is meant by poor quality profit. (3 marks)
4. State three ways in which a firm might use its operating profit. (3 marks)
5. What is meant by the term liquidity? (2 marks)
6. State the rule used by accountants when valuing stocks. (2 marks)
7. Outline three circumstances where a firm may wish to window dress its accounts. (6 marks)
8. Briefly explain why Tesco's very low acid test ratio does not mean the firm is in danger of imminent collapse. (4 marks)
9. Outline two ways in which a firm might improve its acid test ratio without damaging sales levels. (4 marks)
10. Identify three financial efficiency ratios. State the formula for each. (3 marks)
11. Briefly describe the circumstances when a high level of gearing may be seen as perfectly acceptable. (4 marks)
12. Explain how a price cut may cut gross, but improve net, profit margins. (4 marks)

13. State three things with which accounting ratios can be compared to add meaning to this year's ratio values. (3 marks)
14. State three reasons why a firm may be unwilling to accept a profitable special order. (3 marks)
15. What would be the effect on a break-even chart, and the firm's break-even point, of increasing the selling price of its product? (2 marks)
16. What data are all three quantitative investment appraisals based on? (1 mark)
17. Briefly explain why a short payback period represents a less risky investment. (3 marks)
18. Why are future cash flows discounted in the calculation of NPV? (3 marks)
19. Identify two qualitative factors involved in making investment decisions. (2 marks)

Bone china crunchtime

Cohen's Ceramics Ltd have been manufacturing bone china mugs at a factory in Devon for the last 40 years. The firm, owned by the Cohen family, has been financially stable for the last 10 years due to steady demand for its products from a number of loyal, reliable customers. Profit levels are satisfactory, though slightly below industry averages since the plain mugs they produce are priced below the more elaborate designs produced by their rivals. Managing Director Chris Cohen has identified the need for growth as a company aim. In addition he is keen to explore the opportunities offered by the European market, feeling that if any overseas expansion is viable, Europe is the firm's best bet. Meanwhile, his daughter Susannah is keen to boost profitability by adding more value to the mugs currently produced.

Quite unexpectedly, last Monday morning's post included a rather grand envelope displaying some unfamiliar stamps. It contained a formal letter from the Cuban government, ordering 5,000 mugs per month for the next 8 months at a price of £2.25 per mug. This special order is for commemorative mugs celebrating 40 years of Fidel Castro's rule. The mugs would need to have an image of Castro printed on them which would require the hiring of a printing machine. The factory manager pointed out that it would cost £1000 per month to hire this machine.

The Directors plan to discuss today whether to accept the order, which is at a lower price than normal. At this meeting, the Board agrees to consider two separate investment projects.

1. The first suggestion, from Chris's wife, the Sales Director, is to open a factory outlet shop, using a spare building on the factory site. Her logic is that in an area so popular with tourists, a little publicity in the right places could encourage tourist trade and generate an extra source of revenue. Many coach tours pass by the factory during the summer months and they might be interested in visiting a factory outlet. It is therefore important that the outlet opens in time to catch this summer's holiday trade, which begins in 8 weeks' time. Following consultations with several building companies, she has been assured that all preparations should be complete within six weeks. Her cash flow estimates are shown in Appendix B. It is hoped that the firm would be able to borrow the extra £400,000 required to build the shop at an interest rate of 6%.

2. An alternative suggestion is to purchase a colour printing machine to enable the firm to start offering design and print services for all orders. This would allow them to introduce a range of more expensive, decorated mugs in addition to their current plain mugs. An independent consultant has worked out the expected cash flows resulting from this investment (see Appendix B), and is keen to point out that the machine could be funded through the firm's current cash surplus.

Appendix A

Selling price	£3
Current sales per month	10,000
Maximum capacity per month	16,000
Variable cost per unit	£2
Fixed costs per month	£5,000
Average cost per unit	£2.50

Appendix B

Factory outlet shop (Project 1) (£s)	Year	New Machine (Project 2) (£s)
(650,000)	0	(250,000)
250,000	1	50,000
250,000	2	75,000
250,000	3	150,000
250,000	4	150,000

Appendix C Table of discount factors

	4%	6%	8%
Year 1	0.96	0.94	0.93
Year 2	0.92	0.89	0.86
Year 3	0.89	0.84	0.79
Year 4	0.86	0.79	0.74
Year 5	0.82	0.75	0.68

Questions (60 marks; 75 minutes)

1. Calculate Cohen's current break-even point, safety margin and monthly profit. (9 marks)
2. Discuss whether Cohen's Ceramics should accept the order from the Cuban government. (15 marks)
3. a) Calculate payback, ARR and NPV for each project. (12 marks)
   b) Using the results of your calculations in part a) and any other information in the case study, evaluate the two possible investment projects. (12 marks)
4. Assess the usefulness of the investment appraisal methods you have used in this situation. (12 marks)

KEY AS ISSUES IN PEOPLE MANAGEMENT

The AQA specification introduces A2 people management by saying:

> *Candidates are expected to gain an understanding of people at work in an integrated context within the organisation and the wider environment. They are required to understand the interrelationships between organisational structure, leadership style and motivation in a business, and to evaluate the implications of these for the effective planning and management of human resources.*
>
> *Management Structure and Organisation, and Motivation are covered in the People in Organisations section of AS Module 2. Both topics are part of the full A Level specification, though no further content need be taught. The topics should be revisited to provide theoretical underpinning to the new material on Communication, Employer/Employee Relations and Human Resource Management.*

It is clear from this that a thorough understanding of the AS content is crucial to this unit of work.

Motivation

You studied motivation theory and motivation in practice at AS level. You should ensure that you have a good understanding of two motivation theories as you prepare for any A2 examination (one should be either Herzberg or Maslow). These may well be helpful when analysing a question relating to staff morale and the performance of the workforce. Your AS work on 'motivation in practice' will help when you consider the A2 material covered in the employee participation unit (Unit 3.5).

Management and leadership styles

You do not need to write in detail about individual management styles at A2. Yet you do need to be able to recognise autocratic or laissez-faire leadership styles within a case study. The leadership style may be a key underlying problem behind a firm's difficulties with employee performance or customer service. Make sure to remind yourself of the main styles:

- Autocratic;
- Paternalistic;
- Democratic;
- Laissez-faire.

Structure

An organisation's structure will have a deep impact upon levels of employee participation, effectiveness of communication and leadership styles. It is therefore important to consider any information relating to an organisation's structure carefully when assessing A2 case studies. Furthermore, it is crucial to consider structure as something which is decided upon by management rather than taken as given. It can therefore be changed, for example by delayering or decentralising.

Good A2 candidates are able to use with ease terms such as span of control, layers of hierarchy, delegation, consultation and decentralisation. To help you, the following are the definitions taken from the *Complete A–Z Business Studies Handbook,* 4th edition, by Lines, Marcousé and Martin (Hodder & Stoughton 2003).

- *Consultation*: asking for the views of those who will be affected by a decision. These views should then be taken into account by the executive responsible for taking the decision.
- *Decentralisation* means devolving power from the head office to the local branches or divisions. This includes passing authority for decision making 'down the line', thereby accepting less uniformity in how things are done.
- *Delegation* means passing authority down the hierarchy.
- *Layers of hierarchy* means the number of ranks within the organisational structure, i.e. the number of different supervisory and management layers between the shop floor and the chief executive.
- *Span of control*: the number of subordinates answerable directly to a manager. It can be described as 'wide' if the manager has many direct subordinates or 'narrow' if there are few.

HRM

HRM is on the A2 specification too, but this time it is being viewed as a strategic function of a business – a carefully considered, all encompassing plan to derive the greatest benefit from the organisation's human resources. HR strategy will be considered in more detail in Unit 3.3.

Culture

An organisation's culture will play a key role in determining its actions. It is therefore crucial to consider what norms of behaviour are indicated within any case study you are given. Now is the time perhaps to go beyond a generic description of cultures as being role or person based and instead be willing to spot different aspects of cultural behaviour, such as whether an organisation tends to embrace or shy away from risk or innovation.

T Test yourself (60 marks)

1. State the five levels of Maslow's hierarchy of needs. (5 marks)
2. Identify three of Herzberg's:
   a) motivators;
   b) hygiene factors. (6 marks)
3. Explain what is meant by the term 'the Hawthorne Effect'. (2 marks)
4. Briefly explain the benefits of using profit sharing as a financial incentive for staff. (3 marks)
5. Explain what is meant by the term quality circle. (3 marks)
6. Outline two possible problems of an autocratic leadership style. (4 marks)
7. Use motivation theory to explain why a democratic leadership style may motivate subordinates. (4 marks)
8. What is meant by the term span of control? (2 marks)
9. What is the effect on chains of command of delayering an organisation's structure? (2 marks)
10. Explain the meaning of the term 'matrix structure'. (3 marks)
11. Identify the four main functions of HRM. (4 marks)
12. Briefly explain why Herzberg felt that training was such an important factor in motivating staff. (4 marks)
13. Identify three possible determinants of an organisation's culture. (3 marks)
14. Briefly explain how effective HRM can improve productivity. (4 marks)
15. Outline one argument for and one against the proposal that effective HRM will increase a firm's costs. (6 marks)
16. Outline why changing an organisation's culture may prove difficult. (5 marks)

COMMUNICATION

Why is communication so important?

Communication within an organisation is vital to ensure operational efficiency. Communication fulfils three key functions within a firm:

1. Passing instructions – orders need to be passed along the chains of command within a hierarchy so that subordinates know what their managers expect them to do.

2. Sharing information – often staff will need to have access to information in order to make effective decisions. It is therefore crucial that communication systems within the organisation allow them to gain access to all the information necessary to make the best informed decision.

3. Discussion leading to decision making – firms that encourage a participative approach to decision making will need to ensure that those involved are given the opportunity to discuss their opinions fully.

In addition to these practical benefits, good internal communication is fundamental to teamwork and to a positive workplace culture. Gossip and rumours can be damaging, especially if they make some staff feel that secrets are being kept from them.

Communication methods

There are countless methods of communication available to organisations. These methods split into two main categories: written and spoken (oral):

Application – Royal Bank of Scotland PLC – communicating with over 100,000 staff

To communicate within such a large organisation, a wide range of methods are used. Arguably the hardest job is to communicate senior management's goals and objectives to the entire workforce. RBS produces regular CDs and videos sent to all staff explaining the organisation's recent successes and key targets. Newsletters are used to inform bank staff of what is going on elsewhere in the organisation. When announcing news of the takeover of NatWest bank, a live video feed was arranged to communicate it to staff and explain its implications as early as possible.

Problems – Barriers to communication

Amongst the major causes of communication problems are:

- Messages passing through too many intermediaries. This is the problem within large hierarchical structures where a message must pass through many different layers. It opens the door to a range of other possible problems.
- Bias in those passing on or receiving the message may mean that the content is subtly changed. Some who receive messages may be too busy, forget, or are unwilling to pass on the message to those for whom it was intended.

Meanwhile cultural factors may decrease the effectiveness of communication within an

Advantages of written methods	Advantages of oral methods
• A permanent record is available which can be used as proof that the communication took place • The record can be referred back to if clarification is needed – especially useful if the information is detailed and complex • Written communication can carry extra formality and is therefore useful in situations such as issuing a final warning or sealing a major contract	• Oral communication methods such as the telephone allow for immediate feedback • Methods such as face-to-face meetings allow for discussion and further questioning – helping to avoid any misunderstandings • Oral communication conveys emotion far more effectively • The informality of oral methods may enrich the communication

organisation. Bureaucratic cultures may expect all communication to be written – thus slowing communication and decision making or reducing the willingness of staff to communicate with each other. Firms with an autocratic approach will find that communication tends to be used simply for passing down orders and therefore any 'bottom-up' communication disappears. This can cause a 'them and us' divide between workers and managers.

Does size matter?

Yes – effective communication is far harder to achieve within a large organisation.

As organisations grow, their structures need to change to cope with more staff. Extra layers need to be added to avoid overlarge spans of control, and, with these extra layers, comes an extra intermediary for much communication to pass through. This in itself is enough to cause communication difficulties. In addition, lower level staff may be less committed to this huge organisation, reducing their receptiveness to communication from 'on high'. It is clear to see why larger firms often suffer poor communication as a major diseconomy of scale.

Growth can often lead to the need for increasingly formalised communication methods, often a switch from informal oral communication to a reliance on written methods. The reduction in informal chats can have a detrimental effect on effective communication within the organisation.

With more staff, the sheer volume of communication can become a problem as key staff suffer from communication overload. They receive more messages than they can cope with in a working day. Certainly many modern managers complain of the terrifying quantity of emails received each day. Important messages can be lost in a mass of irrelevant information.

As many modern firms rely increasingly on a more flexible workforce consisting of part-timers, temporary staff and subcontractors, the communication challenge becomes even tougher. This is where firms are trying to explore new ways of communicating with those who need to know and battling past the quagmire that many corporate email systems have become.

Application – Solving the inbox problem

A radical measure taken by Churchill Insurance Ltd in 2003, following a period of massive organisational growth, was to nominate email-free days. On one day every month the use of email was effectively banned for all but emergency communication. This gave staff the chance to ensure that they went and spoke to people they needed to talk to, along with the opportunity to reduce the size of inboxes.

Information technology has led to a wide range of new communications methods that bring many advantages. Yet there is an old adage that holds true with communication systems – 'if a bad system is computerised, you speed up the mess'. Communication does not 'just happen'. Managers need to think carefully about how to ensure that all necessary information is available to those who need it, while avoiding overload. This is a tough task and if pressures such as growth or a period of bad trading have dominated management thought, communication systems may have been overlooked. This may cause the business to lose efficiency and therefore competitiveness. The key to judging communication is that however good the system may be, if people are not motivated, they will not care enough to listen to or talk with the management.

E Exam Insight

Carefully consider the firm in your case study. When reading the case ask yourself questions such as:
- Has the firm grown rapidly?
- Has this growth been achieved through adding layers of hierarchy or by increased use of temporary staff?
- Has the growth meant geographical communication issues have arisen, such as the need for different branches to communicate, possibly even internationally?

If the answer to any of these questions is yes then the firm needs to consider how its communication systems will evolve to cope. If it is ignoring communication problems, ask yourself what the medium- to long-term effect might be.

T Test yourself (20 marks)

1. Match the right communication method to the right situation:
   a) Issuing a final warning to a poorly performing member of staff;
   b) Confirming a meeting for tomorrow;
   c) Sharing a new corporate policy with all staff.
   Methods:
   i) Company newsletter;
   ii) Formal letter and meeting;
   iii) Email. (3 marks)
2. Analyse the communication problems caused by a UK retailer setting up branches in three major continental capital cities. (8 marks)
3. Discuss the effect of information technology on communication within business. (9 marks)

HUMAN RESOURCE MANAGEMENT

The introduction to HRM covered by the AS course showed the four main HR functions – workforce planning, recruitment, training and appraisal. At A2, the key HR issue to consider is workforce planning. This deals with ensuring that the firm has sufficient staff with the right skills to achieve its objectives.

Strategic human resource management

A strategic approach to HRM requires consideration of HR issues in constructing the firm's future strategy. A clear HR strategy will form a part of the overall plan for achieving the firm's objectives. This will therefore involve a careful identification of the human resources that will be needed to achieve objectives.

A strategic approach to HRM

Corporate objectives
↓
Strategy – including HR requirements
↓
Audit current skills
↓
Find a way to fill the gap – the HR strategy
↓
Undertake training and/or recruitment as appropriate
↓
Monitor success of strategy

To achieve the corporate objectives, the appropriate human resources must be in place to ensure that other elements of the strategy can be implemented. The corporate strategy should enable the identification of the types of skill required in order to pursue that strategy and the number of staff that will be needed with appropriate skills. In other words, HR must get the right people in the right numbers in the right places at the right time.

Once the strategy has been analysed to identify the firm's future HR requirements, an audit can be carried out on the existing staff. This can be used to identify any 'skills gaps'. What skills will be required in the future that are not currently available within the firm? Quite clearly this is no different from Alex Ferguson planning ahead to decide that he will need a new Paul Scholes (Rooney) or a new Giggs (Ronaldo). Yet there are many firms that fail to see that success is all about their people – football managers can teach many business managers a thing or two about that.

Having made key decisions about future needs, an HR strategy can then be devised to fill the skills gap. This will identify how much and what training and recruitment will be needed to provide the firm with the human resources necessary for its corporate strategy to be successfully implemented. Strategic decisions are required within this process, such as whether the business should promote (and train) from within, or appoint from outside.

Though financial performance indicators such as turnover and profit levels may be used in assessing the underlying success of the HR strategy, clearer indicators will be those identified in Unit 3.4 – performance measurement. These will give a truer indication of the extent to which the HR function is maintaining an effective, positive contribution from staff.

Application – Tesco to China

Recognising the huge potential for growth within the Chinese market, several major British firms, including Tesco, are setting up operations in China. In order to operate effectively, they will be seeking to identify senior or middle managers who can speak Mandarin. Even in such a large company, the likelihood of finding sufficient managers to staff a management structure in China is minimal. This means that Tesco will be looking to rapidly recruit Mandarin-speaking managers with the skills to manage the anticipated challenges in the world's biggest business opportunity. Tesco's HR department faces a major task in either recruiting from the UK or China, or – perhaps less likely – training existing managerial staff to speak Mandarin well enough to take on positions from store manager upwards.

Issues involved in implementing the HR strategy

External skills shortages
In any labour market, there are likely to be certain skills that are in short supply. If a firm needs to recruit

staff with those shortage skills they will probably need to devise a particularly attractive salary and benefits package. If the right staff cannot be recruited, the firm may need to invest in training either for existing staff or training up new recruits, perhaps graduates, in the skills that are missing.

Unforeseen circumstances
Even carefully planned strategies may fall victim to unforeseen circumstances. The effects of competitors' actions may require a total rethink of corporate strategy and therefore the HR element within it. For example, if Top Shop decided to offer a free tailoring service to give their clothes a more personal fit, Next would probably have to train its staff to do the same.

People are humans, not machines
Although a strategy may state that staff are expected to move from London to Glasgow in order to avoid the need for extra recruitment, the people involved may be unwilling to cooperate. They may refuse to move their children out of school, or sell up their house to move to Glasgow. Experienced HR managers learn that you have to earn the right to make decisions about people's lives. Consultation helps enormously.

HR strategy can work both ways – don't be shocked to discover firms developing HR plans that involve reducing staffing levels. With an increase in the amount of subcontracting and outsourcing of various business functions, a corporate plan may require an HR strategy that details how the firm will reduce its head count by 25% in 2 years. These strategies will be markedly different in their content, containing sections covering natural wastage, voluntary redundancies, early retirements or compulsory redundancies.

K Key terms

Human Resource strategy – matching staff performance to the medium–long term needs of the business.

Remuneration – all forms of financial reward received from work, including pay, bonuses and fringe benefits.

Workforce planning – identifying how many staff are needed – and with which skills – in order to meet future business objectives.

E Exam Insight

Consider carefully the approach taken by the firm in the case study. Does the evidence suggest that it takes a strategic approach to planning future HR requirements? Or do managers recruit and train on an ad hoc basis (as and when it seems necessary)? The ad hoc approach does not represent a strategic approach and is likely to lead to a blundering from one HR problem to another.

T Test yourself (20 marks)

1. Analyse the likely consequences for JD Wetherspoons of failing to consider HR issues in designing a corporate strategy for rapid growth.   (7 marks)
2. To what extent should a strategic approach to HRM ensure the success of a corporate strategy?   (8 marks)
3. Explain why an effective HR strategy must be closely linked to marketing and operations strategies.   (5 marks)

PERFORMANCE MEASUREMENT

Performance measurement describes attempts to measure employee performance in an objective way. The result should be quantifiable data on employee performance. This information is important within Human Resource Management, as it provides a factual basis for workforce planning. Also policy decisions such as a move to achieve the 'Investors In People' award can be judged to have been successful or otherwise if key performance indicators improve.

Personnel performance indicators

Name and description	Formula	Causes of problems	Consequences of problems
Labour productivity *A measure of how effectively employees produce units of output*	$$\frac{\text{Output per period}}{\text{Average no. of employees per period}}$$	Motivation, management style, hygiene factors, inadequate resources	Increased cost per unit since labour costs are spread over fewer units, leading to a lack of competitiveness
Absenteeism *Indicates how many days' work are missed by staff in a given period*	$$\frac{\text{No. of days' work missed}}{\text{Total possible days worked}} \times 100$$	Illness, including stress and injuries caused by poor health and safety procedures or workplace bullying. Poor relations with boss or co-workers. Low staff motivation	Reduced levels of output. Costs of covering for the absence, possibly using overtime. Effect on culture of increasing levels of absenteeism being seen to be acceptable
Labour turnover *Measures how many staff have left the firm during a time period*	$$\frac{\text{No. of staff who left work}}{\text{Average total staffing level}} \times 100$$	Lack of motivation, which may be caused by cultural, management style or hygiene issues. Hasty or ill-considered recruitment. Inadequate pay or fringe benefits	Extra costs of recruitment and training of new staff, along with disruption to production. Some labour turnover can be beneficial as it can bring new ideas into the business
Accident levels	No. of reported accidents per month or year	Poor health and safety procedures. Outdated or poorly maintained machinery and equipment. Low skill levels or shortage of appropriate training	Staff absence and the resulting loss of production. Possible damages paid. Problems of recruitment if firm gains a poor reputation

A further indicator that is worth remembering is 'natural wastage'. This means the number of staff leaving the business for natural reasons such as retirement, the wish to bring up a young family or the desire to fulfil a new ambition. In some workforces this may be relatively high. For example, many schools have a high proportion of ageing teachers – who will retire at much the same time. In effect, natural wastage forms part of labour turnover. In some cases it will be a major part and in others it will be insignificant compared with the numbers who are leaving due to redundancy or dissatisfaction with the job or management.

Application

Research on labour turnover in the UK

Brunel University Professor Christopher Martin's findings on labour turnover in the 21st century reveal that the UK's average labour turnover rate is around 12.5%. However, in certain types of firm, rates are far higher. He points to the following three categories as being of particular concern:

- Firms that employ highly skilled labour;
- Firms that provide a significant amount of training for their staff;
- Firms in 'high-tech' sectors.

His main advice is to ensure that effective communication helps to build a mission to which all staff can commit.

The ACAS* guide to absence and labour turnover

As part of its role of promoting better employment practices, ACAS produces a range of booklets for firms. The booklet covering absenteeism and labour turnover concludes that these problems are likely to have multiple causes, which include pay, job evaluation, equal opportunities, communication, management skills, discipline, appraisal, planning, maintenance, procedures, working conditions and hours of work. Effective people management must be viewed as a holistic activity – simply looking at one issue or indicator in isolation is unlikely to give meaningful insight.

* Advisory Conciliation and Arbitration Service

It is important to avoid seeing these numbers as an answer. Just as financial ratios indicate further areas for exploration, so the personnel performance indicators simply raise questions. A high level of absenteeism may have a wide range of causes. These need further investigation. Be clear that these numbers ask questions, they do not answer them.

E Exam Insight

If questioned on any one of the personnel performance indicators, start by clearly defining the term being discussed. This is important because many of the causes overlap. If you are writing about poor motivation, the examiner cannot know whether you are really writing about rising labour turnover or falling productivity.

After defining the key term, carefully examine other information in the case to establish the possible causes of any problems within *this* business. You should also be well equipped to suggest ways in which the organisation in the case might deal with the problems.

S Student howler

'Labour turnover has increased by 5% to 40% so this is good for the firm as new staff will bring in new ideas.'

T Test yourself (25 marks)

1. Analyse the data shown below by commenting on the trend, possible effects of and possible causes of each variable: (12 marks)

	This year	Last year	2 years ago
Labour productivity (units per worker per week)	32	32	35
Absenteeism (%)	12	11	10
Labour turnover (%)	23	18	12
Accidents per month	24	18	15

2. Explain why it might be important to distinguish between natural wastage and labour turnover. (5 marks)
3. To what extent can the quality of a firm's people management be measured in a meaningful way? (8 marks)

Themes for evaluation

The key issue behind this unit is the attempt to quantify the HR function. Just as discussed in Unit 1.3 (the marketing model), businesses continually face the question over whether business activity is an art or a science. Personnel performance indicators give objective (scientific) evidence on issues that can seem quite woolly. Many managers only really treat quantifiable issues as important (they like to say that 'measurement is management'). In this context, people management issues may be overlooked unless the tools to quantify them are in use. Personnel performance indicators allow a firm to evaluate its management policies and foster a culture of continuous improvement, not just in the way products are made, but in the way people are managed.

EMPLOYEE PARTICIPATION AND INDUSTRIAL DEMOCRACY

Attempts to stimulate employee involvement in decision making are referred to as employee participation. Industrial democracy seeks to give all staff a say in key decisions within their workplace.

This unit examines both the advantages and drawbacks of various methods of involving people in decision making.

A number of methods exist for encouraging employee participation in decision making, including worker directors, quality circles and the three methods shown in the table below.

Method	Explanation	Benefits	Weaknesses
Works councils	A group that meets regularly, consisting of management and employee representatives. The works council's main role is to act as a forum for consultation as employee representatives are given access to management information and are consulted over matters affecting employees	Provides a regular forum for consultation, ensuring that staff representatives are fully aware of management issues. Can also offer useful insight into staff perceptions of key issues within the firm	No decision-making power; simply a consultation group. Can representatives be truly representative in huge firms? Aren't the worker representatives looking over their shoulder at their own career prospects?
Employee shareholders	Giving employees shares in the business, or offering them the right to buy shares, perhaps at a reduced price. This means that employees have voting rights at the company's AGM	Employees benefit financially from keeping all shareholders happy – this ties the personal objectives of all staff to those of the business. The result may be a greater sense of 'buy-in' to the firm's mission from all staff	Shareholdings tend to be so small that little influence can be exerted. Individuals may feel that their individual performance has little effect on the business, especially if senior managers seem to make the wrong strategic choices. Offering shares in poorly performing firms may seem a way to avoid offering better wages
Autonomous work groups	A system where groups of employees are fully empowered to make decisions within their own working area. The cells within cell production are frequently run as autonomous work groups	Places decision-making power in the hands of those who best understand the local situation Should motivate staff through added responsibility and more interesting work. Decision making should speed up if the group can solve problems without consulting supervisors	Danger that individual groups' decisions may lead to conflicting approaches within the organisation

Application – John Lewis Partnership – A model of participation and democracy

Unusually for such a large firm, the John Lewis Partnership (including Waitrose supermarkets) is a partnership owned by its employees. This sets the tone for the way in which the organisation involves its staff (owners) in decision making. The partnership has a council of 82 members to supervise the overall activities of the organisation. Five of the twelve Board members are elected by the partnership council. Meanwhile, each

Fig. 3.5A: The Dilbert Principle
© United Feature Syndicate, Inc.
Reproduction by permission.

branch has its own council, elected by staff within the branch. Furthermore, each branch has its own internal newsletter in addition to the organisation's newsletter. These newsletters contain, amongst other things, letters from staff who are unhappy about the way the organisation is run. A final method of participation is a system of 'committees for communication'. These are elected by – and consist exclusively of – staff with no management responsibilities.

Teamworking

Organising groups of employees into teams is now relatively common practice in business. Teams will often be given the authority to make decisions over their own area in the workplace – thus involving all of the team in decision making. The benefits of teamwork can be summarised as:

- Meets employees' social needs;
- A team brings more ideas to a problem than an individual;
- Decision-making involvement can meet esteem and self-actualisation needs;
- Being part of a team may reduce absenteeism as staff do not want to let down team-mates;
- Jobs can be rotated within the team to provide a break from routine.

However, there are potential disadvantages to teamworking:

- Some staff may be more comfortable working by themselves;
- Slower members of the team may hold back faster members from their natural work rate;
- Decision making may be slowed by teamworking;
- There may be an increased potential for bullying within the team if weaker members are disliked by most of the rest of the team;

T Test yourself (20 marks)

1. Analyse the possible problems involved in introducing teamwork within a car dealership. (6 marks)
2. To what extent would the setting up of a works council help to overcome poor morale within the workplace? (8 marks)
3. Explain how offering employees a shareholding in a business can raise individual levels of performance. (6 marks)

- Attempting to introduce teamworking in a culture where autocratic managers dominate is likely to fail because managers will be unwilling to delegate the necessary authority to the team.

Meaningful participation
Many firms make plenty of noises about involving their staff in decision making but fail to actually deliver concrete systems for allowing this to happen. Meanwhile organisations without an appropriate culture will never willingly be interested in giving staff their say. If managers are unwilling to take on board and implement ideas from staff, employee ideas will dry up when they realise that the ideas lead to nothing.

Do the benefits outweigh the costs?
Setting up systems for employee involvement can be expensive, with administrative costs being added to training costs. If the costs of setting up the system outweigh the benefits it brings, the value of that project must be questioned. This can be a significant issue given the difficulty involved in quantifying the benefits that stem from employee involvement.

Mission
The methods of involving staff covered in this unit can all contribute to strengthening an organisation's sense of mission – a shared sense of purpose. If employees feel meaningfully involved in the business, they are more likely to commit to the firm.

E Exam Insight

Employee participation lends itself to scoring analytical marks by using motivation theory to explain the benefits. Maslow's hierarchy offers perhaps the most straightforward chain of logic, as teamworking can present opportunities for staff to progress through the three highest levels of need: social needs, esteem needs and self-actualisation.

When writing case studies, examiners often explore the difference between what managers say and what they actually do. Look critically at any manager's boasts about participation or democracy. Some managers pretend to be democratic, but really only involve staff in trivial issues, not the ones that have a real impact on workers' lives.

TRADE UNIONS

A trade union is an organisation formed to represent the views and interests of employees who have paid to become members of the union. Most of Britain's 100 trade unions belong to the Trades Union Congress (TUC), which acts as the voice of the unions in discussion with government. With around 7 million members, the trade union movement is Britain's largest pressure group.

It is often assumed that unions 'cause trouble' for managers and are therefore a bad thing. In fact many of Britain's most successful and productive companies are enthusiastic about the benefits of union membership. The most prominent is Tesco.

Functions of a trade union

Trade unions provide a range of benefits for their members. These include:
- Negotiating with employers on behalf of their members. In this way, bargaining with employers is collective, rather than on an individual basis. This means that a large group of workers have greater power in the bargaining process.
- Providing legal advice and representation for members who are in dispute with an employer over issues such as bullying, unfair dismissal or discrimination.
- Offering services such as low rate personal loans or discounted travel.
- Lobbying government for changes to the law that will help to protect their members.

Application – Santa's trade union

In late 2004, USDAW – the Union of Shop, Distributive and Allied Workers – lobbied MPs to vote in favour of a bill that would bar all but small retailers trading on Christmas Day. They were fighting to ensure that their members working in the retail trade were able to enjoy at least one day with their families during what is otherwise a hectic time in the industry. The Bill was passed in October and celebrated outside Parliament by, amongst others, several USDAW members dressed as Santa Claus.

Key industrial relations terminology

Term	Explanation
Collective bargaining	Employers will deal with employees in groups when negotiating on issues such as pay rises or working conditions. A trade union provides the organisation for these groups of employees and will often conduct negotiations on behalf of its members. This will save time for management since they can negotiate terms for all staff in one set of meetings
Individual bargaining	Employers negotiate with employees on an individual basis. This means that each employee has less power within the negotiations, but the process will take longer for management since each employee will need to be dealt with individually
Industrial action	Workplace action taken by employees to emphasise their determination to achieve their goals in discussion with management
Go slow	A form of industrial action that involves employees performing their jobs as slowly as possible without breaking their contract of employment
Strike	A form of industrial action involving employees withdrawing their labour for a set period of time. A strike is only legal if organised by a trade union that has balloted its members to find a majority in favour of the action
Work to rule	A form of industrial action where employees fulfil only the minimum requirements of their contracts. No extra tasks will be undertaken. This action may often involve an overtime ban, where staff refuse to take on any overtime offered
Union recognition	In order for a trade union to take any lawful action at a workplace the union must be 'recognised' by the business. This is an acceptance that the management is willing to work with the union on behalf of employees

Term	Explanation
Single union agreement	An agreement confirming that an employer is willing to deal with just one trade union in their workplace
No-strike agreement	An agreement whereby a trade union waives its right to strike, usually in return for certain guarantees relating perhaps to consultation and working conditions

The relationship between trade unions and business

Although many years ago trade unions and employers used to be bitter enemies, their relationship has changed significantly. In business today, trade unions generally try to build a positive working relationship with employers. As a stakeholder group, the union is just as interested in the continued success of a business as its shareholders. Therefore, in order to fulfil its major functions, a trade union tries to engage in a dialogue with management about future plans and any current issues that involve its members. Perhaps trade unions' key role is as a communication channel from the workforce to the management. Given that the hugely successful Tesco supports union membership, it is interesting that the troubled Marks & Spencer does not recognise unions. Perhaps that has made it harder for the company to learn from the shop floor about how to overcome its difficulties.

ACAS

The Advisory, Conciliation and Arbitration Service (ACAS) was set up to provide services that allow businesses to avoid or resolve disputes with their staff. In addition to providing information on how best to avoid problems, ACAS may offer to step into a dispute to act as either a conciliator or – if all else fails – as an arbitrator.

Application – Partnerships between unions and employers

The Airbus plant at Broughton in North Wales is an example of where a genuine partnership works well between employers and unions. In the wake of September 11th many aircraft manufacturers laid off hundreds of staff almost overnight. Airbus, however, sat down with union representatives and managed to find ways to reduce costs that did not involve any compulsory redundancies. It is said that relations have gone from strength to strength with trade unions consulted as a matter of routine on any major decisions at the site.

What are this union's aims?

Protection of members' jobs is the fundamental aim of trade unions. If an excessive pay claim may force redundancies, a trade union is unlikely to put these forward. No matter how vehemently a union may push for a significant pay rise, they would be foolish to do so if they thought such a claim would put members' jobs at risk.

What are this management team's attitudes towards the workforce?

A theory X management team that places little value in the skills and experience of the workforce may be less likely to deal positively with a trade union. Industrial relations are likely to be far better where a management team values the contributions that a trade union can make in consultation and workforce participation. This could be said to be a theory Y approach to management.

How powerful is the union?

Low levels of union membership within a workplace will reduce the power of that union. Meanwhile a firm operating at maximum capacity with full order books will be in a relatively weak position when bargaining with unions given the firm's dependence on its workforce's continued cooperation.

K Key terms

Arbitration – making a judgement in order to resolve a dispute. Often two sides in a dispute will legally agree to accept the decision of an independent arbitrator, who will weigh up all the evidence available to decide on the 'right' outcome

Conciliation – the act of attempting to bring together two sides in a dispute. Conciliation may well involve encouraging both sides to moderate their position so that they become close enough to reach a deal

E Exam Insight

A great problem when answering questions about a trade union dealing with a business is to make over-simplistic assumptions. Despite the possibility of certain tension existing, the trade union is likely to have a working relationship with the firm's management. In many cases there will be an excellent relationship allowing both sides to work together to further their particular interests.

T Test yourself (20 marks)

1. Outline two reasons why a firm might choose to recognise a trade union. (4 marks)
2. To what extent do trade unions add to the costs of running a business? (8 marks)
3. Analyse the reasons why both a trade union and an employer may be willing to sign a no-strike agreement. (8 marks)

UNIT 3.7

INTEGRATED PEOPLE MANAGEMENT

The AQA specification states that:

Candidates are expected to gain an understanding of people at work in an integrated context within the organisation and the wider environment. They are required to understand the interrelationships between organisational structure, leadership style and motivation in a business, and to evaluate the implications of these for the effective planning and management of human resources.

Management Structure and Organisation, and Motivation are covered in the People in Organisations section of AS Module 2. Both topics are part of the full A Level specification, though no further content need be taught. The topics should be revisited to provide theoretical underpinning to the new material on Communication, Employer/Employee Relations and Human Resource Management.

It is therefore plain to see that the content covered in this book must be seen as building on the AS material that you studied last year.

A2 People management

A2 is less about managing and motivating individuals, and more about taking a Board of Directors-level view of the systems needed to get the most out of people.

A strategic approach means planning people management in advance – ideally leaving little to chance. This must involve careful use of the HR function. Recruitment and selection must be viewed as critical. Many firms will prefer to recruit the right attitudes rather than necessarily the most skilled staff. In this way they can be sure that all of their people will be likely to adhere to the organisation's sense of mission. Training should be carefully planned, using a formal system of analysis to pick out the skills required and which staff will need to be trained in those skills to fulfil future requirements. The importance of careful workforce planning is not just in ensuring that we have the right number of staff to implement future strategy but that we have staff with suitable skills.

The culture of an organisation can often be defined by how it treats its staff. A firm with a culture that genuinely values the role that its people play in achieving success may well have an HR director on the Board. This would place the HR function at the same level of importance as marketing or finance.

People and growth

The people management issues tackled at A2 have implications for the troubles of a growing business. Growth throws up many people problems for firms, such as how to ensure communication remains effective, how to avoid industrial relations problems and how to maintain employee participation. Of course, some of the people issues covered at AS also present problems when growing – how to design the organisation's structure or how to maintain motivation amongst a growing staff.

Structural change is a primary cause of communication difficulties – with more layers of hierarchy, more intermediaries can delay or disrupt communications. A 'them and us' situation may occur when a divide opens between management and shop floor staff. Each group may see the other as an enemy, rather than everyone working together for the good of the organisation. There are, of course, steps that can be taken to eradicate such a divide, such as encouraging serious industrial democracy and employee participation, or ensuring that all staff share a single status. However, solutions on paper are far easier to state than to implement and this should be understood if you are to show good judgement when tackling these types of question in an exam.

T Test yourself (60 marks)

1. Briefly explain the effect of poor morale on communication. (4 marks)
2. Briefly explain the effect of poor communication on morale. (4 marks)
3. Identify three possible barriers to communication within a small retail outlet. (3 marks)
4. Outline three particular communication issues faced by large organisations. (9 marks)
5. State two reasons why an employer may prefer to use individual bargaining. (2 marks)

6. Briefly explain why an employer might prefer to use collective bargaining. (2 marks)
7. What is meant by the term 'works council'? (3 marks)
8. Using either Mayo or Maslow, explain why teamworking can motivate staff. (4 marks)
9. List three objectives of all trade unions. (3 marks)
10. State three services that trade unions provide to enable them to achieve their objectives. (3 marks)
11. Distinguish between arbitration and conciliation. (3 marks)
12. Identify two benefits to a business of signing a single union agreement. (2 marks)
13. State the formulae used to calculate the following:
    a) labour productivity;
    b) labour turnover;
    c) absenteeism. (6 marks)
14. Briefly explain the link between decreased productivity and decreasing profit margins. (3 marks)
15. State two benefits of having a low labour turnover. (2 marks)
16. Outline two ways in which a high accident rate increases a firm's costs. (4 marks)
17. Identify three possible causes of a low labour turnover. (3 marks)

Room for growth?

Lauren, Claire and Chelsey had been friends since school days so when the three graduated it was no great surprise that they decided to start up a restaurant together. With Lauren's catering skills, Claire's business degree and Chelsey's degree in hospitality management, the three seemed to have the perfect blend of expertise. Indeed, 'Room 1' proved to be a huge success locally, attracting high-income, young trendies to keep returning to the classiest and hippest restaurant for miles around. Two years on, it was a natural progression to open a second restaurant – 'Room 2' – on the other side of London and within months of that a third in Birmingham. Looking back, Lauren had never been too keen to move to Birmingham in order to manage the third restaurant, which made her decision to quit after 6 months unsurprising. Having recruited a new manager for the Birmingham branch, she moved back to London, where, a few days later, the three founders met up for their first proper strategic discussion since the Birmingham restaurant had opened.

The meeting had originally been called to discuss the final plans for restaurants 4, 5 and 6. It now seemed that there were more fundamental questions to be addressed.

Before the meeting, Claire provided data that had been gathered from the three restaurants:

	Room 1		Room 2		Room 3	
	6 months ago	Now	6 months ago	Now	6 months ago	Now
Staff turnover (%)	8	16	20	18	12	12
Absenteeism (%)	2	6	10	12	5	4
Waste levels (%)	18	24	22	25	14	15

She also reported that takings at the first restaurant were down for the last year. This came as a surprise to both Lauren and Chelsey who had heard little news of Room 1 since the expansion had begun. They had both been very busy running their own branches. Lauren had found it especially difficult to sort out some of the staffing issues that Birmingham had faced, and meanwhile Chelsey had had to hire three different head chefs before she was happy with the quality of the food at Room 2. She had, however, had great success in building up a strong customer base; so much so that the restaurant was full each evening. The rapid success of Room 2 had taken Chelsey by surprise and she had found herself waiting tables far more often than she would have liked on busy evenings due to a shortage of properly trained staff.

Claire's other major concern was that fewer suggestions for improvements were being generated than in the early days of Room 1. Staff there had been encouraged to come up with ideas for improvements very successfully during that first year, without the need of rewards or incentives. Yet now, even Room 1 staff seemed less willing to offer their views.

It was clear that there were changes to be made within the organisation, and by the time the three had finished an excellent lunch, they were all convinced that they had failed to manage their people as effectively as possible during the rapid expansion.

Questions (50 marks; 60 minutes)

1. To what extent were the communication problems experienced by the firm unavoidable? (12 marks)
2. a) Analyse the possible effects of the changes to the personnel performance indicators at the first restaurant. (6 marks)
   b) Evaluate the possible steps that the firm might take to improve these figures. (14 marks)
3. Claire is keen to involve staff more in decision making. Suggest and justify an appropriate way to make this happen. (8 marks)
4. To what extent would a more strategic approach to HR issues have helped avoid the problems faced? (10 marks)

KEY AS ISSUES IN OPERATIONS MANAGEMENT

In your study of operations management at AS level you will have come across three key ideas:

1. Productive efficiency;
2. Controlling operations;
3. Lean production.

It would be useful if you were to review these areas to give you a background for your A2 study of this part of the specification.

Productive efficiency

Efficiency is the ability to manufacture products at as high a quality as possible while keeping the costs of production as low as possible.

Economies/diseconomies of scale

You need to consider the effect the size of the business has on its average costs.

Larger firms have advantages called economies of scale which bring their average costs down as a direct result of being able to operate on a large scale. Examples include the ability to invest in newer, more efficient technology and the ability to bulk-buy, cutting variable costs per unit.

However, larger firms also face problems caused directly by their size, known as diseconomies of scale. These factors lead to increased average costs for larger firms, such as the far greater cost of communications in a large business compared with a small one.

Capacity utilisation

All firms have a limit to the amount they can produce. It would be rare for a firm to be working at full capacity. In fact, it is probably unwise to work at full capacity as this would imply the firm had no ability to increase output to meet any sudden surge in demand.

It would not help the firm, though, if it has too much capacity standing idle. The firm's fixed costs would be spread across a limited output, increasing the average cost of production, perhaps to a level where the firm would have difficulty in competing successfully.

If a firm found itself with too much spare capacity, it has two choices:

1. Reduce its capacity so that the amount being produced represents a high level of utilisation;

2. Increase its usage, perhaps by introducing a new product or carrying through an extension strategy on an existing one.

Methods of production

Whether a firm should adopt job, batch or flow production is likely to depend on the type of product and market with which they are involved. Flow production is usually the most productive in terms of the number of items produced per worker, but job production gives a firm more flexibility, as each task can be tailored to meet the specific needs of the customer. Usually, job production is undertaken by firms small enough to cope with one-off orders. Flow production is used mainly by big firms, such as Heinz in the production of baked beans. Batch production comes in between these two extremes.

Controlling operations

Issues such as economies of scale are theoretical. Far more practical are the day-to-day jobs that control how well the operations work.

Stock control

Stock control is important for managing a firm's working capital. If a firm holds too much stock it will have too many of its resources tied up in an unproductive way, limiting the amount of cash available in the business. However, if too little stock is held, then the firm faces the risk of running out of stock and being unable to meet demand.

A firm must be fully aware of the opportunity cost of stock, in terms of both the financial implications and the alternative uses the resources can be put to.

Application – Getting the operations right

In March 2002 Sainsbury's announced that it would boost its operating profit margins by investing in an IT system that would improve its supply and stock management. It hired management consultants Accenture and outsourced much of its stock distribution management to a software company called Manugistics. The software would forecast sales, order stock and send instructions on deliveries to Sainsbury's depots and truck drivers. Chief Executive Peter Davis was right behind this strategy.

By Autumn 2004 Davis had gone and his successor Justin King said that £3 billion had been wasted on IT systems that led to empty shelves. This had been a major factor in the company's continuing loss in market share compared with Tesco.

Quality control

Quality control is the process of ensuring that work done meets a minimum standard. A quality control procedure can either be imposed by using independent inspectors or by building self-checking into the production process.

Motivation theories would suggest that the second of these would be the more effective method. Giving workers the responsibility for the quality of their own work would, for example, fulfil one of Herzberg's motivators. Total quality management involves the creation of a culture in which everyone throughout a firm is responsible for monitoring and maintaining the quality of their own work.

Firms also need a reliable measure of their own quality level. One way to achieve this is to use benchmarks, which allow a firm to compare itself directly with other firms in its industry.

Lean production

Lean production is the collective name for measures that help to reduce waste throughout a business. This can be waste in terms of time, finance or resources.

Cell production

This is where a flow production system is split into a series of self-contained units. It may reduce the volume of production normally associated with flow production, but may be compensated for by improved worker motivation.

Just in time

This is a way of organising production to minimise the level of stocks held. It depends heavily on close links between the producer and its suppliers. Just in time also requires workers to be flexible in their approach to their jobs.

Time-based management

This is a philosophy that believes that time is the key to business success. Producing products as quickly as possible and getting them to the market first may give a firm a key competitive advantage.

Continuous improvement

This is the process of making many small, gradual changes in the way the firm operates, allowing the production process to evolve as and when necessary. The alternative to this is to keep things as they are for months or years, and then to go through a single large and disruptive change.

Continuous improvement depends on workers being involved enough and concerned enough to make suggestions, as well as their having a certain level of skill and technical knowledge to allow them to make appropriate suggestions.

S Student howlers

'Stock control would be better if a just in time system were used.'
'Lean production aims to use the least possible resources.'

T Test yourself (60 marks)

1. Outline the difference between an economy of sale and a diseconomy of scale. (2 marks)
2. A firm currently produces 6,000 units per week. It has a capacity of 9,000 units per week:
   a) What is its capacity utilisation? (2 marks)
   b) State and explain two ways in which this firm's capacity utilisation could be improved. (6 marks)
3. For each of the following scenarios suggest whether job, batch or flow production is likely to be the most appropriate. Explain your answer:
   a) A producer of a one-off special brew to mark a special occasion;
   b) A producer of cans of beer to meet a regular supermarket order;
   c) A producer of a range of barrels of beer to stock a few local pubs. (9 marks)
4. What is the more important to a firm – always meeting customer orders or carrying a minimum amount of stock to keep costs down? (5 marks)
5. How could a firm use IT to improve its stock control? (4 marks)
6. What do you understand by the term 'lean production'? (4 marks)
7. Suggest how time-based management could improve a firm's marketing position. (8 marks)

INDUSTRIAL LOCATION

A location decision will be made on the basis of the balance between the costs and benefits of the alternatives available.

There are two things to consider in making a location decision. Businesses need to consider:

- Quantitative factors – those that can be expressed in numbers, such as financial data;
- Qualitative factors – those dealing with issues such as quality and values.

When considering quantitative factors it is possible to use several of the techniques covered elsewhere in the course, such as break-even analysis (Unit 2.2) or investment appraisal (Unit 2.9).

Location or relocation?

The location decision can be different if a firm is deciding where to set up or is already operating and deciding where to move to.

For the new firm, a location decision may be limited by factors such as:

- The availability of capital;
- The owner's home location and experience;
- The need to be able to build a market.

Firms wishing to relocate may be more concerned with:

- The availability of labour, or the ability of current workers to move;
- The links with suppliers;
- The speed and reliability of transport links, especially for firms operating on a JIT basis;
- The effect, if any, of the move on customers.

E Exam Insight

Examiners in this area are often more concerned with *how* a decision is made than with presenting a scenario and asking you to make a location decision. Make sure you can see which aspects of decision making are the most appropriate in the specific context of the case study you have been given.

Application of location to business contexts

Manufacturing business

For a manufacturing business it is likely that a major consideration will be the costs of production. If a firm's major cost is its raw materials, then the firm will tend to want to be located as close as possible to its suppliers. Firms reliant on labour will be able to move to any part of the world where these labour costs can be reduced. In general, manufacturing firms are more 'footloose' than service businesses. This means that it is easier for managers to uproot the production site and place it elsewhere, as James Dyson did when moving Dyson Cleaner production from Wiltshire to Singapore.

Service business

For a business providing a face-to-face service, access to consumers is a major consideration. Years ago, customers would make an effort to get to a baker or a dry cleaner. Now, if they are not situated at (expensive) sites by train stations it can be hard to get custom. Nevertheless, improvements in information technology mean that some service businesses are able to locate on the basis of cost. The placing of call centres in India is only possible because of the availability of instantaneous communications. Furthermore, an increasing number of retail businesses sell on the internet and therefore can locate anywhere.

The key factors affecting the location decision of:

- *Dyson*, as a manufacturer of high quality household goods: Customers are concerned with a product that works properly and offers good after-sales service if required. The firm is free to locate wherever there is sufficient skilled labour to put together a quality product, and can choose a low cost environment.
- *Amazon*, as an internet retailer of books, DVDs, games, etc.: The key factor here is to be able to supply customers quickly and efficiently. Amazon requires a large area of land to house a vast warehouse system, so needs this to be as cheap as possible, but close to the motorway or rail network so that 24-hour deliveries can be achieved.

- *HSBC*, as a bank giving a degree of personal service to customers: The banking industry has two areas of operation. The most visible is the high street branch, which must be in a convenient location for its customers. However, much of the operation of a bank is concerned with administration, and these administration centres can be located near sources of labour and available office space. Indeed the growth in internet banking may be making the need for location near customers less of a constraint.

Themes for evaluation

When considering a location decision, you must be fully aware of the specific needs of the firm in the case study. What is really important for this business to succeed? What is there in its history, objectives or competitive position that may make it look for one type of location over another?

Above all else, while a firm will always be concerned with controlling its costs, this won't necessarily be the deciding factor. The Body Shop, for example, was famous for always locating its production plants in deprived areas rather than cheap ones.

K Key terms

Qualitative issues – aspects of a location decision dealing with psychological issues, such as the quality of life for workers, the impact on the environment, etc.

Quantitative issues – aspects of a location decision dealing with numbers, particularly costs

S Student howlers

'A location decision will always be made on the basis of which will be the most profitable.'
'For a footloose business it doesn't matter where they are located.'

T Test yourself (36 marks)

1. List four factors that a business might consider in its location decision. (4 marks)
2. What techniques might a business use to make its location decision? (2 marks)
3. Give two quantitative issues a business might consider in its location decision. (2 marks)
4. Give two qualitative issues a business might consider in its location decision. (2 marks)
5. Explain the impact technology might have on a location decision. (6 marks)
6. Why might the government wish to influence business location decisions? (4 marks)
7. How might the government influence business location decisions? (4 marks)
8. How might a relocation decision differ from the location decision of a new firm? (4 marks)
9. To what extent will the right location decision ensure that a service business proves successful? (8 marks)

INTERNATIONAL LOCATION

International location is an important issue in business decision making. Many firms think globally in terms of markets, production or the outsourcing of specific tasks such as call centres.

Britain has always benefited hugely from international investment. American and Japanese firms have often thought of Britain first when locating in Europe. Foreign firms setting up operations in the UK create many thousands of jobs, directly through the people they employ and indirectly through the other firms that service them.

UK firms also benefit from the ability to locate outside the UK, perhaps through cheaper production costs or more efficient production practices.

The advantages to firms of changing their international location are:

1. *They may gain access to international markets*: The European Union, for example, places trade barriers on overseas firms exporting into the area. This is a major reason why firms such as Toyota and Honda set up car production plants within the EU area.

2. *Government grants may be available*: Within the UK up to a third of the set-up costs can be met by grants from the UK government and the EU. With the multi-million pound investment required to set up large production plants, this can represent substantial cost savings for the firm.

3. *Producing and selling within the same market can remove the problems caused by exchange rate movements*: Sony, for example, follows a policy of locating where they can balance their imports and exports. This means that any exchange rate fluctuation, whether up or down, will have its effect cancelled out. This makes it possible for Sony to plan ahead with much more certainty than other firms who can be drastically affected by exchange rate movements.

4. *Some countries can offer much lower production costs*: This is especially true in developing countries such as China, where the cost of labour may be as little as one-twentieth of the pay levels in the developed world. Largely for this reason, companies such as Dyson have moved their production plants from the UK to other countries.

The disadvantages of moving to international locations are:

1. *Language barriers*: Many managers, especially within UK firms, have limited foreign language skills. They are often reliant on their foreign counterparts being able to speak English. This will often create difficulties if the technical nature of the communication is not understood in whole or in part. Communication may also be hindered by the physical distance from one part of the business to the other.

2. *Cultural differences*: The recent series of television adverts for the HSBC bank, under the slogan of 'The World's Local Bank', has highlighted some of the differences that exist in different parts of the world when it comes to interpreting signs and gestures. The colour red, for example, which often signifies danger in the UK, has a much more positive meaning in the Far East. Firms must take such differences into account in planning their operations.

K Key terms

Exchange rates – the price of one country's currency expressed in terms of another

Globalisation – the growing trend for businesses to be acting on a world-wide basis

Trade barriers – measures taken by governments or trading areas to reduce or stop imports from other countries

International location for manufacturing businesses

A manufacturer would consider moving abroad largely on a cost basis. Labour and raw material costs may be significantly lower in other countries. Against this the firm would need to take into account the availability of supplies and any problems associated with the transportation of goods. The Spanish clothing giant Zara, for example, has kept its clothes production in

Europe so that it can respond more quickly to changes in fashion. Marks & Spencer's Far Eastern suppliers need much longer to respond.

International location for service businesses

Service business can be of two types. Some, such as hairdressers, require direct contact with clients, and so must locate near their market. If the contact is less direct, such as through the internet or over the telephone, this constraint no longer applies. BT recently moved its call centre from the UK to India – the service offered is just as immediate, yet the firm believes the cost savings will be major.

Pros and cons of international location

Toyota
- *Pros*: It avoids the trade barriers imposed on Japanese exports by the EU and the US by producing in those economic areas.
- *Cons*: It has had to re-educate overseas workforces to accept the work practices that made the company so successful when it produced in its native Japan.

Nike
- *Pros*: The company has access to a low wage workforce, reducing its production costs.
- *Cons*: The firm has been the target of campaigns against its apparent exploitation of the workers in the developing world where it chose to locate its production.

E Exam insight

Examiners are impressed with students who can focus on business-related issues rather than concentrating on more general issues such as language barriers. Linking a possible move abroad to a firm's strategic objectives will usually give your answer a sufficiently broad perspective to score highly.

S Student howlers

'Firms will sometimes set up factories in developing countries to exploit the workers.'
'Moving your factory abroad will lead to lower costs for the firm.'
'Foreign firms locating in the UK is a bad thing for British businesses.'

International location is a topic that clearly integrates several different areas of the specification. These links can often be brought out to evaluate a discussion on the topic. Such integration can be through:
- *Marketing*: Product quality, a firm's speed of reaction to changing consumer tastes and the potential for a reduction in price could all affect a firm's marketing strategy if it is considering moving its location.
- *Finance*: If a firm is using investment appraisal techniques such as average rate of return or net present value, it will be placing a heavy emphasis on the costs and projected returns from the investment. It will also need to consider such qualitative issues as the effect of the move on product quality, its existing workforce and even the brand loyalty of its consumers who may turn against the company if it makes large numbers of UK workers redundant.
- *People*: Issues such as trade unions and motivation will need to be considered before such a move is made. The task of human resource management will take on a new perspective as the firm attempts to use as effectively as possible workers in different locations around the world.

T Test yourself (40 marks)

1. Explain what is meant by globalisation. (2 marks)
2. Outline two benefits a UK firm may obtain from locating its factory abroad. (4 marks)
3. Outline two benefits a Japanese firm may obtain from locating its factory in the UK. (4 marks)
4. Analyse the case for and against the EU having some trade barriers against the rest of the world. (6 marks)
5. How might a firm set about making the decision to locate abroad? (4 marks)
6. Explain how the growth in home internet access may affect the location of a retail business. (6 marks)
7. How important is location to the success of a business? (6 marks)
8. To what extent can a government influence the location decision of a global company? (8 marks)

PLANNING OPERATION (INCLUDING CRITICAL PATH ANALYSIS)

Planning a project helps to ensure that customer expectations can be met on time and cost effectively. Well-run firms will produce a single, coherent strategic plan. This will point all aspects of the firm's operations, in the same direction.

Planning by itself, however, is insufficient. It must be communicated effectively and implemented accurately by the workforce and their supervisors.

One technique for monitoring and control of an operational plan is critical path analysis.

Critical path analysis

Critical path analysis is a method of planning a complex project. The CPA can also be used to monitor the progress of a project once it is underway. It involves:

1. Breaking the whole project down into a series of activities;
2. Deciding the order in which the activities must take place;
3. Deciding which can be carried out at the same time;
4. Identifying which activities are *critical* for the whole project to finish on time.

A critical path diagram will look something like Figure 4.4A, where each activity in the project is shown by a line, while the circles, usually called nodes, show a point in time. The nodes will contain three numbers, which show the number of the node in sequence on the left of the node, the earliest possible time the next activity can start (called the earliest start time, or EST)

and the last possible moment the previous activity can end if the whole project is not to be delayed (called the latest finishing time, or LFT). See Fig. 4.4B.

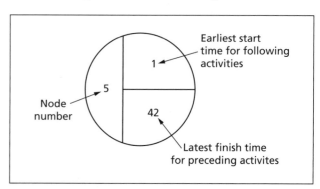

Fig. 4.4B: Diagram of a single node

Rules for drawing a critical path diagram
1. Networks must start and end with a single node.
2. The activity lines must never cross.
3. Don't add any lines that don't represent an activity.
4. Make sure the nodes are large enough to write in all three figures.

Calculations on the critical path
ESTs are calculated from left to right. You must identify any activities that feed into a node from the left and, for each, add together the EST from the previous node and the duration of the activity. From all the activities going into a node, the largest answer you have worked out will give you the EST for the next node, since all the activities have to be completed before any activity following the node can be started.

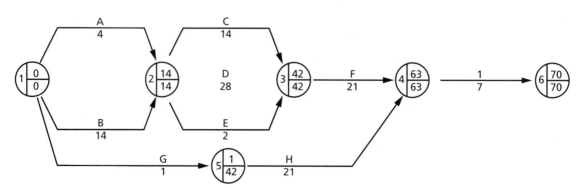

Fig. 4.4A: Critical path analysis

The LFT works the other way, from right to left. This time the duration of an activity is taken away from the LFT on the following node to find the LFT on the preceding node. Again, if there is more than one activity feeding into a node from the right, you must calculate them all. This time you will choose the lowest figure to fill in the node.

The critical path can be identified as the activities which must start and finish at a set moment in time if the whole activity is not to be delayed.

Float

Activities that aren't on the critical path will have some extra time in which they can be completed. This is called the float time. The total float available on an activity is the amount of time that activity can be delayed without causing the whole project to be delayed. It can be calculated by the formula:

$$LFT - duration - EST = total float$$

Note that the LFT will be found in the node at the end of the activity, and the EST will be in the node at the start of the activity.

Pros and cons of critical path analysis

Tesco
- *Pros*: It can assist in the development and building of new stores.
- *Cons*: Main areas of the business, such as the ordering of stock, are done in a routine way and so CPA would not be appropriate.

Nissan
- *Pros*: New product developments could be speeded up so that the firm may be able to implement technological advantages before competitors.
- *Cons*: The scale of the process may lead to the firm adopting tried and trusted methods rather than developing a new CPA for each new development.

Strengths of critical path analysis

- It forces the firm to undertake detailed planning into the timing of activities and their sequencing.
- By identifying activities that can be undertaken simultaneously, it shortens the overall time taken to complete the project.
- The firm will know exactly when resources will be needed, and so can adopt a just in time policy.
- If any part of the project is delayed, the network diagram allows the firm to work out the most appropriate course of action, such as switching staff to concentrate on critical activities.

Limitations of critical path analysis

The diagram is just a starting point for the successful management of the project. It must be clearly communicated to all staff involved and they must be motivated to achieve its outcome.

Some very large projects may be too complex to allow the construction of usable diagrams, although computers may be able to complete the task and allow users to zoom in on various components of the plan.

Critical path analysis emphasises the need for plans to be practical and usable if they are to allow the firm to achieve its operational goals. Ultimately the success of the business does not rest with how good the planning process was, but with how the plan is translated into action by the workforce.

Nevertheless, as *time* becomes more crucial to business success, planning activities through CPA is necessary for success for any firm involved in complex projects.

T Test yourself (40 marks)

1. Explain what is meant by critical path analysis. (3 marks)
2. What do the three figures in a node tell you? (3 marks)
3. How can you identify the critical activities in a project? (2 marks)
4. For each of the following, draw the network diagram, identify the critical path and state the shortest possible time to complete the project:
   a) (6 marks)

Activity	Preceded by	Duration (days)
A	–	3
B	A	4
C	A	2
D	B,C	3

   b) (8 marks)

Activity	Preceded by	Duration (weeks)
A	–	1
B	–	4
C	A	5
D	B,C	2
E	D	3
F	D	3
G	F	4

5. For each activity in questions 4a and 4b that isn't on the critical path, calculate the available float. (3 marks)
6. Give two advantages of using critical path analysis for a firm using lean production techniques. (4 marks)
7. Why might the use of critical path analysis not be appropriate for a firm involved in research and development? (3 marks)
8. Evaluate the statement that 'managers need only concern themselves with critical activities'. (8 marks)

RESEARCH AND DEVELOPMENT

Research and development (R&D) refers to scientific research and technical development. It can be applied either to new products or to new production processes. It means applying science and technology to improve product performance and thereby add value.

By itself R&D is not sufficient to improve the performance of a business. The process of R&D must be followed by innovation to ensure that new findings are translated into practical ideas. There was, for example, little benefit in inventing a new but not very sticky glue, until the 3M Company used the idea to develop the 'Post-It' note.

Many firms see R&D as an essential part of a strategy of keeping one step ahead of the competition. Ideally, the R part (scientific research) will lead to patents that give a supplier 20 years of monopoly rights to a new way of making something. In the cosmetics business, L'Oréal is a huge spender on R&D; in electronics Apple has enjoyed huge success from its R&D spending. Apple's iPod music player has transformed the profitability of the whole business, even encouraging iPod fans to buy Apple computers. By keeping ahead, a firm is able to use a price skimming approach, rather than price on a competitive basis.

Of course some firms will not see R&D as a key part of their strategy. They will prefer to see what developments are being made elsewhere and then either copy or purchase the new technology from the developer. This way may not allow such firms to be market leaders, but will mean that they can maintain a healthy market position.

The process of R&D

There are several ways a firm can undertake its R&D:

1. Market-led R&D: start from market research to find out what the customer wants, then find ways to develop these needs.
2. Product-led R&D: either undertake pure scientific research and then look for ways to use the findings, or look for ways to improve existing products.

Firms that are leaders in the development of new products are likely to use a combination of both to find their new, winning ideas.

Application of research and development to business contexts

Manufacturing business

Large manufacturers see R&D as a way to maintain their market position, but also realise that major market breakthroughs are also usually a result of new technology. For instance, Walls re-introduced adults to the lollipop via the (patented) smooth ice coating on the *Solero* brand. The product has achieved sales worth over £1,000 million worldwide! The importance of R&D has increased in recent years as the rate of development of new technology has increased and product life cycles have shortened. If a firm is not prepared to take on new ideas it may get left behind.

Service business

Service providers also have to keep abreast of new developments. High street banks have had to adapt to customers using telephone and internet banking, both of which entailed huge changes from their normal means of operating. Much R&D spending was needed to ensure systems were efficient, reliable and secure. Nevertheless, for service firms R&D spending is rarely as important as for manufacturers.

Pros and cons of research and development

BMW
- *Pros*: Keep their cars at the forefront of technology, adding to their status.
- *Cons*: A business culture dominated by R&D may mean customers' views (market research) may be undervalued.

Heinz
- *Pros*: New recipes, new packaging ideas and new production methods keep the business at the forefront of the market.
- *Cons*: Little scope for product breakthroughs when customers value traditional Heinz products.

R&D in the UK

UK firms typically spend far less on R&D as a percentage of sales revenue than companies in other leading economies. The average UK figure is 2.3% while in Japan the figure is closer to 5%. This suggests that in the long term UK firms will be less competitive than their foreign rivals.

Analysts who have tried to identify reasons why UK firms are behind their international rivals suggest two main factors:

1. UK firms often adopt short-termist views, particularly as a result of the power of shareholders and their demand for profits.
2. R&D requires a risk-taking culture. Failures must be allowed to happen if R&D is eventually to end in success. Traditionally, UK firms have been risk averse, and mistakes punished. If a firm dismisses a manager responsible for an unsuccessful innovation, other managers will be cautious – timid, even – in future.

Strengths of research and development

R&D's main purpose is to improve the firm's competitive position. If a firm can produce new ideas that meet customer needs or use new production processes to improve the quality of their products, then they will immediately be ahead of their competitors.

Additionally, the long-term consequence of successful R&D is likely to be a reduction in production costs and increases in efficiency. Both of these ought to give a firm cost advantages against rivals and strengthen its market position.

Limitations of research and development

R&D is expensive. There will be no guarantee that the research will produce a successful product, although it is likely that there is a positive correlation – the more a firm spends on R&D, the more likely it is to develop winning ideas.

Themes for evaluation

Not all businesses will be in markets where R&D is essential. The general characteristics of a market where R&D is likely to be needed are:
- The market depends on technology;
- The marketplace has a rapid rate of change;
- There is a high degree of competition.
A firm must balance the overall cost of R&D against the potential benefits it may bring. In an exam, you may have to judge whether a firm is as innovative as it should be.

K Key terms

Competitive position – how well a firm is able to win customers ahead of their rivals

Risk averse – the tendency not to want to take risks

Short-termism – looking at the near future rather than taking a broader view, especially in terms of wanting as large a profit as possible now rather than investing for the future

E Exam Insight

Keep remembering that the 'research' part of R&D is scientific, not market, research. R&D develops products; market research would be needed to test them out.

S Student howlers

'Research and Development involves finding out what your customers want.'
'All firms would benefit from undertaking a programme of R&D.'
'A firm that doesn't undertake R&D will not be competitive.'

T Test yourself (35 marks)

1. Outline the difference between invention and innovation. (2 marks)
2. Distinguish between R&D by product and R&D by process. (2 marks)
3. Explain the difference between R&D and market research. (4 marks)
4. Assess both the likely short-term and long-term effects of UK firms investing less in R&D than their main international rivals. (6 marks)
5. Describe three problems a firm may face as a result of an unsuccessful R&D programme. (6 marks)
6. A firm has developed a successful product from its R&D programme. Discuss whether or not it should it continue with its R&D spending. (8 marks)
7. How far does product innovation guarantee success? (7 marks)
8. 'Process innovation may look good on paper, but in reality it will be too disruptive to the workers to be worthwhile.' Do you agree with this statement? (5 marks)

APPLICATION OF IT

Over the last 10–15 years there has been a rapid growth in the use of IT within business. Thirty years ago the application of IT in a business context was extremely limited; today it can be seen in almost every aspect of business life.

The most obvious forms of IT use in a business are concerned with communication (internet, mobile technology) and in production (robotics, computer controls). However, IT will also have an impact on many aspects of business life, such as accounting (record keeping and analysis), personnel (again, record keeping and the possibility of teleworking) and marketing (consumer databases and the analysis of up-to-date research results).

One specific area in which IT has had a major impact on businesses is in stock control. In a large supermarket such as Tesco, each store keeps a detailed record of the stock being bought by customers through the EPOS (Electronic Point of Sales) equipment, the till. These data are fed directly to the storeroom where the workers know instantly which items of stock need replenishing on the shelves.

The store also knows when they need to re-order material from external suppliers, and IT can help them process requests on a just in time basis so that the new delivery arrives when it is needed.

The sales till will also, through the use of loyalty cards, help the store build up a large database on the buying habits and preferences of each customer, allowing the firm to more precisely target their needs.

Application: I.T. flop at Sainsbury's

Although there are many advantages to the use of IT, it still remains just one tool of business activity. Just having the technology doesn't improve a business. The crucial factor is to use the technology to give your firm a competitive advantage. In 2003 and 2004, Sainsbury's invested £3 billion in improved IT systems, and the net result was worse stock management than before they started. It certainly is not enough to spend money on IT – it has to be spent well and managed effectively.

Using IT to gain a competitive advantage

Firms can develop a competitive advantage in many ways, from the quality of their marketing activities to their ability to react to changing circumstances. IT can help a firm gain a competitive advantage through:

- *Improved efficiency*: Work done with the aid of IT may be more accurate and more consistent. A robotic production line, such as that used by many large car producers, will have fewer errors and therefore less waste, reducing the overall costs of the firm.
- *Improved quality*: The accuracy of IT-controlled robotics will allow products to be more suited to their purpose and so will meet consumer requirements more often.
- *Quicker response time*: If most of a firm's production processes are computer controlled, the speed of response is greater, limited only by the time needed to change a computer program. Land Rover can adapt its production line almost instantaneously to meet the requirements of a particular customer in terms of colour, trim and additional features.
- *After-sales service*: IT allows a firm to keep better data on its sales, spare parts, recurring problems and so on. This allows the firm to serve the specific needs of individual customers.

IT Problems in practice

Using IT can also be a source of problems for a firm. These could be:

- Employees resisting the changes being made. In particular some employees will be scared of the new technology if they don't understand it and aren't familiar with it.
- New technology will bring with it a need for training which could be expensive for the firm in terms of the cost of training, the lost production while staff are training and the potential mistakes as people get used to the new technology.
- New technology can rapidly become out of date. What was 'state of the art' last year is likely to have been superseded this year by newer versions or advances in technology.

- Once firms have purchased their new technology there is a common tendency for them to rely too heavily on it.

By itself, technology does not solve business problems or produce an advantage for any firm. The benefit to a firm can only come through the correct application of IT to each firm in its own particular context.

K Key terms

Competitive advantage – something which allows a firm to compete more effectively in the market

Simultaneous engineering – the process of developing new products where each aspect is undertaken at the same time rather than in sequence

Teleworking – using IT to work from home while still remaining in close contact with the office

Application of IT

Manufacturing business

Manufacturing firms can revolutionise their whole production process by introducing IT. They must, however, be aware of the cost implications of doing so and be very clear as to the reasons why they are investing in it. They must carefully consider the effect on factors such as their capacity utilisation, the quality of their product and their ability to react to changes before making a commitment to the new technology. Most of the US giant motor manufacturers such as Ford and General Motors are buying fewer production robots today than 10 years ago. Humans have proved more flexible.

Service business

Although service businesses are less likely to make use of the production technology and robotics, they could benefit greatly from improvement in areas such as telecommunications, stock control and the ability to be more international in their location decisions.

Pros and cons of IT

Virgin Rail
- *Pros*: IT will allow the firm to keep better control of its network of trains, their location and status, helping them to respond to changing situations more appropriately.
- *Cons*: IT will not prevent issues such as speed limits, closed lines and so on from disrupting the service offered to passengers.

RS McColl (a chain of small newsagents)
- *Pros*: IT allows centralised ordering of newspapers and magazines and can respond instantly if a customer changes their order.
- *Cons*: For small firms it is very difficult to keep up to date with the latest technology and they may find it difficult to integrate their systems with those of their suppliers.

Within the context given, you must try to give a balanced view of the costs and benefits of the new IT. Important questions to ask could be things like:
- How important is it that this firm can respond quickly to changes?
- What will the short- and long-term impacts be on the firm's workforce?
- Will the introduction of IT change a firm's USP?

Morgan Cars, for example, prides itself on the hand-built nature of its cars. If it introduced a fully automated system along the lines used by Nissan, not only would it lose its current USP, but it would also find itself massively outmatched by the scale of production other car manufacturers can use.

E Exam Insight

Examiners like to see students who can keep a mature, balanced perspective in their writing. The use of IT doesn't by itself give a firm success. Used wrongly, it can lead directly to a firm's collapse. IT must be an integral part of a wider business strategy if it is to aid success.

S Student howlers

'The use of IT will always give a firm a significant advantage over its competitors.'
'Robot workers will always be better than humans.'
'IT introduces a greater degree of flexibility into a production line.'

T Test yourself (40 marks)

1. List three ways in which IT can help to improve a flow production system.   (3 marks)
2. List three ways in which IT can help to improve the service provided by a dentist.   (3 marks)
3. Explain both the positive and negative effects new technology may have on a firm's workforce.   (8 marks)
4. Explain how IT might give a firm a competitive advantage over its competitors.   (6 marks)
5. Explain why IT might fail to give a firm a competitive advantage over its competitors.   (6 marks)
6. Explain what is likely to be the impact of investing in new technology on a firm's costs, in both the short and the long term.   (8 marks)
7. What factors ought a firm to consider before investing in new IT-based technology?   (6 marks)

INTEGRATED OPERATIONS MANAGEMENT

The AQA specification for this unit says:

Candidates are expected to gain an understanding of operations management in an integrated context within the organisation and the wider environment ... The material should be related to that of the AS Subject Content, especially the Operations Management section of module 2. Candidates are required to analyse and evaluate the use of different operations management tools to enhance decision making in order to improve efficiency and quality.

As you study the topics within operations management it is important to see that each individual topic is one part of an integrated approach to the management of the business as a whole. A location decision, for example, cannot be taken in isolation from considerations of marketing or personnel.

In the examination paper you will be sitting, you will need to consider operations management issues within the context of a business case study. High marks can only be achieved if your consideration of operations management takes into account the marketing, financial and personnel issues as well.

Your consideration of operations management issues should ultimately centre on how the business can improve the *quality* of its work and its *efficiency* in carrying out its work.

- *Quality* can be thought of as 'fitness for purpose'. Ask yourself whether or not the issue under discussion will enable the firm to best meet its objectives. This will depend on what the firm's objectives are. Is the business attempting to increase its market share, or develop a reputation for innovative products? Is entering an overseas market important to this firm, or is the firm in a difficult enough position to make survival the main objective? In all of these cases, what makes a desirable level of quality will be different.
- *Efficiency* refers to how well a business uses its resources, and can be summed up as getting the most out of the business for putting the least in. There is a direct financial cost in being inefficient – waste, idle machinery and under-employed workers all drain a firm's resources. However, there will often be a financial cost to improving efficiency as well. Better, more up-to-date

machinery may reduce waste, but will require a financial investment. The initial cost will need to be outweighed by the long-term benefits if the investment is to be worthwhile.

The various topics within operations management – planning through critical path analysis, research and development, location decisions and the use of IT – should all be considered in terms of their impact on a firm's quality and efficiency, if meaningful judgements are to be made.

T Test yourself (50 marks)

1. Explain what is meant by Research and Development. (2 marks)
2. Give three examples of recent innovative products. (3 marks)
3. At what point in a product's life cycle should a firm begin developing a replacement? Explain your answer. (3 marks)
4. Explain what is meant by a critical path analysis. (2 marks)
5. Explain what is meant by the term 'float' on a critical path diagram. (2 marks)
6. Explain two ways in which a critical path analysis can help a business improve its efficiency. (4 marks)
7. Explain the difference between the 'Earliest Start Time' and the 'Latest Finishing Time' on a critical path analysis. (4 marks)
8. State three applications of IT within a service business. (3 marks)
9. State two advantages for a manufacturing firm of using IT to control stock levels. (2 marks)
10. Explain one advantage and one disadvantage to a firm of introducing teleworking for staff at its head office. (4 marks)
11. Outline two reasons why using IT may adversely affect communications within a business. (4 marks)
12. State two quantitative techniques for making location decisions. (2 marks)
13. Explain why the government may wish to influence a business location decision. (4 marks)

14. Outline two potential advantages of a UK manufacturer moving its production abroad. (4 marks)
15. Outline two qualitative disadvantages of a UK manufacturer moving its production abroad. (4 marks)
16. State three ways in which a business can measure its efficiency. (3 marks)

Now try the following data response questions. Allow yourself 35 minutes for each set of questions.

Data response: Virgin's tilting trains

Britain's railway tracks do not run straight. Still largely based on the first lines laid down in the 19th century, many tracks, even on mainline routes, follow a weaving path through the countryside.

This is a problem for UK train operators, as the numerous bends reduce the top speeds possible for trains. In an era when cheap air fares and toll motorways offer ever quicker travel, railways need to find a way to compete against the speed of their main rivals.

The solution is not a new one. Trains that are flexible enough to lean into a curve would allow trains to maintain a higher speed. Research into the technology to achieve this was undertaken in the UK in the 1970s, and prototypes were tested in the early 1980s. The early trials, however, were failures. The tilting movement spilt drinks, rolled pens off tables and caused many passengers to feel a kind of sea-sickness.

In September 2004, a new generation of leaning train finally went into service. Sir Richard Branson's Virgin Group introduced the tilting *Pendolino* train on its London to Manchester route. The normal travelling time for this route is 2 hours 20 minutes. The special service put on for the launch of the service made the journey in 1 hour 54 minutes. It is thought unlikely, though, that this time will be met by the new regular service.

Source: *The Independent*, Tuesday 21 September 2004

Questions
1. Explain what is meant by the following terms used in the article:
   i) technology;
   ii) research. (2 marks)
2. Explain how the development of the tilting train is an example of consumer orientation. (4 marks)
3. Outline the main stages that the development of the tilting train is likely to have gone through. (4 marks)
4. 'Research and Development spending guarantees a good return.' Discuss this statement. (10 marks)

5. The development of the leaning train is thought to have cost millions of pounds. To what extent is such spending on product development justifiable? (10 marks)

Data response: The First 'Walkman'?

In 2004, the German inventor who pioneered the technology behind the Sony Walkman won a multi-million pound payout, nearly 30 years after dreaming up his invention.

Andreas Pavel's original 1970s concept of the 'stereobelt' revolutionised portable listening and Sony's version – The Walkman – became a global hit. Now, the 57-year-old stereo enthusiast is threatening to use his payout to sue Apple Computer, whose iPod portable music player is the digital successor to the Walkman.

Sony said the long-running dispute, which has gone on for 25 years, was settled 'in friendly agreement' with Mr Pavel, who applied for a patent in 1977 for a 'portable small component for the hi-fidelity reproduction of recorded sound'. He called it a 'stereophonic production system for personal wear' – shortened to 'stereobelt'. The key idea was that it could be clipped to a belt or handbag, and produce sounds to be played back through headphones.

Though Pavel produced prototypes, none reached the market. Two years later Sony began marketing the Walkman. The payment by Sony, which does not reverse previous court decisions in their favour, follows the death in 1999 of the company's co-founder, Akio Morita, who was often cited as a driving force behind the invention and popularisation of the original cassette-playing Walkman.

Source: *The Independent*, Thursday 3 June 2004

Questions
1. Explain what is meant by the following terms used in the article:
   i) prototype;
   ii) patent. (4 marks)
2. Outline two possible sources of new products for a manufacturing business. (4 marks)
3. Assess whether or not a large manufacturer is able to produce more efficiently than a small manufacturer. (6 marks)
4. How far do you think it is true that a large firm can produce a better quality product than a small one? (6 marks)
5. To what extent is it ethically correct for a large business to develop individuals' innovations into successful products? (10 marks)

KEY AS ISSUES IN EXTERNAL INFLUENCES

In your study of external influences at AS level you will have come across three key ideas:

1. How the economy affects businesses;
2. How the government affects businesses;
3. How society affects businesses.

It would be useful if you were to review these areas to give you a background for your A2 study of this part of the specification.

How the economy affects businesses

The business cycle

This is a regular pattern of fluctuations in demand and output within the economy. Boom periods, when demand is high and unemployment relatively low, are followed by recessions and slumps as demand falls and unemployment begins to increase. Remarkably, the UK economy had no economic downturn between 1992 and 2005; serious recessions occurred in 1980–1982 and 1990–1992.

Within the business cycle the key economic variables are:

- Interest rates – the cost of borrowing money, which is used by the Bank of England as a main tool of economic management. If the general level of prices appears to be rising, the Bank of England is likely to increase interest rates. This reduces the disposable income of everyone who has a loan and encourages people to save instead of spend. So consumer demand falls.
- Exchange rates – the price of one currency expressed in terms of another. The changes in exchange rates will have a direct effect on any firm that trades in other countries or competes against firms from other countries. A strong pound, when one pound buys more of a foreign currency, makes imports cheaper and so benefits a firm buying raw materials from abroad, but disadvantages a UK firm trying to sell abroad.
- Inflation – a sustained rise in the general level of prices and wages due a fall in the value of money. At low levels, the rate of inflation has little effect on firms or households. At high levels (say 8%+ per year) inflation erodes the value of savings but

also reduces the real value of debts. Firms with heavy borrowings will find it easier to repay their debts if inflation has been high for a few years.
- Unemployment – the number of people in the economy who are unable to find jobs. Rising unemployment can start a downward spiral in the state of the economy – as people lose their jobs, demand in the economy will fall causing other firms to shed more workers.

The market and competitors

The way a firm operates will be directly affected by the type of market it is in. A firm with a monopoly position, where it is the largest supplier of a product or service, can act differently from one in a highly competitive market.

Firms with monopoly powers are able to exercise a degree of control over the prices their products are sold for, or the level of supply of the product. They may be able to set up effective barriers that can prevent new firms from being able to enter the market and compete effectively (Microsoft has often been accused of that). By using the benefits of economies of scale a large firm may be able to reduce their prices below the level a new, smaller firm can afford.

How the government affects businesses

Legal constraints

Businesses are directly limited by the laws passed by the governments of both the UK and the European Union. Four key areas of legislation are:

- Health and Safety – looking after the well-being of employees within the workplace;
- Employment protection – looking after the rights of employees in areas such as discrimination, minimum wages, maximum working hours and unfair dismissal;
- Consumer protection – protecting consumers from the unscrupulous actions of some firms, such as selling goods that can harm consumers or that don't do what the business claims they can do;
- Competition legislation – to ensure that markets retain a degree of competition that will ensure a balance between 'fair' prices for consumers and 'fair' profits for businesses.

How society affects businesses

Stakeholding

A stakeholder is anyone who is affected by the operations of the business, whether they are internal to the business, such as managers and employees, or external such as suppliers, bankers or the government.

A key problem for a business is balancing the different needs of each of these stakeholder groups. One view is that since shareholders are the owners of the business, their needs ought to be taken first in any decision. Many others, however, argue that firms need to look more widely than this and try to accommodate the needs of as many stakeholders as possible. They argue that by considering the needs of the local community and consumers, the business may spend more, but benefit from a better public image.

Business ethics

Ethics are the moral issues that underpin decision making. Many business decisions have an ethical dimension that may be considered by managers in making the decision. To many people there is a direct link between ethical decisions and an increase in costs. As with looking after the needs of stakeholders, however, there may be a trade-off between short-term costs and long-term benefits.

Technology

New technological developments will give firms both the opportunity to develop new products or production processes and the threat of being left behind as other firms are able to work more efficiently.

In addition, the introduction of new technology will require careful management. Many employees may be reluctant to adapt to changes in technology. They may resist training on new techniques or be concerned that the new technology may leave them redundant.

T Test yourself (35 marks)

1. Sketch a typical business cycle. (4 marks)
2. Explain why an increase in the exchange rate for the pound against the euro may help a UK firm that imports raw materials. (4 marks)
3. Explain why unemployment and inflation often have an inverse relationship. (4 marks)
4. Analyse the likely impact of a sharp rise in interest rates on a house-building company. (5 marks)
5. In terms of competition law, what do you understand by 'a level playing field'? (3 marks)
6. List three internal stakeholders for a business. (3 marks)
7. List three external stakeholders for a business. (3 marks)
8. Explain the meaning of the term 'business ethics'. (3 marks)
9. Outline two benefits for a firm of new technology. (4 marks)
10. Outline one possible disadvantage of new technology. (2 marks)

STRATEGIC IMPLICATIONS OF THE BUSINESS CYCLE

Introduction to the business cycle

The business cycle is the pattern of ups and downs in the level of demand and output within the economy. Boom periods will be followed by a downturn in demand called a recession. Ultimately this will level off in a slump, followed by an upturn in demand called the recovery, leading back to a boom.

Unusually, the UK economy had no true recession between 1992 and 2005 (with national output falling for two successive quarters). The rate of growth slowed down in 2002 especially, but not sufficiently to cause a sustained rise in unemployment. When the economy is growing, but too slowly to keep people in work, this can be called a 'growth recession'.

The model of the business cycle is a very complex one, and it is important to remember that the shifts in the business cycle will have different effects for all firms. Nevertheless, some general ideas can be put forward.

Although the general pattern of the business cycle is identifiable, and economists try to predict future movements in demand, it is very difficult to say exactly when a slump will become a recovery, or even how deep a recession will fall before it levels off. This is why it is important for firms to be prepared for any possible economic future. There is no excuse for being 'wiped out' by a recession. Good managements have strategies for coping with anything as inevitable as a rocky economic spell.

The impact upon firms

In general terms, the recovery and boom periods should give most firms the opportunity to expand their level of sales, although some firms with a cheaper range of products may find that their existing customers shift demand to more expensive brands.

The likely impact on firms will differ depending on the individual characteristics of each firm. In a recession, the general level of demand for a product is likely to fall. This will not happen to all firms within an industry. Some may have brand names that are trusted and respected by consumers – they may not lose out as the total demand in the market falls. They may even benefit as consumers switch spending from other brands.

If a recession hits the UK next year, it would cause severe problems for:
- Fast-growing firms that had borrowed to finance extra capacity to meet expected extra demand, i.e. highly geared firms;
- Firms selling luxury consumer goods or services – high priced perfumes, sports cars, posh restaurants and top hotels;
- Firms selling investment goods to other firms – lorries, company cars, office space, expensive machinery and equipment.

Income elasticity of demand

One key factor for a firm in a recession is the level of income elasticity of demand. This is the extent to which demand for a product changes as people's income changes. A recession is characterised by falling levels of income as firms cut back on production owing to falling demand. If a firm's products have high income elasticity then it is likely to be hit hard by a recession. Luxury goods or more expensive brands will often fall into this category. The basic necessities of life which are more likely to have a low income elasticity of demand will be in demand even when times are bad.

What other factors are likely to determine how a firm is affected as economic conditions change? The following table highlights some key factors:

Market dominance	Market leaders may be less affected by a downturn than those with a lesser presence
Reliance on the home market	A firm may be able to balance the adverse effects of a recession at home with the positive effects of a strong overseas market
Degree of diversification	Firms with a diverse portfolio of products may survive a general recession more easily than ones with a limited product range
Type of product	Consumers may switch to cheaper products instead of dropping demand altogether. The manufacturers of such products could well benefit in a recession

Strategies to be prepared

For a boom

Booms sound like a time when everything goes well for everyone. Not necessarily. Boom conditions in the world steel industry in 2004 caused steel prices to virtually double. Electrolux found its profits hit by rising production costs on its fridges and washing machines. Nissan suffered because steel shortages forced it to cut car production in Japan in the 2004/05 winter. As part of a cost-cutting programme, Nissan had cut long-standing ties with Japanese steel producers, preferring to look to China. Then, when Nissan wanted more steel from Japan, the suppliers said no.

To be prepared for a boom, a firm should build good relationships with its suppliers, but also its staff. In a boom, jobs are plentiful so good staff will leave unless they have grown loyal to their employer.

For a recession

Every director should know that, one day, a recession will hit. But it may not be for another 5, even 10 years. Yet whenever it happens the firm should be able to cope. The Japanese giant Toyota will cope, as it has more than £5,000 million in cash in its balance sheet. That may be excessive, but a strong liquidity position is a great protection against any shock. So is a gearing level that is modest enough to mean that high loan repayments will not strangle a firm that is going through a bad period. A firm with a strong balance sheet can finance its way out of difficult trading.

Other key strategies for coping with recession include:

- A diversified product portfolio, not reliant solely upon luxury goods or services;
- A human resource strategy based upon three-quarters permanent staff and one-quarter temporary or contract workers. Then the permanent staff can be unaffected, while the flexible staff provide the scope for cost-cutting;
- A flexible production system, capable of switching quickly and efficiently to different, cheaper models or to a different product entirely.

Themes for evaluation

It is important to remember that it isn't possible to identify the current position of an economy on the business cycle. We have reliable data telling us what has happened in the past, but only forecasts for what may happen in the future. Like all forecasts, questions can always be asked about where the forecasts have come from and how reliable they are likely to be. The great economist J.K. Galbraith said: 'There are only two types of [economic] forecasters: those who don't know and those who don't know that they don't know.' So be prepared – always.

T Test yourself (30 marks)

1. What are the four stages of the business cycle? (2 marks)
2. What factors may determine how severely a firm is affected by a recession? (4 marks)
3. What is meant by income elasticity of demand? (4 marks)
4. Why might a firm not change its strategy if a recession is forecast? (4 marks)
5. Is a large or small firm more likely to be adversely affected by a recession? Explain your answer. (4 marks)
6. Why might a firm with a differentiated product portfolio be more likely to survive a recession than a single-product firm? (4 marks)
7. At what point in the trade cycle might it be most appropriate to use a strategy of 'market development'? (4 marks)
8. Does the existence of the business cycle suggest firms should spend more or less on product development? Explain your answer. (4 marks)

INTEREST RATES AND INVESTMENT

Introduction

The interest rate is often defined as the cost of money. It tells a firm how much it has to pay if it wishes to borrow money from banks or other financial institutions. For a business, the interest rate will often have a direct impact on its investment plans.

All businesses will invest from time to time. The setting up of a business will involve the firm in investing in things like premises, machinery and vehicles. Established firms will be investing money in the development of new products or new premises. They may be investing in training for their workforce, or in community projects for their local community.

Interest rates

The price a firm pays for these investments is determined by the prevailing rate of interest. This can be looked at as a straightforward cost, or may be manipulated in a calculation such as net present value (see Unit 2.9, Investment appraisal).

In the UK, interest rates are set by the Monetary Policy Committee of the Bank of England. They have been given the task of managing the economy to meet certain targets for the level of inflation and the growth of the economy. To do this, a monthly meeting is held to consider the level at which the interest rate should be set.

For a business, the decisions of this committee can have far reaching effects. From 1997, when the Bank of England was first given this responsibility by the government, up to 2003, the general trend of interest rate movements was downward. This meant that it was cheaper for firms to borrow money to invest, and as such was a main motivating factor in promoting economic growth.

Between 2003 and early 2005, interest rates moved upwards. The Bank of England was concerned that there was too much demand in the economy and so tried to reduce demand without starting a recession. For firms, it became slightly more expensive to borrow money.

Determinants of investment

It would be too simplistic, though, to say that the rate of interest is the only determinant of the levels of investment. A firm may take into account many other factors, such as:

- *Need*: At times a firm will feel that a new investment is important to achieve its strategic aims despite the cost of doing so. The launch of a successful new product may well be worth more to a firm than the financial cost of making the investment in the first place.
- *Gearing*: A firm's gearing ratio measures how much of its capital employed is provided by long-term loans. A firm may well judge a potential investment on how it impacts their whole financial structure.
- *Investment appraisal*: The various techniques of appraisal, such as payback, average rate of return and net present value, take into account other factors as well as the rate of interest in judging the worth of potential investments.
- *Future expectations*: A firm will judge investments on what it expects to happen to interest rates. If businesses expect interest rates to fall, they will be more likely to invest their money. As well as the specific cost, businesses will also see the movement of the interest rate as an indicator of how the economy is expected to perform. It will affect business confidence.

Effect of interest rate changes

For all businesses, changes in the interest rate affect a firm in two ways:

1. There will be a direct effect on the business, centring around the costs they have to pay for borrowing money;
2. There will also be an effect on the firm's consumers. The majority of people in the economy will find they have less disposable income. They may have more money to pay on mortgages or on other loans, or may be tempted to save more money to earn a higher rate of interest.

For manufacturing businesses there is likely to be a fall in the level of domestic demand for most products. Consumers may switch from expensive brands to cheaper ones rather than stopping purchasing altogether, benefiting some producers. It may be that foreign producers have a competitive edge over domestic producers as their costs may be lower – this could be reflected in the comparative prices.

For service businesses there may be less of a direct effect on demand. Some services, such as banking, involve a continual commitment that wouldn't be easily changed in the short term. Other services are seen by customers as 'little luxuries', such as a visit to the hairdresser's. It may well be that consumers continue to take advantage of these services, even if they are cutting back on spending elsewhere.

Themes for evaluation

The effect of changes in interest rates and their impact on investment will vary dramatically between one business and another. It is important that the effect of changes in interest rates is seen in a wider context of a firm's competitive position and its objectives. These will all help to determine how a firm will act. A firm with a strong market position and strong balance sheet, such as Next, may choose to ignore the effect of a sharp rise in interest rates.

E Exam Insight

Examiners will want to see a balanced approach to your consideration of the effect of interest rates on a firm and its investment plans. It is important that you don't overemphasise one aspect, just because that is the focus of the question you have been asked. Don't ignore the other issues that a real business will consider in making such decisions.

S Student howlers

'A rise in interest rates will stop a firm making new investments.'
'A firm may stop an investment it has made if interest rates go up.'
'An increase in interest rates will increase a firm's gearing ratio.'

T Test yourself (26 marks)

1. List three ways a firm may assess if an investment project is worthwhile. (3 marks)
2. Explain how interest rates are set. (3 marks)
3. What is more important for a firm's investment decision – the current rate of interest or the expected future rate of interest? Explain your answer. (4 marks)
4. In what two ways can a change in interest rates affect a firm? (2 marks)
5. Apart from the rate of interest, give two other factors that will help to determine a firm's level of investment. (2 marks)
6. Why would it be expected for demand to fall as interest rates rise? (4 marks)
7. Explain why some services may prosper even if interest rates increase. (4 marks)
8. What is the likely effect on a firm's gearing ratio of an increase in interest rates? (4 marks)

UNEMPLOYMENT AND INFLATION

Unemployment and inflation are two key measures by which the performance of an economy is measured.

Unemployment is when there are people who are willing and able to work but who cannot find jobs. A government may base its economic strategy around minimising the number of people unemployed as a way of promoting a healthy standard of living across the country. In reality it is unlikely that a situation of zero unemployment would be reached as there will always be people who are moving from one job to another or whose skills are no longer required as the nature of industry changes. Firms should find that workers are available to them when they are needed, but it may be that these workers are in the wrong place, tempting a business to change its location, or have the wrong skills, implying the need for a training programme.

Inflation measures the change in the general level of prices from one year to the next. At present, the government has a set target for inflation of 2% per year. The government believes that if inflation was too high (prices rising too quickly) this would damage many aspects of business, particularly the international competitiveness of UK firms.

The correlation of unemployment and inflation

As a general rule, unemployment and inflation have an inverse relationship. The factors that cause inflation to rise, such as an increase in demand within the economy, will also cause the number of jobs available to rise as firms want more staff to produce more output. So the level of unemployment ought to fall.

Unfortunately this is not a perfect relationship, and it is difficult for firms to use this knowledge to help them plan for the future. A time-lag will exist between a change in one factor, such as a rise in prices, and its impact in the market and on unemployment.

E Exam Insight

Students are inclined to think that 'a recession' means that every aspect of the economy is going badly. In fact, jobs will be lost in a recession, making unemployment rise. The slight consolation is that this should help cut inflation.

The effects of unemployment on businesses

Unemployment affects the workforce available to the firm and the level of demand it receives. If there is a high level of unemployment, there will be more workers available from which to recruit new employees as required. People who wish to work will be willing to accept relatively lower wages, since if they demand too much they can be replaced by others who will work for less.

In the past, high unemployment levels have rarely hit the South-East of England, so it is important to check the local economic conditions. Nationally high unemployment might not matter much to a firm in the South-East. It is important to pick up as many clues as possible about local economic and business conditions.

High levels of unemployment may also reduce the overall level of demand in the economy, perhaps leading firms to reduce output. Again, this conclusion is very generalised. Some products or services will face a fall in demand, while others may be unaffected or even see demand switch to them from other areas.

The effects of inflation on businesses

There are two levels of impact to consider. In times of high inflation, prices and wage levels are usually rising at around the same pace. So consumer demand may be unaffected, except among those (including pensioners) whose income is not based upon rising wages. Despite the relatively low direct impact on living standards, many people look more carefully at prices when they are rising, so firms can suffer from greater price sensitivity on the part of consumers.

Inflation may also affect the firm's running costs. This could be more significant for a firm's competitive position. If one firm receives its supplies from a country with a high level of inflation while its competitors are sourced from another country with lower price rises then the second will find itself in a stronger competitive position.

The main benefit firms receive from inflation is that it reduces the real value of the firms debts.

Themes for evaluation

A business ought to keep a careful watch on economic factors, assess their likely impact and devise appropriate strategic responses. However, economic measures are very generalised. They give a picture of the whole of an economy, whereas a business may be more concerned with conditions in their own market, whether that is considered geographically or by market segment. It is important always to contextualise answers to the specific conditions faced by specific firms in their given circumstances.

K Key terms

Correlation – a measure of how far two factors are connected

Time lag – the difference in time between a cause and an effect. In an economy, there may be as much as 18 months between a change in one factor and its impact in another area

E Exam Insight

You will often be presented with economic data, perhaps in the form of forecasts, within a case study. The examiner will want to see three things:

1. Do you understand the data presented? This goes further than being able to describe the data. How do the different patterns of unemployment and inflation (and perhaps growth and interest rates) fit together? What are they telling you about the economy's position on the business cycle?

2. How will these data affect the firm described in the case study? Which of the economic factors is most important for this specific firm in its specific circumstances? How should the firm deal with the changes it faces in the economy?

3. Do you appreciate the nature of the information? If the data are forecasted, how reliable are they? What source has been used? It is likely that a firm wouldn't use a single forecast alone as the basis for its future business strategy.

S Student howlers

'Since unemployment is rising it will be easier and cheaper for firms to hire new staff.'
'A fall in inflation is a good thing for all businesses.'
'A firm must respond immediately to any change in economic conditions.'

T Test yourself (28 marks)

1. Outline two ways in which increasing inflation may affect a business. (4 marks)
2. Outline two ways in which increasing unemployment may affect a business. (4 marks)
3. Last year inflation was at 2.5%. This year it is at 2.0%. Are prices rising or falling? Explain your answer. (4 marks)
4. The latest figures show an increase in the rate of inflation in the UK. What do you expect to be happening to the level of unemployment in the UK? Explain your answer. (4 marks)
5. Demand in an economy is falling. Would you expect unemployment to be rising or falling? Explain your answer. (4 marks)
6. Demand in an economy is rising. Would you expect inflation to be rising or falling? Explain your answer. (4 marks)
7. Would you expect changes in the UK economy to affect a local sole trader or a multinational company the most? Why? (4 marks)

EXCHANGE RATES AND INTERNATIONAL COMPETITIVENESS

An exchange rate measures the value of one currency in terms of another. It will have a direct impact on any firm that buys or sells goods from abroad. If the £ is rising, each £ will buy more $s or €s, e.g. from £1 = $1.50 to £1 = $1.80. When the £ goes up, UK exporting firms will find it harder to stay competitive and profitable.

Broadly, what happens is that:

	Increase in exchange rate	Decrease in exchange rate
Imports of raw materials	Raw materials will be cheaper, so the firm's costs will fall	Raw materials will be more expensive, so the firm's costs will increase
Exports of finished products	Foreign consumers will find the products more expensive, so demand is likely to fall	Foreign consumers will find the products cheaper, so demand is likely to rise
Imports of competitors' products	Domestic consumers will find foreign products cheaper, so the demand for home produce products may fall	Domestic consumers will find foreign products more expensive, so the demand for home produce products may rise

There are other, more complex, factors that need to be considered.

1. There is a growing trend for UK firms to base their production facilities abroad. Often, the primary reason for this move is financial. Labour and resources are often cheaper and this benefit outweighs the extra transportation costs. Changes in the exchange rate may impact this benefit, but in the short term a firm will have little option but to continue producing there. In effect, firms who make this move are gambling on exchange rates staying favourable.

2. If a firm imports raw materials and exports finished products, a change in the exchange rate may broadly balance out in terms of its overall effect.

3. If the UK enters the common European currency, the euro, then the effect of exchange rate changes will be lessened, particularly for firms whose main areas of trade are within the Eurozone.

Strategy for coping with exchange rate uncertainties

When the £ rose sharply against the dollar in 1980 and again in 1990, many UK exporters were pushed close to bankruptcy. Those who survived resolved never again to be pushed into such a corner. They adopted strategies such as:

*   Diversifying by country, ensuring that production was spread among a number of countries, instead of just one. Honda, for example, has major production plants in Japan, America and Europe. A fall or rise in the yen is therefore a minor matter, because if the yen falls against the $, the $ is rising against the yen, so extra costs in one country are balanced by lower costs in another.
*   Reducing dependence upon one export market. Wedgwood pottery gained over 50% of its export sales from America in 1990, making the high £ a crippling burden. By 2004 it had reduced its dependence to 25%, making the latest rise in the £ against the $ a less serious issue.
*   Selling off subsidiaries that produced price elastic products such as bulk chemicals or white paint. The UK giant ICI sold off most of these businesses, as it knew that currency changes could make production crushingly unprofitable. Today the firm focuses on niche chemical products that can hold their prices on international markets.

International competitiveness

A firm's ability to compete with overseas rivals is known as its international competitiveness. This is affected by the exchange rate, as a high £ will make it tougher for a British firm to compete with foreign companies. There are also other cost factors to consider, especially the productivity levels. British firms' productivity lags behind many in Germany, Japan and – especially – America. This causes labour costs per unit to be higher for British producers – which may encourage some firms to outsource to factories in China or Eastern Europe.

Apart from costs, there are several other factors affecting a firm's international competitiveness. These include:

1. The quality of the product;
2. The image of the product;
3. The existence of a USP;
4. After-sales service.

In short, whether a business is competing in its domestic market or in foreign markets, the basic principles need to be right to give a firm a chance of success.

Nevertheless, competing on the international market does bring its own particular issues. Different markets have different features which the firm needs to consider. HSBC has been running a series of television adverts highlighting the need for understanding local customs and culture. If a firm doesn't understand the market in which it is operating it is unlikely to be successful. Communication problems, because of distance and language issues, can be more acute for a firm trying to operate in overseas markets.

Application – The effect of exchange rate changes

Top Shop – importing clothes
As Top Shop exports virtually nothing but imports nearly everything, a rising £ would boost profits, as it would make the imports cheaper, and therefore lower the retailer's variable costs.

BMW – producing the Mini
Some of the parts for the Mini are imported, but a much more significant part of the output is exported from BMW's Cowley plant in Oxford. Overall, therefore, a higher £ will make the car plant less profitable, as it makes it harder for Minis to be exported profitably.

Themes for evaluation

Firms that are operating in more than one country will have to carefully consider the match between their strategies and the different requirements of each market. The basic principles for competition are same whether they are in the domestic market or across international ones.

The key issue is the increasing complexity of operating in different markets where there are different demands being placed on the firm. Can the firm really manage this increased level of complexity? Do the skills exist within the firm? Is the organisational structure strong enough to cope with the increased stresses?

K Key terms

Eurozone – the group of countries with the European Union that share a common currency – the euro

International competitiveness – the ability to compete profitably with overseas firms.

E Exam Insight

Examiners will be looking for student answers that hold a truly international perspective. They will want to see answers that can balance the differences and similarities between domestic markets and international markets. Why is it that some firms can create international brands while others find it difficult to enter a second market?

S Student howlers

'An increase in exchange rates is a good thing.'
'If a firm has a successful product in the UK it should be able to sell it abroad as well.'

T Test yourself (27 marks)

1. What is meant by international competitiveness? (3 marks)
2. Explain how a UK exporter of goods may be affected by a fall in the value of the pound. (4 marks)
3. If the value of the pound is expected to rise in the long term, will UK firms be more or less likely to move their production abroad? Explain your answer. (4 marks)
4. Outline the factors that might determine if a firm will be able to successfully compete abroad. (6 marks)
5. How far will globalisation benefit all firms who trade abroad? (6 marks)
6. What are the characteristics of a firm that benefits from a decrease in the exchange rate of its domestic currency? (4 marks)

GOVERNMENT POLICIES AFFECTING BUSINESS

Governments attempt to control the economic environment for business in order to meet a range of objectives. They may have targets surrounding the level of unemployment or the rate of inflation. Given the complexity of the business environment, it is sensible to try to simplify the issues involved by taking them individually.

Intervention or laissez-faire

Different governments approach the task of managing a country in different ways. At times, governments feel they need to keep tight control of many aspects of the economy and adopt an interventionist approach. They pass many laws and take direct control of many areas of economic life. On the other hand some governments take a more laissez-faire approach and have less direct control of events. This does not mean, however, that they don't apply policies and measures that shape events.

One area where this is clear has been the growth and decline of nationalisation and its counter-measure, privatisation. Nationalisation occurred when the government identified key industries that it wanted to have direct control over, such as the production of steel, shipbuilding, gas and coal. This control was exercised through the management structures set up, the appointment by the government of key personnel and the setting of targets to match government economic policies. Whatever the benefit of such systems, it came to be seen that such nationalised industries were generally inefficient and expensive.

To counter this, a policy of privatisation was followed. The nationalised industries were returned to the private sector through the selling of shares to re-form them as public limited companies.

Fiscal or monetary policy

Governments have two major types of economic policy that they can use to achieve their objectives: fiscal policy and monetary policy. Fiscal policy works through the government's budget. The government spends money on running its services, and raises money through taxation. By altering its plans the government can affect the level of activity in the

economy. Increasing government spending will increase the demand for goods and services, e.g. giving schools more money to buy textbooks. This should encourage firms to increase their output and so create more economic activity and more jobs. It would be hoped that this will stimulate economic activity and so increase the level of economic growth.

Alternatively, if the government feels that excessive consumer spending threatens an increase in inflation, it can increase taxes to cut into people's spending power. It can increase the amount it raises in tax from businesses through corporation tax or individuals through income tax. The aim would be to reduce the amount of money available for spending, reducing the overall level of demand and so taking some inflationary pressures out of the economy. This is likely to reduce the rate of inflation, but may come at the cost of increasing unemployment.

The government's other major influence on the economy is monetary policy. If a government wants to restrict demand in the economy, it can reduce the money supply which will increase interest rates. This will cut people's spending on credit cards, hire purchase or overdrafts. A 'tight' monetary policy clamps down on credit spending because the interest rate is too high for comfort.

Although governments around the world value their ability to make monetary decisions, in 1997 the Labour Government handed over decisions on interest rates to an independent committee of the Bank of England. The Monetary Policy Committee meets monthly to decide on the interest rate that is compatible with a target inflation rate of about 2%.

If interest rates are increased, people and businesses with loans or mortgages will be paying more in interest. This means they have less disposable income and so demand in the economy is likely to fall, reducing the level of inflation but also increasing unemployment. Conversely, reducing interest rates will allow more spending and create an increase in economic activity.

The effect on businesses

A firm may cut back on its investment plans if it finds that the cost will be too high or if it thinks it will have less disposable income because of tax rises. This may impact on its ability to compete, especially with foreign firms who may not be facing the same economic conditions.

The extent to which a business is affected is likely to be determined by its products' income elasticity of demand. If this is low then a large fall in the general level of people's income will only cause a small change in the demand. On the other hand, if interest rates fall, these firms wouldn't benefit as much as others.

Themes for evaluation

As well as the direct effect on a business, there is a need to take a wide view. This may include:

1. Firms taking into account the expected future interest rates as well as their current level.

2. Firms looking at the economic conditions in relation to their plans, objectives and market conditions. An investment may be expensive, but a firm may still feel that the benefits to be gained outweigh the extra cost.

3. Firms taking a more global view of their situation, and perhaps moving their operations to other countries if they think conditions in the domestic market will not help them.

K Key terms

Inflation – a general rise in the level of prices in an economy

Unemployment – workers in an economy being willing and able to work but not being able to find jobs

E Exam Insight

The difference between an E grade answer and an A grade answer in this area rests upon the ability to relate economic ideas to the circumstances of a particular firm. As elsewhere, application is usually the key skill. The economic policies of the government need to be assessed in combination with the firm's specific objectives and market situation.

S Student howlers

'Multinational companies aren't affected by the policies of government.'
'The government no longer controls the economy because they told the Bank of England to change exchange rates.'

T Test yourself (26 marks)

1. What is meant by fiscal policy? (3 marks)
2. What is meant by monetary policy? (3 marks)
3. Explain the difference between nationalisation and privatisation. (4 marks)
4. What economic conditions might lead a government to increase taxation and reduce its spending? (4 marks)
5. What economic conditions might lead the Bank of England's Monetary Policy Committee to reduce interest rates? (4 marks)
6. Outline two possible effects on a UK business if the government increased the general level of taxation. (4 marks)
7. Outline the effect of a fall in interest rates on a firm whose products have a large income elasticity of demand. (4 marks)

BUSINESS IN EUROPE

The European Union as a single economic body came into being in November 1993 when the 12 member countries signed the Maastricht Treaty. Since then, 13 more countries have joined, including 10 in 2004. These 25 economies operate a single market, allowing many freedoms between the member states.

Economic freedoms within the EU

1. Free movement of capital between companies;
2. Free movement of people to live and work in any EU country;*
3. No tariffs or quotas to restrict trade between firms in EU countries;
4. Working towards common technical standards within every EU country.

* In fact, countries such as Britain and Holland have placed restrictions on free movement of labour from the lower wage East European countries that joined the E.U. in 2004.

Business opportunities

By introducing a single market, it is hoped that efficient businesses will be able to benefit from massive economies of scale. The EU has a population of around 400 million people – larger than that of the United States.

This huge market offers terrific opportunities to innovative or highly efficient firms. L'Oréal has boosted its European market share hugely over the last 10 years from its base in France. For less efficient British firms, there is an increased threat from overseas businesses that are free to enter the UK market.

Part of the purpose of creating a substantial EU market is to attract world-leading firms that might think of individual European economies as too small. Companies such as Toyota, Honda and Samsung have set up factories in Britain as a stepping stone to the EU. Although there are limits on the import of some products from outside the EU, these restrictions don't apply to firms that produce within the EU. This is why many firms from the United States and the Far East have opened production plants within the EU, often choosing the UK.

The extension of the EU in 2004 from 15 to 25 members has opened up even more opportunities for businesses. Many of these new member states are less economically developed than the existing members, but it is expected that membership of the EU will help them to rapidly catch up to their neighbours. In order to do this it is necessary for there to be a huge amount of investment. Tesco, for example, is one of the top 10 overseas investors into Hungary. For manufacturing firms, the relatively low production costs and wages make these new member states an attractive proposition.

Application – More car exports than Japan

A 2005 report by the management consultancy KPMG pointed out that 'We have real strength in the UK (car sector). We have the most diverse manufacturing base in the world. We export more cars than Japan – with the Japanese manufacturers in particular seeing the UK as the best footprint to get into Europe.'

Britain's big 3 car exporters (Nissan, Toyota and BMW Mini) all sell mainly to Europe.

Single currency

The move towards a single market also brought the opportunity for European countries to join a single currency system, known as the Euro. Having a single currency provides transparency as customers can more easily compare prices across national frontiers and buy from the cheapest supplier. Firms benefit because they do not have to pay banks to convert one currency into another and, more importantly, it removes the risks of foreign exchange losses when dealing with another country.

S Student howler

'Because the UK isn't a member of the Euro, firms can't deal directly with other firms in Europe.'

Of the 15 members of the EU when the euro was introduced, three, including the UK, didn't join the single currency. This has implications for UK firms. A Dutch manufacturer knows that supplies bought from France will cost the agreed number of euros. If the Dutch firm buys from the UK, the eventual size of the bill will depend on the value of the £ against the euro on the day the bill is settled. Business is uncertain enough without opting for this extra problem.

Benefits of a single currency for UK firms:
- Trade may be easier and cheaper;
- Financial forecasting may be more certain without exchange rate fluctuations;
- It may encourage a firm to operate in a wider market, benefiting from economies of scale.

Although the benefits of membership are substantial, many feel that staying outside the Eurozone allows the UK government to keep more control over its own economy. Between the euro's launch in 1999 and the time of writing (2005) Britain's economy has enjoyed more favourable conditions than most of the Eurozone.

Limitations of a single currency for UK firms:
- Economic policy decisions may not be the best for UK firms;
- Most UK firms are small service businesses that have no direct trade with overseas; such firms have no wish to spend time and money converting their systems and prices to euros.

European legislation

As a member of the EU, the UK government is required to implement legislation passed by the EU. This can cover all aspects of the law. In terms of business, some of the relevant legislation includes:
- The Social Chapter – this harmonises working conditions in all EU states, such as trade union rights and equal opportunities;
- Works councils – all firms with more than 50 employees are required to set up a works council, a committee of employer and employee representatives which discusses company-wide issues.

K Key terms

Strategy – a medium- to long-term plan for achieving a set objective

Works council – a regular forum for discussion between managers and representatives of workers for looking at the company's plans and ways of improving the work done

Pan-European strategies

Although the EU now forms a single market, different parts still have very different characteristics. The market is fragmented and differentiated. Different firms have adopted different strategies to take advantage of the opportunities offered.

1. Adopt a pan-European marketing strategy – treating the market as a single entity and selling the same product in the same way in all states. Mega-brands, such as Kellogg's and Coca Cola, successfully impose themselves on mass markets without appearing to cater for regional differences.
2. Engage in joint ventures with more local firms. This allows each firm to use its local knowledge and expertise to the benefit of the whole group. This may be done through offering production licences to overseas producers, engaging in a joint venture with other producers or even merging with or taking over other producers.
3. Differentiate the product range to be appropriate for different market conditions, e.g. cosmetics sold in hot countries such as Italy may have different ingredients from cooler countries such as Sweden.

Themes for evaluation

There is a clear need for all firms to balance the opportunities offered by the EU against the threats it brings. A firm needs to look at its operations and resources, its current trading position and its objectives before it is able to decide on its European strategy. A model such as Ansoff's Matrix points out the risks of developing into new markets. Firms such as Marks & Spencer and Tesco have had their fingers burnt when running stores in France.

E Exam Insight

Whenever you are suggesting a strategy for a business an examiner will be keen to see that you can justify your suggestions for a specific firm. This means you need to pull together several strands of the case study, perhaps considering objectives, the competitive position and economic forecasts.

T Test yourself (26 marks)

1. Explain what is meant by a 'single market'. (3 marks)
2. List three features of the European Single Market. (3 marks)
3. How might a UK firm benefit if the country joined the Euro? (4 marks)
4. Give two potential benefits to UK firms of the expansion of members of the EU. (4 marks)
5. What is meant by a pan-European strategy? (4 marks)
6. How else might a firm approach its Europe-wide marketing? (3 marks)
7. Is European legislation more likely to help or hinder UK firms? (5 marks)

SOCIAL RESPONSIBILITIES

Social responsibilities are a firm's duties to its employees, customers, society and the environment. Some firms may accept these responsibilities willingly; others may find them a hindrance.

There are laws that protect these groups from the actions of socially irresponsible businesses. Social responsibility can be seen as how much further than the mere legal requirements the firm is prepared to go.

Social responsibilities or profit?

Some managers feel that their sole objective is to generate profit for the shareholders of the business. This is the approach taken at the electrical retailer Dixons. Anything that doesn't lead to an increase in profit is seen as being against the owners' interests and therefore rejected by managers. Recent years have seen an increase in public discussion about wider responsibilities of business, and some firms say that they put social responsibilities before profit.

Possible reasons for this change have been:
1. The growing wealth of advanced economies allows consumers greater freedom of choice. Amongst other things, consumers now are more likely to ask how products have been made and where the raw materials came from than they were in the past.

2. The growth of global brands has made the marketplace much more competitive. One way of differentiating your product from others, along with product features and price, is how the product was made.

It is argued, though, that accepting social responsibility and working to fulfil wider obligations may not harm a firm's profits in the long run. A firm that does the 'right' thing may lose profit in the first instance, but may find its improved public image may bring future rewards. It may even give the workforce a feel-good factor which may motivate them and develop a greater commitment to the firm. The Coop Bank decided 10 years ago to refuse to do business with firms such as arms manufacturers. Since then, the bank's responsible stance has attracted customers and boosted its profits.

Some commentators would say that there is no choice to be made between social responsibility and profit. They would argue that the choice is between short- and long-term profits.

Social issues

Some of the social issues that have concerned people in recent times are:
- Over-enthusiastic marketing of fatty foods, often targeting children;
- Protecting the environment, such as global warming and deforestation;
- Animal welfare, such as dolphins caught in tuna fishing nets and the use of real fur;
- The exploitation of workers, especially children, in less economically developed countries.

S Student howlers

'A firm need only take ethical decisions if it is going to be caught.'
'A firm will only accept its social responsibilities to give a good public image.'

Social audits

A social audit has been described as the ethical equivalent of the financial audit. An independent group is allowed to investigate the workings of a firm and produce a public report assessing the impact that the firm's actions have on wider society.

A social audit is not a legal requirement, but can be a valuable exercise as it may allow the firm to promote a positive public image that could attract employees, customers and potential investors. If anything is found to be wrong or of concern, then the audit may provide early warning before anything disastrous can happen. For example, a social audit might reveal that the number of workplace accidents in a factory has risen 15% since last year. A responsible manager might investigate, remove the underlying cause, and prevent further (perhaps fatal) accidents from happening.

Just doing a social audit, though, does not necessarily mean that the firm is acting responsibly. The audit needs to be followed up by positive action to improve the firm's activities if they are found wanting at all. If the audit is undertaken just so that the firm can show it has been done, it would be a waste of time, money and effort. Managers must be prepared to take action and put sufficient resources in place to solve any shortcomings the audit may uncover if the whole process is to be worthwhile.

Ethics

Ethics refers to the degree to which a firm considers what is morally right and wrong in its decisions. Almost all decisions have an ethical dimension, but only rarely will the 'right' answer be obvious. Some issues facing businesses today that have large ethical dimensions are:

- Should the production of a UK firm take place in the UK, where the firm pays UK taxes, employs UK workers and provides a direct input to the economic growth of the nation, or should it move production abroad where labour and land may be much cheaper?
- Is it acceptable to continue producing a product such as tobacco that is widely believed to be connected with severe health problems? What about the thousands of people who work in the industry and would lose their jobs if production was stopped? Thousands of investors would lose their money. The product, after all, is still legal.

K | Key terms

Ethics – the notion of there being moral right and wrong in business decisions

Social audits – an independent investigation into how a firm's activities affect wider society

What determines how socially responsible a firm is likely to be?

A firm's acceptance of its social responsibilities will be affected by many factors. The individual views of the owners and managers may impact on the decisions made, as will the nature of the market in which the business operates and its standing within it. The company's objectives may help determine the firm's attitude. If the firm is attempting to make quick profits it is less likely to accept its social responsibilities willingly. On the other hand a firm striving for long-term growth and a dominant market share may well be more prepared to accept its responsibilities to the broader society.

Responsibility or public relations?

One thing that clouds the issue of social responsibility is the way that some businesses appear to accept their responsibilities in order to generate favourable publicity. It can be no coincidence that the firms who shout loudest about their social consciences are firms such as BP and Shell, both of which have many question marks about their business behaviour. One way to judge if a firm is genuinely socially responsible is to examine its record over the longer term.

A firm may wish to consider the impact that accepting social responsibilities may have in both the short and long term. It is likely that short-term costs need to be balanced against long-term gains. How does this match up to the firm's objectives? There will need to be a balance struck between these factors to decide how the firm ought to react. It also shows good judgement to distinguish clearly between ethics and ethical trading. The latter may just be a way of marketing your product in a differentiated manner.

E | Exam Insight

Examiners are aware of the difficulties this topic can pose students, and so will not be looking for a perfect philosophical answer. Instead, they will be impressed by a clear outline of the broad issues, provided it is applied to the specific case study set in the exam. There will be clues in the case as to the important issues – the personal view of a key character or a clear statement of the firm's objectives. Your answer should clearly take account of these factors. This area provides a great deal of scope for evaluation; it is therefore tested very regularly by examiners.

T | Test yourself (26 marks)

1. What is meant by social responsibility? (3 marks)
2. What is meant by ethics? (3 marks)
3. What are the two main purposes of a social audit? (4 marks)
4. Give two arguments for a country like the UK allowing companies to continue the production of fighter aircraft. (4 marks)
5. Give two reasons why firms may be becoming more socially aware. (4 marks)
6. Explain the statement that 'accepting social responsibilities may bring short-term losses but long-term gains'. (4 marks)
7. Give two factors that may determine whether or not a firm will accept its social responsibilities. (4 marks)

THE ENVIRONMENT AND PRESSURE GROUP ACTIVITY

Business activity has an impact on the environment that surrounds it. Increasingly businesses are taking more notice of the effect they have and are trying to minimise any negative impact. Pressure groups are one reason why this issue is becoming more and more important. A pressure group is an organisation formed by a group of people with a common interest who try to put pressure on the government or businesses in an attempt to pursue their goals.

A business will often take environmental issues into account when planning its activities. Issues of concern to the public and the media include:

- Waste and waste disposal;
- Recycling;
- The use and source of energy;
- Emissions into the atmosphere.

It is likely that many businesses will have policy statements covering these areas and may proclaim loudly their commitment to protecting the environment. It is, though, possible that such things come as much for the need for a good public image as from a real commitment.

Application – Tesco, Every Little Helps?

Tesco's website has a substantial section on corporate responsibility. It includes Chief Executive Sir Terry Leahy stating: 'We focus our efforts on practical activities that make a difference, maximising the benefits we bring and minimising any negative impacts.' Local people in Kew, west London, might doubt this. After Tesco converted a small store they had bought into a Tesco Express outlet, locals were shocked to find up to 10 huge lorries a day using a local school bus stop as their unloading bay. Deliveries started at 6 a.m. and went on to 11.00 p.m. The previous store owners had just two deliveries a day, but Tesco's just in time delivery system required far more frequent arrivals. A local resident said that: 'The bus stop has become a truck park in the mornings.'

Environmental audits

Businesses may open up their operations to external scrutiny in the form of environmental audits. These documents will often be used by businesses to highlight how much they have done in this area. Critics will often point out that an environmental audit should be the start of the process, not the end. If carried out thoroughly the audit should highlight areas where improvements are possible and form the basis of an action plan for the business to improve the care it gives the environment.

The benefits to a business of improving in this area are:

1. The effective management of resources can reduce their costs and give the firm a larger profit margin or an improved ability to compete on prices;
2. There may be positive media coverage which could lead to more customers, more motivated workers and interest from potential investors.

There are also some drawbacks, such as:

1. Putting into place measures to reduce pollution or improve energy efficiency can be expensive, especially in the short term;
2. The work done may be seen as the norm rather than anything special, so there may be no extra benefit for the firm directly (although they may not fall further behind their competitors).

There are also benefits to firms operating in the area of environmental protection, a market that has seen tremendous opportunities for growth. Such firms have faced the challenge of maintaining market share during a period of rapid growth and the entrance of many new firms into their market.

K Key term

Environmental audit – an independent check on the levels of pollution, wastage and recycling of a firm

Pressure group activity

Pressure groups operate by trying to persuade decision makers to decide in their favour. These decision makers can vary from the government to local councils or from businesses to their customers. They can aim to:

- Have laws passed that force businesses to act in a certain way;
- Raise public awareness of an issue through the media to bring pressure to bear on firms;
- Influence consumer behaviour, perhaps by organising a boycott of a firm's products.

Businesses will respond to pressure groups only if they feel it is in their interests to do so. A pressure group is more likely to be effective in changing business behaviour if it can attract a large amount of public support, perhaps by obtaining wide-scale media coverage. If successful, the pressure group may have a major impact on business activity, even to the extent of encouraging the firm to change its objectives.

Themes for evaluation

Environmental issues can appear simple, but as the issues are developed complexities may arise. It may help the environment to produce electrical goods that last longer and work more efficiently, but a firm that produced such products may find its available market dwindling as people stop replacing old purchases. Where would this firm's duty lie?

Pressure groups can usually only be effective if they can persuade large numbers of people to support their cause. How possible is this likely to be when the group may be taking on the resources and marketing ability of large, successful multinational companies?

S Student howlers

'Large firms can ignore pressure group activity.'
'Firms will always create waste as part of their production process.'

T Test yourself (31 marks)

1. What is meant by the term pressure group? (3 marks)
2. What is the purpose of a pressure group? (4 marks)
3. What determines the extent to which a pressure group is likely to be successful? (4 marks)
4. What actions by a business might an environmental pressure group be interested in? (4 marks)
5. What might be the benefits for a firm of adopting environmental policies? (4 marks)
6. What might be the costs to a firm of adopting environmental policies? (4 marks)
7. Will all firms involved in the waste disposal industry benefit from the increased concern with environmental issues? Explain your answer. (4 marks)
8. What is the purpose of an environmental audit? (4 marks)

E Exam Insight

It is easy when discussing emotive subjects such as the environment to lose sight of the fact that you are writing a business studies answer. Always try to keep your focus on the case study and its scenario, and apply your thoughts to the business situation described. Dramatic black and white condemnation or praise of a company is rarely appropriate; more commonly the issues involve shades of grey.

INTEGRATED EXTERNAL INFLUENCES

The AQA specification for this unit says:

This module section comprises external business influences which affect decision making and the ability of organisations to meet their objectives. It builds on all the AS Subject Content, especially the External Influences section of AS Module 3.

As you study the topics within external influences it is important to always remember to build your arguments within the context of business studies. Many of the topics in this section touch on other subject areas, such as economics or geography. Take care to restrict your answers to business situations and business theory. No matter how passionately you may feel about, say, the use of animals in product testing, a case study that touches on this area will need approaching from a strictly business point of view. Within that business perspective, though, it is perfectly acceptable to argue on moral or ethical grounds.

The key to producing high quality answers for this part of the course is to identify the connections between the external influences and the firm's objectives and strategies. A firm is very unlikely to be successful if its direction is at odds with the external environment in which it finds itself. Firms pursuing a profit at any cost may find themselves increasingly isolated from their market if more emphasis is placed on issues such as social responsibility, ethics and environmental concerns.

When you are considering economic data in a case study it is important that you can:

1. *Interpret the data accurately*: Beware of mistakes such as muddling a fall in the rate of inflation with falling prices. Similarly, if figures show consumer spending to be rising, but at a slower rate (e.g. 3.5% last year and 3.0% this year), don't describe it as a fall in consumer spending.

2. *Read the data in relation to the business cycle*: An increase in the rate of inflation and a fall in the level of unemployment can usually be taken as a sign that the economy is approaching a boom period in the business cycle. Good candidates would acknowledge this and suggest strategies appropriate to a boom. Weaker answers tackle these two issues in isolation without seeing the bigger picture.

3. *Understand the limitations of the data*: Economic forecasts need to be used carefully since, as with any forecast, they could turn out to be inaccurate. A famous saying is that 'economists have predicted eleven of the last three recessions'.

It is always important to remember that the most significant external influence remains the marketplace. Customers' needs change, their tastes change and the level of competition changes.

Application – Coke's C2 disaster

In early 2004, with the Atkins Diet taken up by more than 20 million Americans, Coca-Cola launched C2 – a low-carb Coke. By the time of the summer sales peak for soft drink sales, the Atkins Diet was becoming less trendy. Not only did this leave Coca-Cola with an embarrassing sales flop, but the effort and marketing spending that was put behind C2 distracted the business from its core brand. Coca-Cola sales fell by 3% and in early 2005 Chief Marketing Officer Javier Benito was fired.

T Test yourself (50 marks)

1. Explain what is meant by the business cycle. (2 marks)
2. What are the four stages of the business cycle? (3 marks)
3. How is the income elasticity of demand for a product calculated? (3 marks)
4. Outline two factors that may determine the extent to which a firm is affected by a recession. (4 marks)
5. What are the four strategic options outlined by Ansoff's Matrix? (4 marks)
6. What is meant by the rate of interest? (2 marks)
7. Who sets the rate of interest in the UK? (2 marks)
8. Apart from the rate of interest, list three other factors a firm may take into account when making an investment decision. (3 marks)

9. Explain the statement 'inflation and unemployment have an inverse correlation'. (3 marks)
10. List four factors that will help to determine how well a firm can compete internationally. (4 marks)
11. Explain what is meant by 'fiscal' policies. (3 marks)
12. Explain two benefits to UK firms of the UK joining the Euro monetary system. (4 marks)
13. What is meant by the term social responsibilities? (2 marks)
14. List four areas in which a business can affect the environment. (4 marks)
15. What is meant by a pressure group? (3 marks)
16. List four factors outside a business that could influence its success. (4 marks)

Now try the following data response questions. Allow yourself 35 minutes for each set of questions.

Data response: An ethical dilemma

In late 2004 a local newspaper ran the tragic story of a local teenager who committed suicide. While this is a sad story and worthy of coverage, it is all too common and would usually have had a limited time within the newspaper. This case, however, turned out to be different.

The police investigation found out that the girl had been reading books on how to kill yourself. The paper began a campaign to make such books harder to obtain. Locally they met with success. Local bookshops and the county library service all readily agreed to remove these books from their shelves.

However, when the paper approached the giant internet book-seller Amazon, they received a different response, highlighting the difficulty with ethical issues.

Amazon believes in supporting freedom of speech, and while very sympathetic towards the girl and her family, the management felt that withdrawing these sorts of books would be counter to their principle of free speech.

One group's view of what is ethically correct seems to be balanced against an alternate, but equally worthwhile view.

Questions

1. Explain what is meant by the following terms used in the article:
   i) ethically correct;
   ii) internet. (6 marks)
2. Explain how the newspaper was acting as a pressure group in this case. (4 marks)
3. Outline the reasons why both firms, the newspaper and Amazon, were acting ethically in this case. (7 marks)
4. To what extent should a firm such as Amazon change their policies on the basis of public opinion? (8 marks)
5. Discuss the view that 'acting ethically would benefit all businesses'. (10 marks)

Data response: easyJet profits rocket

In late 2004 the low-cost airline easyJet unveiled a 21% improvement in annual profits, but at the same time warned that it expected harder times to follow. Despite the company's excellent performance, it remained concerned for the future, owing to a number of factors:

1. There is pressure on the firm's overheads as a result of having to pay 22% more for fuel compared with the preceding year.
2. Increased competition from other firms entering the market. In 2001, there were just seven low-cost operators in Europe. By 2004 this had grown to at least 47.

In response to these pressures, the business has been following a strategy of cost saving through investing in newer, more fuel-efficient aircraft and by withdrawing from poorly performing markets or airports it considers over-priced.

The firm said it believed that these measures had helped it to become more efficient and more able to compete within its own particular market environment.

Source: *Lancashire Evening Post*,
Tuesday 23 November 2004

Questions

1. Explain what is meant by the following terms used in the article:
   i) overheads;
   ii) market environment. (6 marks)
2. Apart from price, explain what other forms of competition easyJet are involved with. (4 marks)
3. Outline the factors that may have caused the large increase in fuel prices. (5 marks)
4. Discuss the extent to which easyJet's strategy matches the external forces acting upon it. (10 marks)
5. 'A firm can either set its objectives, or follow the market. It can't do both.' Discuss this statement. (10 marks)

KEY AS ISSUES IN OBJECTIVES AND STRATEGY

In your study of objectives and strategy at AS level you will have come across three key ideas:

1. Starting a small firm;
2. Business objectives;
3. Business strategy.

Starting a small firm

Different businesses will uncover different needs, problems and opportunities when setting up. The fundamental issues, however, will remain the same. A business will need to:

1. *Identify an opportunity*: The new entrepreneur may start from what seems to be a good idea, but it would be foolhardy to expect a single good idea to lead to a successful business. There will be a need for some market research, however small scale that may be. All businesses need to carefully consider the market they will be entering. In addition, if the business is based on a new or innovative idea, it may be necessary to protect the idea by taking out a copyright or a patent.

2. *Choose an appropriate legal structure*: Most new businesses start out as sole traders by default – it never occurs to the entrepreneur to consider other forms of business. Yet there may be advantages to starting as a partnership or limited company. The legal structure of the firm ought to be considered carefully if the most appropriate form is to be chosen.

3. *Overcome the practical problems*: The main cause of business failure is cash flow problems. A new business needs to plan its finances carefully in terms of both where the initial capital will be coming from and how the firm will be kept liquid. It is usually important that a new firm draws up a business plan to ensure such things are carefully considered before they become a real problem for the firm.

Application: PERATECH and the Eureka Moment

In 1996 research engineer David Lussey discovered a material that could transform itself from a conductor to an insulator and back again, depending on whether or not it was touched. He named the substance Quantum Tunnelling Composite (QTC), but had only the vaguest idea as to what the commercial applications might be. "I didn't realise what I had was special straightaway," says Lussey, "It wasn't so much a eureka moment as a eureka fortnight." He turned to professional design agencies to come up with ideas. The result was more than 80 patents for QTC and a workable manufacturing process. He formed a company called Peratech and soon attracted large investments from venture capital firms.

As at February 2005, the Peratech website boasted innovations based on QTC including:

- Switches that work without sparks (ideal where there is gas or petrol, i.e. dangerously flammable substances)
- 'Wearable electronics' (!), e.g. a jacket with an MP3 player built in, with the buttons built into the sleeves (but they need not be visible); this would have no electric wires
- Cables that act as switches can now be installed as fire alarms that can be pressed in any part of a building (vital where fire risk is high, e.g. a chemicals factory)

All these applications have huge worldwide potential. It is expected that 90% of Peratech's income will come from overseas.

Business objectives

New businesses are often started by people who have an aim (to get rich, perhaps), and have a strategy. Often they lack clear objectives, such as to achieve a 5% share of the local market by the end of the year. Ideally, firms should consider both their short- and long-term objectives. Survival may be the key objective at first, but entrepreneurs should soon have an eye to the future.

The key thing about an objective is that it should drive decision making. In other words, if the objective is to boost market share from 30 to 40%, it might be right to launch a big selling, but low profit margin, product rather than a highly profitable niche product. The same point is true in managing a football club. If the objective is to win the Premiership this year, this might be very expensive to achieve (as Chelsea has found). Yet if that is the objective, it would be absurd for a managing director to try to cut the players' wage bill in order to boost profit. Many students write about different business objectives, yet think that all decisions are based on profit. They are not.

Business strategy

A strategy is a medium- to long-term plan for achieving an objective. A business is more likely to be successful if it is able to plan with a full view and understanding of the market it is in and the competitive forces it faces.

A key method for achieving this is by undertaking a SWOT analysis. If done thoroughly, this will give the firm a clear picture of its internal strengths and weaknesses and its external opportunities and threats. This picture ought to allow the firm to prepare a strategy that is appropriate to all its circumstances and realistic to the position in which it finds itself.

S Student howlers

'If a firm prepares a SWOT analysis it will be successful.'
'All businesses start as a sole trader.'

T Test yourself (26 marks)

1. Give four things that would normally be in a business plan. (4 marks)
2. Explain what is meant by limited liability. (4 marks)
3. Explain the difference between a private limited company and a public limited company. (4 marks)
4. Explain the term liquidity. (3 marks)
5. Give four examples of different stakeholders in a business. (4 marks)
6. What is involved in a SWOT analysis? (4 marks)
7. Explain what is meant by 'patent'. (3 marks)

SWOT analysis of McDonalds UK

STRENGTHS	WEAKNESSES
• Reputation for quick, efficient service and reliable, consistent food • Effective market segmentation, e.g. Happy Meals, burgers, salads • Great locations in High Streets and main roads	• Reputation for high fat and high calorie food • Value added is restricted by the image of mass-produced food and unskilled staff • Weak presence on motorways and in railway stations

OPPORTUNITIES	THREATS
• More segmentation, e.g. a strategic move into vegetarian food • Devise a new product as powerful as the Big Mac or McNuggets • Fight Burger King for all future Motorway Services burger outlets	• Further diet fads as dramatic and as punishing as the 2004 Atkins Diet • Legislation to ban TV advertising aiming fatty foods at kids • Law suits by people blaming McDonalds for their own obesity

CHANGES IN SIZE

One of the toughest challenges facing a business is the management of growth. If a new business survives its first few years, it will find that its circumstances change. A successful business will face the opportunities for developing its operations, but coping with the new situation may be the hardest challenge facing managers.

The problems caused to managers by a growing business can be split into four key areas:

1. Financing growth;
2. The speed of growth;
3. The reorganisation of management;
4. The changing nature of the business.

If a business is to continue being successful, each of these issues will need addressing.

Financing growth

In one sense, the problems of financing growth are similar to the more general issues of financing a firm. There is a wide range of sources of finance available to a firm, whether they are internal or external, short term or long term. It is important that the firm chooses an appropriate source of finance that matches its needs. In other words, long-term capital requirements need long-term financing (a machine with an expected 4-year life should be financed by a 4-year bank loan).

When a firm is growing, it will need to look especially carefully at its capital structure and the level of gearing. Too much borrowing from external sources may force the firm to pay more interest than it can afford and lead to huge capital repayments. On the other hand, too little external finance may leave the firm with insufficient funds to take full advantage of the opportunities available. For example, in January 2005 the 150-year-old Scottish carpetmaker Stoddard went into receivership. Suddenly there was an opportunity for other carpetmakers to buy up the assets, even the brand name, very cheaply. But many of the key UK rivals lacked the finance to be able to do so.

The speed of growth

A firm also needs to carefully manage the speed at which it is growing. Rapid change can take on a life of its own, leaving the firm to establish its own shape almost without guidance from management. Even if it is responding to a sudden opportunity, managers still need to give the firm a clear sense of direction.

Along with the possibility of losing control, rapid growth has severe implications for a firm's financial position. A firm runs the risk of overtrading, which occurs when a firm expands without the long-term finance it needs. This brings pressure on to the firm's short-term cash position as well, as there will be a need for more and more cash to pay the current liabilities of the firm.

Source of finance	Internal	External	Short term	Long term
Sales of assets	X		X	
Cash flow management	X		X	
Retained profit	X			X
Trade credit		X	X	
Bank overdraft		X	X	
Leasing		X		X
Factoring		X	X	
Loans		X		X
Shares		X		X
Debentures		X		X
Venture capital		X		X

The reorganisation of management

As a firm grows it may well have to change the way it organises its management. A sole trader, for example, may have grown used to being involved in every decision made in the firm. This becomes less possible as the firm grows, so the entrepreneur has to adopt a degree of delegation, thereby relinquishing some control.

The growing firm is more likely to suffer from the problems caused by diseconomies of scale. These are the factors that cause the cost per unit of the firm to rise as the firm grows. The main factors are:

- Poorer communication – due to the increased number of workers, greater distance between different levels and the increasing use of communication methods other than face to face.
- Weaker coordination – as more and more people are given the authority to make decisions there is a growing risk of different directions being taken by different decision makers.
- Weaker motivation – as more people are brought into the business there is a greater chance that they will be just doing a job, rather than committing themselves to the mission of the firm.

The changing nature of the business

As firms grow they are likely to change their legal status. A sole trader may take on a partner, or a private limited company may go public. Each change of this nature brings a different set of pressures and expectations on a business. Limited companies have to abide by much more legislation than a sole trader business, and the change in ownership from personal to shareholders can effectively change the whole direction of the business. Entrepreneurs have to be prepared for such changes and be willing to accept them if the business is to continue being successful.

Application – Triumph at Tesco

For the retailer that was once in awe of Sainsbury, Tesco has come a long way. In 2005 its share of the UK grocery market is likely to reach 30% – nearly double that of Sainsbury. And its £2 billion profit will be a record for any UK retailer.

Although its very size is attracting more criticism, Tesco has shown that rapid, persistent growth can be achieved successfully. It once flopped in France, but has since achieved great success in Eastern Europe and South East Asia, in addition to its UK domination. Good financial, people and operations management have been at the heart of this.

K Key term

Overtrading – allowing sales growth to outstrip the firm's financial resources, putting working capital and cash flow under severe strain

Allowing a firm to grow in size is an important step in the development of any firm. It is possible that such growth can happen without real planning – opportunities arise to which a business may respond without looking at the longer term implications for the business or the interests of the owner.

Often an entrepreneur will find that s/he loses control of the business as a result of it being too successful. This is especially true for entrepreneurs who find it difficult to adapt to or even accept their own changing role. Failed growth may often be due to owners not changing their own management style to fit their new circumstances.

E Exam Insight

Case studies will often highlight the personal characteristics of managers or entrepreneurs to provide clues as to why things may be going wrong with their seemingly successful business. It is important that there is a suitable match made between the firm's situation and the management style and organisational structure to be adopted.

S Student howlers

'A firm should never borrow money to finance an expansion.'
'Larger firms will always be more efficient than smaller ones.'

T Test yourself (20 marks)

1. List four problems that could arise for a growing business. (4 marks)
2. Give two internal sources of funds for financing growth. (2 marks)
3. Give two external sources of funds for financing growth. (2 marks)
4. Give two short-term sources of funds for financing growth. (2 marks)
5. Give two long-term sources of funds for financing growth. (2 marks)
6. Explain what is meant by overtrading. (3 marks)
7. Explain what is meant by diseconomies of scale. (3 marks)
8. Give two examples of diseconomies of scale. (2 marks)

CHANGES IN OWNERSHIP

During its life a business will often change hands as a result of either internal or external decisions. Woolworths was divested from Kingfisher, i.e. floated onto the stock market, as a separate business. This was an internal decision. Other changes in ownership come about as the result of competitive decisions, such as the 2004 purchase of Safeway Stores by Morrison's. Two firms may merge, or one may take over another, as a means of improving its position in the market.

Takeovers and mergers are two ways in which different firms can get together to become a single enterprise. A merger involves an agreement between both firms to come together under a single board of directors. Usually, the two firms will be of a similar size. A takeover involves one firm obtaining at least 50% of the shares in the other business, thereby allowing them to control it and run it as they wish. The new owners may leave the existing managers to get on with things as they always have, though it is more common that new owners bring in a new management team.

The case for corporate integration is usually based on synergy, i.e. that the two firms will be more successful together than alone. Certain benefits are easy to identify, such as greater bulk-buying bargaining power, e.g. if Next bought Top Shop.

Over many years, research has consistently found that most takeovers are financial and economic failures, i.e. combining two firms leads to lower growth and profit prospects for the two together rather than the two separately. Why, therefore, do mergers and takeovers have waves of corporate popularity? Partly it is because successful bosses have the arrogance to believe that they will succeed where others have failed. It is also because it is easy to identify synergies – especially cost savings – but much harder to anticipate the problems of combining two distinct corporate cultures.

▎Forms of integration

Whether the firms are integrating through a takeover or a merger, there are four forms of integration that can happen, depending on the place each business has in the chain of production (Fig. 6.3A).

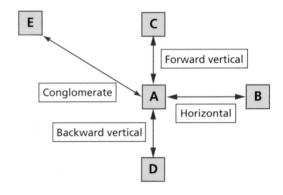

Fig. 6.3A: Forms of integration

Horizontal integration

Horizontal integration (Fig. 6.3A, A–B) is when the two firms that are getting together operate at the same stage of the production process. They are likely to be competitors although they could be separated geographically. The key benefit is likely to be that the new firm will immediately acquire a larger market share. The new, larger firm will probably be able to take advantage of economies of scale. On the other hand there may well be problems as the two firms will have different way of operating. Integrating the two systems may cause resentment at the changes, especially if it causes redundancies.

Application – at the Last Minute

Internet retailer Lastminute.com carried out a series of acquisitions between 2000 and 2004. It began by buying a French internet site for over £50 million. City analysts suggested that this would help Lastminute make its first operating profit within 6 months. It went on to buy 'Destination', 'Travel Price', 'First Option' and its German sister 'Lastminute.de', plus many other companies. Then, in 2004, it blamed its poor profit performance on problems in integrating all these companies! For shareholders, it must have seemed like the last straw.

Forward vertical integration

Forward vertical integration (Fig. 6.3A, A–C) is when one firm integrates with another that is further on in the production process. A manufacturer may join with a retail outlet. This is likely to give the producer more control over how its products reach the customer and this control may give the firm an advantage over other producers. However, this could cause resentment amongst customers who dislike outlets that are dominated by one firm's products and it may cause complacency that could lead to inefficiency.

Backward vertical integration

Backward vertical integration (Fig. 6.3A, A–D) is when one firm integrates with another that is earlier on in the production process. A manufacturer may join with a supplier of raw materials or components. This is likely to give the producer more control over the quality and quantity of supplies and, especially if just in time is being used, over delivery schedules. It does, however, keep the firm dependent on this one industry. Also, the modern trend for firms is to 'outsource', i.e. buy supplies or services from outside the business to keep the management focused on the core tasks. Backward vertical integration is therefore currently out of fashion.

Conglomerate or diversifying integration

Conglomerate or diversifying integration (Fig. 6.3A, A–E) is when the integration occurs between two firms with no clear connection. This may be a strategy used to spread risk and increase a firm's overall profit potential. Although the objective is to spread risk, Ansoff's Matrix points out that diversifying is the riskiest business strategy.

A further spur to conglomerate integration is the attempt by a mature company to buy growth prospects. – in effect, to buy a rising star to set alongside its own cash cows. Whitbread did this successfully when buying the David Lloyd health club chain.

E Exam Insight

Examiners will always be keen to see that you can develop a balanced argument for and against any proposed strategy of integration.

Management buyouts

Another way in which the ownership of a business can change is through a management buyout. This is when the managers of a business buy sufficient shares to become the majority owners and hence have control of the business. Management buyouts often happen when a firm is struggling, or when a large company feels that one part or division of the business is holding the others back.

Managers often believe that they have the knowledge and expertise to improve operational performance, and that holding a significant stake in the fortunes of the business will help to motivate and focus their decisions. However, management buyouts are often starting from a disadvantageous position if the firm or division is struggling, and it may be difficult for the managers to obtain sufficient finance

to avoid problems of excessive gearing. The buy-out of the Allders retail chain led to its 2005 collapse for just this reason.

There are no certainties in business. It is important to always consider both sides of a proposed integration or change in ownership of a business. Important questions could be asked such as: Will the cultures of the two businesses be compatible? Are the management styles similar, or will the integration involve significant changes for one of the two businesses?

Generally, the merger of the two weak businesses rarely works.

K Key terms

Acquisition – to purchase, e.g. Morrison's acquired Safeway

Integration – to bring together, either through merger or takeover

Synergy – that the whole is greater than the sum of the parts, e.g. that 2 + 2 = 5; this is the justification for most takeovers, though research shows it is very hard to achieve

S Student howlers

'Bigger firms will always perform better than smaller ones.'
'Conglomerate integration will spread a firm's risks and so make them safer.'

T Test yourself (19 marks)

1. Explain the difference between a takeover and a merger. (4 marks)
2. In what four ways can a firm integrate with other firms? (4 marks)
3. The following are examples of what forms of integration?
   i) a jeweller integrating with a gold mine; (1 mark)
   ii) a brewery integrating with a chain of pubs; (1 mark)
   iii) a football club integrating with a television company; (1 mark)
   iv) a mobile phone network in the UK integrating with a German mobile phone network. (1 mark)
4. What do managers need to do to effect a management buyout? (3 marks)
5. What are likely to be the two main problems facing a management buyout? (4 marks)

AIMS, MISSION AND CULTURE

Aims

An aim is the long-term ambition of the business, stated in general terms. It is often used to create a common vision which everyone in the organisation should target. If this vision is inspirational, it can turn the aim into a mission. For example, people working for Innocent Drinks (makers of fresh fruit 'smoothies') are genuinely passionate about the aim of the business which is 'doing good things'. They are proud of the product and proud of the firm's social and environmental work among their suppliers in developing countries. A sense of mission can add motivation to staff and create a positive, 'can-do' culture.

Corporate aims ought to give a clear direction to a business in the long term. They provide the framework upon which objectives can be set. The strategies of the firm can then be constructed with the objectives clearly in mind. The aim ought also to help build team spirit, encourage commitment to the organisation and cooperation within it. This will particularly be the case if the aim is agreed by all people within the organisation, rather than it being imposed from the top down. Many motivation theorists will point to involvement as being central to being motivated.

Application to Tamara – an 18-year-old A-Level student

- Aim: To get rich
- Objective: First £250,000 in the bank by 25
- Strategy: Start own business at 18; keep reinvesting profits to build it up, then sell it; go to Uni at 25 ('in my Merc')

Mission

The mission may be written in the form of a mission statement which must then be communicated to staff (in some firms it's a poster on the wall in every room). This may work well, but if the workplace culture is sceptical or suspicious of management, it may mean nothing.

Some mission statements used by world famous companies are:

Firm	Mission
The Body Shop	Tirelessly work to narrow the gap between principle and practice, whilst making fun, passion and care part of our daily lives
Coca-Cola	Our mission is to get more people to drink Coke than water
Pret a Manger	Our mission is to sell handmade extremely fresh food
Unilever	Raise the quality of life

Source: *Business Studies*, 2nd edition, edited by Ian Marcousé (Hodder & Stoughton 2003)

A mission statement will often be put together by a firm with the best of intentions. In many firms, though, it will have little practical use. It is unlikely that it will be used as a practical means of assessing potential decisions for the day-to-day running of the business. Nevertheless, if the mission really means something at Innocent Drinks, a manager who suggests saving some money by diluting the fruit juice should be howled down by others.

Culture

If they are to be of practical use, the aim and mission statement of the business must be supported by the culture of the organisation. Culture is the unstated attitudes and behaviours that affect the way things are done in a business. It is 'the way we do things round here'. It may be bureaucratic, negative and conservative – or entrepreneurial, positive and innovative. The culture affects (and is affected by) the attitudes of the workers, how decisions are made and the management style adopted.

Areas where the culture can affect a business include:

- *Attitude to risk and blame*: A risk-taking business will be more tolerant of employees whose decisions don't pay off. If an employee feels that any failing on their part will be instantly criticised then they will be more inclined to play safe. This may mean missing opportunities for the firm to succeed and grow, rather than risk failing.
- *Resistance to change*: Some businesses will be able to respond to changes in their environment much

more quickly and with much less resistance than other firms could. If workers are welcoming of change and used to the excitement and challenge of new ideas the firm will be much more responsive. In firms where the prevailing attitude is one of 'THAT'S how we've always done it', change management will be a difficult, costly and time-consuming exercise.

- *Success at any price or a commitment to stakeholders*: Some firms expect their workers to stand or fall on the basis of their generation of sales, revenue and profits. There will be no incentive for such workers to look at the needs or requirements of wider stakeholders. If they can persuade a customer to pay over the odds then they will do so, whatever the rights or wrongs of doing so.

The foundation for a firm's culture will be found in several practical areas of the firm, such as:

- The organisational structure and the power structure;
- The formal rules laid down by the firm;
- The way everyday decisions and tasks are carried out;
- Communication within the firm.

Themes for evaluation

It is important that the mission, aims and culture of a business all give a single, coherent message. If the behaviour norms point in one direction while the written mission statement and aims point in another, then there will be confusion or cynicism. It is most likely that the reality for the business will be shown by the behaviour of the workforce, and the written statements will be little more than decorations on the office wall.

Since culture is so significant within a business, this is the area that needs to be addressed if real change is to be achieved. Unfortunately, because it is likely to be so ingrained and accepted by the workforce, it is also likely to be the one area that is hardest to change as well. Famously, when Alex Ferguson took over at Manchester United, he had to fight against the drinking culture within the first team squad. It took him 3 years to achieve success, and that was after replacing many senior players with keen youngsters, in order to break the culture.

K Key terms

Bureaucratic culture – where paperwork and systems are designed to avoid mistakes, not to achieve innovation or change

Entrepreneurial culture – encouraging risk-taking and initiative within all levels of the workforce

Mission statement – a written document setting out the firm's aims in a way intended to inspire staff

E Exam Insight

An examiner would be very impressed with a candidate who was able to comment intelligently on the divergence between a company's stated aim and mission and its actions within a case study. Evidence could be gathered to show that the actions of the workers are speaking louder than the mission statement and then the implications of this for the business, both internally and externally, could be highlighted.

S Student howlers

'Once written a firm's mission statement should never change.'
'A firm's culture cannot be changed by managers.'

T Test yourself (28 marks)

1. What is meant by the term 'mission'? (2 marks)
2. Would you expect a mission statement to include numbers? Explain your answer. (4 marks)
3. What is the job of a corporate aim? (3 marks)
4. How might an 'aim' help improve the company? (4 marks)
5. What is meant by a corporate culture? (3 marks)
6. Explain two examples of ways in which the corporate culture may affect a business. (4 marks)
7. Give four practical influences on a business culture. (4 marks)
8. What is most likely to actually determine the way a firm operates – its culture or its mission? Explain your answer. (4 marks)

CORPORATE STRATEGY

A corporate strategy is a plan of action which, it is hoped, will lead to the achievement of the organisation's objectives. The setting of corporate objectives ought to allow the business to coordinate its actions towards a common goal. For a small firm, where a manager has daily contact with every employee, the long-term direction can be communicated clearly from day to day. Where the firm is larger, however, this personal contact may not exist, so there is a greater need to formalise the strategy.

Although corporate objectives can take many forms, a number of targets are widely adopted, such as:

1. Maximising profit;
2. Maximising shareholder wealth;
3. Growth in the size of the firm;
4. Diversification;
5. Improving the market position.

Once the corporate objectives have been determined, a firm can consider the strategy it would like to use to achieve them. For a strategy to be realistic, it needs to be based on:

1. The objectives;
2. The resources available to the firm;
3. The results of an analysis of the market.

Of particular importance is the impact of the firm's environment on its strategy. The business guru, Michael Porter, developed a systematic way of analysing a firm's competitive environment. It is called the 'Five Forces' model. The five forces that determine a firm's competitive position are:

By assessing the market in a structured way such as this, managers have a clear model to use to assess their marketplace. Each of the five elements can provide useful information to help the firm decide what its overall strategy ought to be.

Ansoff's matrix

A key writer on the importance of firms adopting a strategic perspective is Igor Ansoff. Ansoff stressed the importance for a firm to work on not only developing a strategy, but also being able to respond to changes in its competitive environment as well.

Within this general picture, Ansoff identified four broad strategies that a firm may adopt, dependent on its aims and its competitive position. This is usually pictured in the form of a matrix. Although split into four 'boxes', it is important to recognise that within each box there will be different degrees of position at which a firm can be placed. For example, Tesco opening outlets in Europe would be a minor market development, but setting up in an undeveloped country such as Cambodia would be a very new venture (Fig. 6.5A).

- *Market penetration*: When a firm concentrates on selling more of an existing product in its current market.
- *Product development*: A firm stays with the current market that it knows well, but tries to introduce new product ideas. These could be developments of existing products or innovative new ideas in the same field.

Force	Strategies to minimise the threat
The threat of new competitors entering the market	Barriers to entry can be created by investing heavily in capital equipment, promoting products intensively or patenting key products and processes
The level of rivalry between established companies	Develop differentiated products, or reach an agreement with competitors (without breaking the law on things such as cartels)
The power of the purchaser	Integrate with distributors or encourage current buyers to rely on your product or product range
The power of the supplier	Integrate with a supplier or buy from a variety of sources
The threat from substitute products	Spoil the market for substitutes by dropping prices or developing your own substitutes first

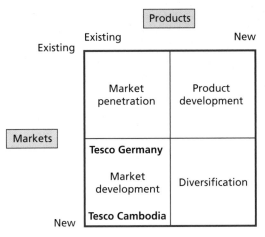

Products

	Existing	New
Existing	Market penetration	Product development
New	**Tesco Germany** Market development **Tesco Cambodia**	Diversification

Markets

Fig. 6.5A: Ansoff's Matrix applied to Tesco

- *Market development*: A business with a successful product may try to find a new market in which to sell. This new market could be geographical or just into a new market segment.
- *Diversification*: When a firm develops a new product and tries to sell it in a different market than the one in which they normally operate.

There are different degrees of risk associated with each of these strategies. In general, the more closely a firm stays with its current products and markets, the less risk it is likely to carry. It may also bring lower rewards. Successfully launching a diversified product into a new market opens up many new possibilities for a firm, whereas market penetration can offer only a limited level of future development.

Corporate strategies should not be set in stone. Since the business operates in a dynamic environment that is constantly changing, so its strategies must constantly change as well. A new product idea may give a firm a short-term competitive advantage, but competitors will soon adopt this new idea, and may also develop new ideas of their own. A firm's strategy has to be adapted to meet these changing circumstances.

K Key terms

Barriers to entry – any measure that makes it difficult for new businesses to enter a firm's market and compete effectively

Integration – the joining together of two businesses

Themes for evaluation

The most important criterion for assessing a business strategy is its suitability for the circumstances and environment for a specific firm. A firm that is a market leader in a stable market faces very different challenges and opportunities than a business with a weak position in a growing market. The chosen strategy needs to reflect each firm's individual position.

E Exam Insight

At A2 level, examiners like to see students who can adopt a strategic approach to their answers, rather than a group of individual actions the firm can take. Whatever specific area a question may be asking about, make sure that your answer considers the strategic position of the whole firm, especially in your evaluation.

S Student howlers

'A corporate strategy tells a manager what to do in all circumstances.'
'If a firm adopts a strategy of market penetration it is not taking any risk.'

T Test yourself (34 marks)

1. Explain the difference between objectives and strategy. (3 marks)
2. Give three common business objectives. (3 marks)
3. Give three factors that should be considered when setting the business strategy. (3 marks)
4. List Porter's Five Forces. (5 marks)
5. What is measured on the axes of Ansoff's Matrix? (4 marks)
6. List the four broad strategies from Ansoff's Matrix. (4 marks)
7. Explain why diversification is usually thought of as being a riskier strategy than market penetration. (4 marks)
8. Explain why corporate strategies should change regularly. (4 marks)

DECISION MAKING AND DECISION TREES

Decision making is important within a manager's job and vital for a director of a business. However, even the best decision makers will make some wrong decisions. Some of these may prove expensive for the firm and may call into question the competence of the decision maker. What then becomes important is that others can see the logic behind the decision. Even better is if colleagues and bosses have been part of the decision-making process and therefore knew the reasoning from the start.

'Ad hoc' decisions

An 'ad hoc' decision is one made without reference to plans or research data. It is a one-off decision in response to a sudden problem or opportunity. Managers who make ad hoc decisions are relying on two things:

1. Experience – if the manager has dealt with similar issues many times before, his/her own knowledge and background may suffice to make an appropriate decision.
2. Knowledge – both of the market and firm's objectives in relation to the market.

However, in a crisis, if a decision is needed immediately, a good manager will take the responsibility, relying on judgement rather than detailed gathering of evidence.

Scientific decision making

Scientific decision making is the use of a formal, set process to make sure that decisions are arrived at in an objective manner. The basis of scientific decision making is the analysis of factual data in a set, logical way. The process is a continuous cycle, including elements of review and evaluation, which aims to bring an element of continuous improvement to the decision-making process (Fig. 6.6A).

By following a process such as this it is likely that the decision made will be the most appropriate one taking into account the current market situation and the aims and objectives of the business. Although this method may be slow, this may be compensated for if the decision is a high quality one.

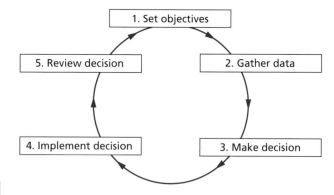

Fig. 6.6A: Scientific decision-making cycle

Decision trees

A decision tree is a diagram that sets out the options available to a firm together with the possible outcomes and the likelihood of them occurring. By using these data it is possible to calculate the expected outcome of each alternative. The firm may then choose the alternative likely to give the greatest expected outcome.

The diagram comprises two elements:

1. Squares, that show where a decision (or choice) has to be made;
2. Circles (or nodes) where chance takes over. You cannot choose success or failure, just as you cannot choose good or bad weather.

Having drawn the diagram, it should be labelled by showing the probabilities of each event occurring. If there is a 50/50 chance of one outcome or another, each one has a probability of 0.5. Similarly, if there is a 1 in 4 chance of an outcome, that has a probability of 0.25. Note that all the outcomes from a chance event must add up to 1.

Take the following example:

• Top Shop must decide whether or not to open its first branch in Paris. The set-up costs are £2 million. Research forecasts operating profits in Paris of £10 million in the next 4 years. But the experience of other British retailers suggests only a 1 in 4 chance of success (Fig. 6.6B). Should they go ahead?

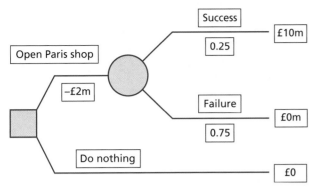

Fig. 6.6B: Decision tree for Top Shop Paris store

Having set it out, you can see that the diagram shows all the information provided beforehand. Now it is time to calculate the expected value of opening in Paris. In decision trees, all calculations are from right to left, so:

£10m × 0.25 = £2.5m
plus £0m × 0.75 = £0
Add both together = £2.5m (this is the 'expected value' or EV)
Subtract initial cost of £2m to make £0.5m (the 'net expected value' or NEV)

The data show, therefore, that on average the investment of £2 million in Paris will yield a total profit of £0.5 million over the next 4 years. That's better than doing nothing, though Top Shop management might decide to look at other uses of £2 million before going further.

The following is a more complex example of a decision tree, the complete diagram for which is shown in Figure 6.6C:

• A firm has to choose whether or not to launch a new product. If the launch goes ahead it will cost the firm £250,000. There is a 0.7 chance that if the firm launches a major competitor will respond. If there is a response from a competitor the income from the new product is expected to be £350,000, whereas if there is no response the likely income is £550,000.
• Alternatively, if the firm decides not to launch a new product but a competitor does, the firm may

lose £250,000 income as customers switch to the new product. It is thought that there is a 0.3 chance of competitors launching a new product in this way. If there is no launch from competitors, the firm's income is expected to rise by £250,000. The calculations for this tree are:

Decision 1 – Launch
	£350,000 × 0.7	= £245,000
	£550,000 × 0.3	= £165,000
	Expected value	= £410,000
minus	launch cost	= £250,000
equals	net benefit	= £160,000

Decision 2 – Don't launch
	–£250,000 × 0.3	= –£75,000
	£250,000 × 0.7	= £175,000
	Expected value	= £100,000

On financial considerations alone, this firm would then decide to launch the new product, since this is expected to bring an extra net benefit of £160,000 to the firm. However, there may also be other, qualitative factors that the firm may wish to take into consideration as well, such as the impact on existing products or the long-term aims of the business.

The use of decision trees has advantages and disadvantages:

Advantages	Disadvantages
• Problems are set out clearly and logically • Managers can use the decision tree as a starting point for a discussion on the decision • The inclusion of probabilities gives a more realistic picture than just using possible returns	• The data used may not be accurate. It is very difficult in reality to give precise figures for either the probabilities or the expected outcomes • The person drawing up the decision tree may, deliberately or not, introduce an element of bias into the data

T **Test yourself (28 marks)**

1. What is meant by an ad hoc decision? (3 marks)
2. How is an ad hoc decision made? (4 marks)
3. What are the possible problems of making a decision on an ad hoc basis? (4 marks)
4. What is meant by a scientific decision? (3 marks)
5. What are the five stages of a scientific decision-making process? (5 marks)
6. What is meant by a decision tree? (4 marks)
7. What are the advantages of using a decision tree? (3 marks)
8. What are the disadvantages of using a decision tree? (2 marks)

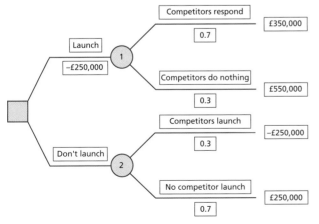

Fig. 6.6C: Complex decision tree for new product launch

STRATEGIC THINKING

Strategic thinking is developing a plan for achieving the firm's objectives. Strategic thinking will give the firm a clear direction for its future decision making. The strategy ought to be regularly reviewed to allow the firm to take into account changes in the external environment. For example, when the Atkins Diet faded from popularity in 2004, many of the food and drink companies had to re-think their low-carb strategies.

Strategic thinking ought to be based on both internal and external data. These data will be obtained by undertaking audits to find all the needed information.

External audit

An external audit will involve looking at the general business and economic conditions around the firm and an investigation into the state of the market in which the firm is operating. The business and economic environment can be investigated through a PEST analysis. This looks at four key issues:

P:	The political environment. Government policies can have a major impact on businesses. Unit 5.6 looks at the impact of monetary and fiscal policies. Another important factor constraining business behaviour and strategies is legislation.
E:	The economic environment. As the state of the economy changes there will be a clear impact on consumer demand and a firm's international competitiveness.
S:	The social environment. Consumer behaviour reflects changes in society. Businesses today are under growing pressure to take issues such as the environment into account because they matter more to their consumers. As the population in the UK is ageing over time, firms will need to build this into their strategic planning.
T:	The technological environment. Technology affects both the products that are demanded by consumers and the processes by which they are produced.

In addition a firm needs to undertake a market analysis. The firm has to be constantly aware of how things are changing within its market, both in terms of consumers and competitors. Key factors that need to be considered are:

- Market size, whether measured by value or by volume;
- Market growth, if any;
- Market trends, including the launching of new products by competitors or the shift in product positioning by competitors;
- Market share, for both the firm in question and competitors.

A key measure for firms within their market audit will come in the form of benchmarks. A benchmark is based on the standards of the most efficient businesses in a firm's market. These benchmarks are used to set targets for performance.

Application – Cut price Star

In January 2005 the cover price of the *Daily Star* was cut from 35p to 15p. This 60% price cut was in response to a 2004 sales decline of just over 1%. On the face of it, an astonishing over-reaction. Yet the owner, Richard Desmond, knew that the market trend for newspapers was downwards. Even *The Sun* was fading. Desmond was determined to increase his market share to compensate for the falling market size. His only worry over this strategic move would be if it forced *The Mirror* and *The Sun* to follow with big price cuts.

Internal audit

An internal audit will consider the firm's strengths and weaknesses in relation to competitors. It ought to be objective, and as such will normally be based on factual data such as costs and revenues.

The internal audit will culminate in a full SWOT analysis for the firm. A realistic SWOT analysis will give a firm a framework within which to make appropriate decisions that help to move the business forwards.

By combining the results of both the internal and external audits it will be possible to develop appropriate strategies to enable the firm to achieve its objectives.

Porter's strategic matrix

Michael Porter developed a model that he called a strategic matrix. It assesses strategy on two criteria:
- Is the business aiming at cost leadership or product leadership?
- Is the business in the mass market or a more focused market segment?

These two issues lead to four possible generic strategies that a business can adopt (Fig. 6.7A):

1. To become the lowest cost supplier within a mass market;
2. To have highly differentiated products within a mass market;
3. To become the lowest cost supplier within a focused market segment;
4. To have highly differentiated products within a market segment.

Porter argues strongly that a firm needs to decide which of these strategies it wishes to adopt, making sure that consumers will accept this strategy and that everyone in the firm fully accepts the strategy and directs all decisions at achieving it. Firms need to be careful that they are not putting mixed messages out to consumers. Attempting to offer highly differentiated products at low prices will not meet any of Porter's strategies and runs the risk of consumers becoming confused and so not trusting the firm.

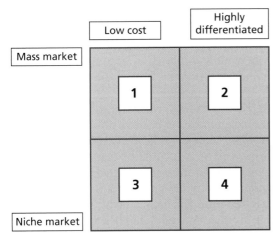

Fig. 6.7A: Porter's strategic matrix

Application – Marks & Spencer

For many years Marks & Spencer was a byword for product quality, product innovation and impressive, committed staff. The company was proud to boast that 95% of all products were made in Britain. It never offered high fashion clothing for 16–21-year-olds, but women from 22 to 62 bought their clothes from M&S. It was a highly differentiated supplier to the mass market; never cheap but always seen as value for money.

Then, in the late 1990s, a new chief executive made changes that pushed Marks & Spencer into the place that Michael Porter warns against. Today it is a mass market retailer that is neither low cost nor properly differentiated. Staff are no better than elsewhere, the

food and clothing are no more innovative or significantly better in quality. This huge business has become a byword for failure in strategic thinking.

> Porter's model provides a framework for analysing a firm's current and potential future strategies and allows you to make a judgement about the quality of the firm's strategies.
>
> The hardest strategies to judge will be those that lie between the extremes of lowest cost and highest differentiation.

K Key terms

External environment – the circumstances within which a firm operates that are outside its control

SWOT analysis – an assessment based on a firm's strengths, weaknesses, opportunities and threats

E Exam Insight

At A2 level you will be expected to be able to analyse the strategic choices that a firm has made or which are facing the firm. A model like Porter's can be used to give your answer structure, proving to the examiner that you can make realistic judgements rather than just making assertions.

S Student howlers

'Once decided on, a firm shouldn't change its strategy.'
'Porter's strategic matrix tells a firm what strategy it should select.'

T Test yourself (18 marks)

1. What are the four elements of a PEST analysis? (4 marks)
2. Give three things a market audit may look at. (3 marks)
3. What is meant by a 'benchmark'? (3 marks)
4. Explain how a benchmark may be used. (4 marks)
5. What are the four elements of a SWOT analysis? (4 marks)
6. What four general strategies are suggested by Porter's strategic matrix? (4 marks)

CRISIS MANAGEMENT

A crisis can be any event that threatens to damage a firm, either directly or through one of its brands. Usually crises are unexpected.

There are several common types of crises that can arise, such as:

- Physical damage, such as a fire or other accident;
- Environmental disasters, such as an oil spillage from a tanker;
- Hostile takeover bids;
- Major customers withdrawing their order;
- Prolonged strikes by the workforce.

Although these events are unpredictable, the fact that a firm is aware that they *could* happen allows them to prepare for them in case they occur. Such preparation is called contingency planning.

A contingency plan will allow the firm to make a timely and appropriate response should any of the foreseeable crises arise. Contingency planning is often shown as a five-stage process.

1. Recognise the need for a contingency plan;
2. Catalogue as many crisis scenarios as possible;
3. Search for ways to prevent each crisis;
4. Formulate plans for dealing with each crisis;
5. Run simulation exercises of the crisis and its handling.

At the heart of this process is a 'what if?' analysis. By asking itself as many 'what if?' questions as possible the firm will have a better appreciation of the possible crises it faces and the severity of the risks it is running.

Application – The tsunami

In 2003 and 2004 the main governments of countries around the Indian Ocean met to discuss whether to set up an early warning system for tsunamis (powerful waves caused by earthquakes that can reach speeds as high as 400 miles an hour). As tsunamis had rarely hit the Indian Ocean in the past, the governments decided that it was not worth the money. This left the coastal populations unprotected. There would be no system for gathering information and therefore no basis for contingency planning.

When the huge earthquake of 26 December 2004 caused tsunami waves to rush across the oceans, no early warning system warned people to head for the hills. Even though the waves travelled 2,000 miles to Sri Lanka and India (taking several hours), the crisis hit without warning. The massive losses of life throughout the region are well documented.

By mid-January 2005 the United Nations and the United States were both expressing their willingness to support financially an early warning system in the Indian Ocean. Needless to say, crisis management is about anticipating problems rather than responding to them.

Managing a crisis

If a crisis actually occurs the firm needs to be prepared to deal with it as efficiently as possible. By their nature, crises damage a firm. The first priority of crisis management has to be to limit the damage done. The firm can work within each of its functional areas to try to minimise the negative impact the crisis has on the firm. This could include:

- *Marketing*: Limit the damage to the firm's image through generating positive public relations.
- *Finance*: Most crises have a major impact on the firm's cash flow. It could be that products have to be withdrawn from shop shelves, so the firm faces a period of limited revenue. A firm with a healthy acid test ratio will be in a better position to survive a crisis than one that relies heavily on its immediate cash flow.
- *Personnel*: Despite the generally accepted ways to motivate workers, in a crisis it is likely that the best management style to adopt will be authoritarian. This provides for the quickest decision-making model and ensures that all decisions can be coordinated to achieve an immediate goal.
- *Operations*: The way a firm controls its operations could impact in a crisis situation. If the firm uses just in time production, a crisis which impacts on its supply will be more devastating than for a firm that maintains a buffer stock.

Throughout a crisis, it is important that a firm maintains strong communications both within the organisation and with its customers and suppliers. This can stop misinterpretations from being accepted as truth and worsening the position for the firm.

Application – Tsunami 2

Although the tsunami disaster was unexpected, UK tour operators have a great deal of experience in handling crises. They have learnt the importance of good communication with relatives and acting decisively in bringing home surviving clients who feel stranded or frightened. From an ethical point of view they should give all the help they can; from a self-interested business point of view, they must do the same. Any tour operator seen to be mean-spirited or unhelpful would take a battering from the media.

Having dealt with existing clients as best they can, the operators then have to deal with the many customers who want to change their holiday plans. It is time-consuming and expensive for the businesses to offer money back or a switch to a different destination. Yet they have learnt that there is no other acceptable way to respond to crisis.

When an unexpected crisis hits, the firm's style of leadership becomes important. Crises demand quick, decisive leadership in which people do what they are told without questioning. This may be natural within a business run on autocratic lines, but more problematic within a democratic style of leadership (especially if it is laissez-faire). It follows, therefore, that leaders who have a democratic approach should be especially careful to get training on how to act in a crisis. It is often said that the best leaders can use different styles, as appropriate to the situation.

In a case study you may be required to assess a firm's response to a crisis. You could ask yourself two things: How prepared for the crisis was the firm? How effectively was the crisis handled? Be alert to ethical issues, such as that the business could have done more, but chose to do as little as it could get away with. Be willing to criticise on moral grounds.

E Exam Insight

An examiner is likely to want to know that you are able to assess the advantages of contingency planning in a given situation and that you can evaluate a firm's response to a crisis situation.

S Student howlers

'Since a crisis is unpredictable it is pointless to try to prepare for one.'
'A contingency plan means a crisis can't happen.'

T Test yourself (25 marks)

1. Explain what is meant by a crisis. (3 marks)
2. Give three examples of possible crises for a firm. (3 marks)
3. Explain what is meant by a contingency plan. (3 marks)
4. Explain one marketing action a firm could take to limit the damage of a crisis. (3 marks)
5. Explain one finance action a firm could take to limit the damage of a crisis. (3 marks)
6. Explain one personnel action a firm could take to limit the damage of a crisis. (3 marks)
7. Explain one operational action a firm could take to limit the damage of a crisis. (3 marks)
8. Explain why it is important to keep effective communications during a crisis. (4 marks)

INTEGRATED OBJECTIVES AND STRATEGY

The AQA specification for this unit says:

This module section draws together all the Subject Content Areas, and the items given below should be seen as integrating themes which emphasise the interactive nature of the business world. The material set out below builds on all the Subject Content for both the AS and the A2. The topics in the Objectives and Strategy section of AS module 3 should be revisited when covering the following material. In relation to various business situations, candidates are required to recognise potential conflicts between the objectives of different stakeholder interests, and to suggest and evaluate resolutions to such conflict. They are also required to recognise the interrelationship between objectives and an uncertain business environment, and to devise and evaluate strategies which aim to anticipate, respond to and manage change.

As you study the topics within objectives and strategy, the following should be borne in mind.

Business Studies is a single subject. The way it is covered in textbooks, classes and even in this revision guide may make it seem like a series of separate chunks: marketing, finance, etc. It is important, though, that it is seen as a single, whole subject. The glue that holds it all together is business objectives – specifically, the way that different firms have different objectives depending on their circumstances and on the people who own and run them. Stemming from the objectives are the strategies and the decisions made at all management levels.

All business decisions have implications across the whole of a firm. A marketing decision will affect not only the marketing function of the firm but will also have implications for finance, personnel and operations. Any decision made must take a broad perspective across all the functional areas if is it to be an effective one.

Some of the common questions that a business needs to explore and understand are:

1. Costs vs revenue – increasing sales bring increasing costs. Which is the more important for a firm to control?
2. People vs capital – does the firm have a moral stance on its obligations to its employees, or can the workers be replaced if it is financially justified?

3. Marketing vs production – does the firm find out what consumers want and then produce them, or does the firm produce its products then find a market in which to sell them?
4. Does the business have the ability to anticipate the impact of external changes such as an economic downturn or a change in fashion? Does it have the flexibility to be able to respond quickly to different customer tastes or expectations?

The solution of such disputes will often depend on the firm's objectives and strategy. The firm's aims and objectives must underlie everything the business does. All decisions ought to help the firm move towards its ultimate goals. The strategy the firm decides upon needs to be consistent with the aims and objectives, just as all the decisions taken to carry out the strategy need consistency too.

The key to the successful attainment of set objectives lies in adopting an appropriate strategy and making decisions consistent with it.

T Test yourself (50 marks)

1. List four problems that could arise for a growing business. (4 marks)
2. Give two possible sources of funds for financing growth. (2 marks)
3. Explain what is meant by overtrading. (3 marks)
4. Explain what is meant by diseconomies of scale. (3 marks)
5. Explain the difference between a takeover and a merger. (4 marks)
6. In what four ways can a firm integrate with other firms? (4 marks)
7. What is meant by a corporate culture? (3 marks)
8. Explain two examples of ways in which the corporate culture may affect a business. (4 marks)
9. Explain the difference between objectives and strategy. (3 marks)

10. Give three common business
    objectives.   (3 marks)
11 Give three factors that should be considered
    when setting the business strategy. (3 marks)
12. List Porter's Five Forces.   (5 marks)
13. What is measured on the axes of Ansoff's
    Matrix?   (4 marks)
14. What is meant by a scientific
    decision?   (3 marks)
15. What is meant by a 'benchmark'?   (2 marks)

Now try the following data response questions. Allow
yourself 30 minutes for each set of questions.

Data response: Where good food costs less

During the 1980s and into the 1990s, Sainsbury's
was the dominant supermarket in the UK. It was
the market leader and a model of good practice
within the marketplace.

Since then, however, Sainsbury's has seen its
dominant position decline and it is now far behind
the new market leader, Tesco. One reason that
commentators have put forward for the decline has
been Sainsbury's confused message to customers.
The advertising line they used for many years was
'Where good food costs less'. The promise of good
quality food at low prices seems ideal, but gives
consumers a mixed message. Are they really going
to be getting a high quality product, despite the
low price? Or will the quality of the food match the
price being asked?

A clearer strategy might have helped Sainsbury's
stay at the top of the market.

Questions

1. Explain what is meant by the following terms
   used in the case study:
   i) market leader;
   ii) strategy.   (4 marks)
2. Outline two factors, other than advertising, that
   could affect the performance of a supermarket.
   (6 marks)
3. Using Porter's strategic matrix, assess Sainsbury's
   advertising slogan 'Where good food costs less'.
   (10 marks)
4. Discuss the extent to which an advertising
   slogan determines a firm's performance in the
   marketplace.   (10 marks)

Data response: A tale of two strategies

Two firms in the same market have adopted quite
different strategies for their growth. Two engine
builders, Cummins and Caterpillar, operate in
slightly different segments of the engine market.
Cummins focuses almost entirely on engines,
whereas Caterpillar not only sells diesel engines but
also earth-moving equipment.

When it comes to moving into new markets,
Cummins uses a strategy that involves joint
ventures with other firms, whether they are
competitors or customers. Caterpillar, on the other
hand, prefers to work by itself, and grows by
acquiring new firms.

This difference extends to other areas of the
businesses as well. Cummins can operate on a
smaller financial base and adopts a corporate
culture that is based more on collaboration.

Both firms, however, are successful in their own
areas. This is largely because they are both playing
to their own strengths and circumstances.

Source: Adapted from *Objectives and Strategy*
by Andrew Gillespie and Simon Harrison
(Hodder & Stoughton 2000)

Questions

1. Explain what is meant by the following terms
   used in the case study:
   i) joint venture;
   ii) corporate culture.   (4 marks)
2. Outline two potential problems Caterpillar
   could face in its strategy.   (6 marks)
3. Assess the advantages and disadvantages
   of Cummins' strategy.   (10 marks)
4. To what extent does this case show that there
   is no single, best strategy for a firm? (10 marks)

A2 EXAM SKILLS

In many ways A2 is a natural progression from AS. The subject matter may be harder – for instance learning in detail about company accounts and ratio analysis. Yet it is easy to see how this follows on from learning about profit, break-even and cash flow. Exams may require longer, deeper answers, but high marks still hinge on your ability to build up arguments that are applied to the case material and focused on answering the question. More, and better supported, judgements are required (evaluation), yet again this is a follow-up on the AS year.

Despite these similarities, there are fundamental differences in the approach needed for success. A2 is not only a higher academic standard than AS, it also requires a change of perspective. This is most obvious in the final 'synoptic' paper taken in June. This paper (worth 40% of the A2) relies upon you being able to rise above the middle management perspective adopted throughout most of the course. For the synoptic paper, you need to think as a company director – as a leader, not just a manager.

This point becomes clearer by referring to some of the AS subject content. The first year includes detail on motivating staff, on recruitment and training, on advertising and distribution, on stock and quality control (and much else). These issues are the concerns of middle managers, supervisors and 'shop floor' staff. Broadly the AS explains what a business is and how middle managers make decisions that determine the day-to-day running of firms.

Most A2 courses start in a similar way, though with more complex decision making or management methods such as investment appraisal or critical path analysis. As soon as possible, though, you need to start thinking beyond the individual concerns of specific managers and think from the Boardroom. Most important decisions require an overview of the impact upon the whole business, not just the marketing department or the factory.

In practical terms, success in A2 exams rests upon the following.

1. Reading and understanding the case material

Exams involve time pressure, so it is natural to rush through the reading to get onto answering the questions. Yet the essence of case study exam success is to show the ability to apply your answers to the business context. So give yourself time to digest the material properly. Generally, A2 exams allow 10 minutes' reading time, but be willing to give yourself a little longer if necessary. You need long enough to know what's distinctive, unique even, about this firm – the one in the case. Ideally, you should make sure you get from the case:

- Two distinctive features of the firm's external environment (Fierce competition? Boom conditions? Falling £? Rising minimum wage? etc.)
- Two distinctive features of the company and its products (Poor communication between departments? Struggling with stock control? Great new product success? Etc.)
- Two distinctive features of the people or the leadership (Boss lacking experience or indecisive? Marketing manager dislikes the operations manager? Overall leadership style seems overly autocratic? etc.)

2. Reading the questions at least twice

Far too often, good students get poor exam results because they do not answer the question set. They answer a question that's similar, but not the same. Or, they start by answering the question set, then drift off towards textbook descriptions. The June 2004 AQA Unit 4 exam asked students:

'Analyse how the new HR Director might encourage participation by the employees appointed to the Riverside restaurants.'

This required an answer focused on topics such as works councils, kaizen groups or leadership style. In fact, many students answered as if the question was:

'Analyse why the new HR Director might encourage participation by the employees appointed to the Riverside restaurants.'

Only one word is different, but now the answers were focused on reasons why you might introduce participation, such as low morale, high labour turnover or low productivity.

So make sure to read every word of the question with care.

3. Boost your marks

All A Level Business Studies exams require you to show four skills:

i) Knowledge and understanding;

ii) Application;

iii) Analysis;

iv) Evaluation.

At A2, the most important are analysis and evaluation. Yet the reality is that you rarely get high marks on evaluation unless your answers are well applied to the case. So evaluation depends on application.

3i. Knowledge and understanding

Knowledge and understanding can be shown quickly and easily. This hinges on defining the terms you use, then building your answer upon the definition. If the question is on workforce planning, quickly state what you understand by the term, then build your answer from there. Business Studies, like every other A Level, has a language of its own that you have to learn. To help you, take a copy of the *A-Z Business Studies Handbook** to every business lesson, and look up every term the teacher uses. You will soon find that you have mastered the language of business.

3ii. Application

Application means directing your answer at the particular business in question, not just any business. Even if you know masses about the marketing strategy of McDonalds, if the exam case study is about Ryanair,

* *Complete A–Z Business Studies Handbook*, 4th edition, by Lines, Marcousé and Martin (Hodder & Stoughton 2003)

make sure to relate your answer to the low-cost airline business. The key thing is to go for it. Don't say to yourself 'I don't know anything much about Ryanair but I sure know a lot about McD'. Examiners simply don't care about what you know, unless it's relevant. Remember that examiners do know that Ryanair was not on the syllabus, therefore there's no reason you should know anything more than is provided in the case study. So don't worry, just do your best to focus on the business in question.

3iii. Analysis

Analysis is looking into a topic in more depth by breaking it down into its component parts. To analyse the performance of a British Olympic team, you might break it down into track, field, swimming and other sports. If analysing a firm's poor profit performance, you could break profit down into revenue and costs, then break costs down into fixed and variable. Within most A2 answers, the skill of analysis will be shown by sequences of thought, i.e. a build-up of argument – 'If this happens, that will happen because …' Within paragraphs of analysis, make sure to incorporate relevant business theory into your arguments.

3iv. Evaluation

Evaluation means judgement. It can be shown openly, by drawing conclusions that incorporate and justify the views you have. For instance, in answer to a decision-making question you may wish to suggest that the quantitative evidence supports going ahead, but your reading of the key directors makes you doubt whether they share the right objectives and commitment to make it a success. This is a clear judgement, but it would have to be backed by evidence. In A2 exams, evaluation counts for up to 40% of the marks available.

AQA A2 UNIT 4 EXAMINATION

The shortest written question you are likely to see on the AQA's BUS4 exam will require content, application and analysis. Do not expect questions to be worth less than 6 marks. You will find 80 marks' worth of questions on the paper. These will be evenly split into 20 marks on each of the four modules being assessed – marketing, finance, people management and operations management. There is a good chance that you will face a 20-mark question within the paper. You can also be assured of at least one if not two numerate questions.

Possible sources of numerate questions include:
- Sales forecasting;
- Setting marketing budgets;
- Correlation and extrapolation;
- Investment appraisal;
- Break-even;
- Contribution and special order decisions;
- Ratio analysis or profit and loss accounts and balance sheets;
- Critical path analysis;
- Personnel performance indicators.

There is no guarantee that the finance question will involve numbers, so ensure that you have thoroughly revised the other numerate techniques listed above. In fact numerate questions can be an advantage to you. If you know how to tackle them, you should be able to get full marks, and possibly save yourself a little time too.

The skill that carries the highest marks on this paper is analysis (one-third of total marks for the paper). This is a far higher proportion than you met at AS level and your lines of argument should reflect this. Not only should paragraphs be longer but they should develop the points you make carefully and logically. It is from the depth of argument rather than the quantity of strands of argument that high marks will be earned.

Despite the clear assessment focus on analysis it can be very dangerous to overlook other skills. Knowledge needs to be well learned. Each question should be started, where appropriate, with a definition of the key term in the question. Inaccurate definitions on terms could lead to 20-mark questions producing zero marks if the examiner is not convinced of your knowledge of that particular topic. Here we hit the major snag that you have twice as much knowledge to learn for this

paper than for any other. With the exam assessing two of the three modules of A2 content there is a need for extremely thorough revision.

Although it is not pre-issued, this exam is a case study of a business. Therefore answers must be about the business in the case, not business in general. Application ought to flow naturally from answering questions in relation to *this* firm. Yet you only have 10 minutes to study the case. This may seem disconcerting at first, but that 10 minutes of reading time is built into the 90 minute 80 mark exam. Some candidates hurt their chances by answering questions after a brief look through the case. This is a foolish approach.

Although it will take a certain amount of courage, you should not open your answer booklet until 10 minutes into the exam. Those first 10 minutes must be spent reading and making brief notes on the case study itself. Without a careful appreciation of the type of business involved, its current position and future plans, your answers may be irrelevant to *that* business and therefore score poorly.

Using the 10 minutes

Start by reading the case study, making notes in the margin about any key business points (e.g. 'USP' or 'Autocratic') and making observations about *this* firm. It also makes sense to work a little with any numerical data given. If you are provided with company accounts, calculate the gearing, the acid test and the return on capital ratios. They will give you insight into the firm's financial health and profitability.

Then, and only then, read all the questions. Then before answering each one, read it again, carefully.

It's a case study

You must ensure that all of your answers are about the business in the case. You will not be asked broad, theoretical questions about businesses in general. All questions on this paper will relate to the firm in the story. Root all of your answers in the context you have been given to gain not just application marks, but evaluation too. Ask yourself: is it big or small; manufactring or service; profit-focused or with a different objective?

Timing

The timing on this paper is clear. You are expected to spend 10 minutes reading and annotating the case study which leaves you 80 minutes to answer questions worth 80 marks. Stick carefully to the time allocations for each question. Spending too long on an early question may not produce many extra marks and will damage your chances of a decent score on a later question. It is helpful to briefly note the latest finish time for each question before you begin.

Be selective

You are unlikely to have enough time available to write down everything you can think of. If you think of five different points to make for each question, thin these out to just two or three before you begin. Eliminate those with the least relevance to this particular business. Higher marks are awarded for the depth of analysis of the points you make. Analysing many points briefly will do you no favours.

The Own Figure Rule

Examiners marking your paper will be using what is known as the 'own figure rule'. This means that if you make a mistake on a numerate question, you will only be penalised once for that mistake. Having seen the error, the examiner will then check to see that you have used your wrong answer in the right way and award marks for this. Not only is this important when tackling numerate questions – show all your workings clearly – but it also helps on written questions that follow on from a numerate question. If, for example, you have been asked to calculate payback and NPV for a project, you may be asked as a second part of the question to recommend which project should be chosen. Just because you made an error calculating NPV does not mean you will lose marks on the follow-up. The examiner will assess your answer considering the figure you calculated, not the right answer. This means that even if you have a horrible feeling about a numerate answer you must push on with follow-up questions and answer them as best you can. If you are unable to attempt a numerate question with a written follow-up, make and state an assumption about the answer to the numerate question and base your answer on that assumption.

The route to success on BUS 4

You have to score on every question. The first marks for each of the four skills are the easiest to get, since they require only simple or low level knowledge, application, etc. Students managing to score an average of 5/10 on each question will be comfortably getting a C grade on this paper. To achieve an A you need to average 6/10. 10/10 is fine, but very hard to achieve regularly. What is important for your average score on this paper is that you make a valid attempt at every single question. If you then score Level 1 marks for all four skills on each question you will achieve at least a C grade.

It all sounds so simple now but do not be fooled. You will not be able to answer every question unless your revision has focused on ensuring that you know the syllabus content well – your knowledge must be spot-on. BUS 4 is a really tough challenge, because instead of examining just two modules of work it tests four. The key to success is to start by revising thoroughly the relevant units of this book, i.e. all those in sections 1–4.

SUCCESS AT AQA UNIT 5

The Unit 5 exam has two parts, both worth 40 marks. In 90 minutes you have to answer a numerical report and also write an essay in a choice of one out of four titles. Both parts of the exam are based on an integrated understanding of the whole course. Therefore the essays are not about specific areas such as motivation or marketing. They are general questions about broad business problems, opportunities or issues.

The Numerical Report (Section A; allow 45–50 minutes)

Section A of the exam paper has three components:

1. A brief written introduction to the business and its issues or problems (this will be no more than 10 lines).

2. A question, in bold print, that asks you to write a report on a topic or decision. The question will say what role you play in the business, who the report is for, and what the report is supposed to cover.

3. Five appendices of data, mainly presented in figures, though some may be presented diagrammatically (e.g. a critical path network) or as a graph or bar chart.

Your task is to go through the introduction and the appendices, identifying the information that will help answer the question. The intention is that there will be more data than you can use effectively in the time available, therefore you need to be selective. You may have been given the stock turnover ratio, and you may know what it is, but if you cannot see how it helps you tackle a marketing problem, just ignore it. There is no requirement to even mention all the appendices in your answer.

Do
1. Be selective, as mentioned above

2. Keep a tight focus on the question
Beware of ending up describing the contents of each appendix, or writing a general 'report on the strengths and weaknesses of the XYZ Company'. The key is to answer the question.

3. Make a quick assessment of the big picture
As you look through the appendices, consider whether the business seems successful or not; well managed or not; a rising star or a bit of a dog. What are its future prospects? If it is thriving, that will affect the answer to almost any question.

4. Look for links between the appendices
Examiners are impressed if you show that you can see that, for example, the low labour turnover figures shown in Appendix B may relate to the high repeat purchase rates shown in Appendix D.

5. Write in report format
There are marks available for writing in report form. More importantly, though, the structure of your report will have an impact on the marks awarded for synthesis and evaluation. The ideal is numbered points within subheaded sections – but make sure to make some of your points detailed enough to generate good marks for analysis.

6. Make recommendations and justify them fully
A report is a business document focused upon a particular decision. Just as all essays should end with an evaluative conclusion, so a report should end with well-justified recommendations.

Don't
1. Overuse your calculator
This exam requires you to select and interpret data, not calculate it. If the examiner anticipates that a calculation would be useful, s/he will provide it for you. Of course, there may be calculations that you think are helpful, but the mark scheme will not require them from you.

2. Describe each appendix in turn
Good exam answers are structured around the question, not the appendices. For example, the report structure may be:
- Introduction;
- Reasons why the firm should move to London;
- Reasons why the firm should not move to London;
- Conclusions and recommendations.

Relevant material should be selected from the appendices; the appendices should not structure the answer.

3. Make your points too brief
Choose relevant material that you can write something about. If the firm that might move to London has a gearing ratio of 50%, you may be in a good position to explain the risks involved in further borrowings to finance the costs of moving.

4. Take too long
Don't over-run on time. A good essay needs 40 minutes, so spend no longer than 50 minutes on the numerical report.

The Essay (Section B; allow 40–45 minutes)

The essay questions are hard to prepare for, as they are not focused upon specific syllabus topics. The key, therefore, is to practise past questions. Usually, these questions can be tackled by asking yourself four main things:

1. What are the firm's objectives? (If they are not known, then a standard part of your essay will be to consider how the answer would differ for a firm targeting rapid growth compared with one demanding profit maximisation.)

2. What impact does the question/issue have on the four functional areas of the firm: marketing, finance, people and operations?

3. What are the internal and external constraints upon the business in question? (Useful, here, to prepare by making yourself aware of at least two key economic trends affecting the economy in the months leading up to the exam.)

4. What are the priorities? These may be in relation to time (in the short term … in the longer term …) or in unpicking the underlying problems from the immediate ones. For example, Sainsbury's immediate problem may be falling market share, but the underlying issue may be an over-centralised management.

In your essay, as in the report, make sure to allow time for a thoughtful, rounded conclusion. Evaluation marks are 40% of the total, so a conclusion could be as long as a whole side of A4.

BUS 6 – EXAMINER'S COMMENTS

The Unit 6 examination serves two purposes. First of all it tests your knowledge of Section 6 of the specification, covering the A2 material on External influences and Objectives and strategy. Secondly, it is a synoptic paper, which means that it is designed to test your understanding of the whole course. Above all else in Business Studies, it is about the business as a whole, not the individual parts or departments of the business.

This has implications for the way you are expected to approach your answers on this paper. Questions will be rooted in part of the specification section 6, and you will need to show the examiner that you fully understand topics such as takeovers. It is usually a good idea to start your ideas with a clear, concise definition. Straightaway you will be helping the examiner to give you content marks. However, to show that you have a good all-round understanding of the topic area, you ought also to try to make clear links to other parts of the specification. The impact of a change in economic conditions, for example, may well depend to an extent on the firm's current financial position.

- Do:
    — give a clear definition of the topic from the question;
    — make links to other parts of the specification.
- Don't:
    — latch on to a single word/topic and just write all you know about it;
    — try to cover too many issues, or you will struggle to build up strong, detailed arguments

Paper 6 is based on a case study of around 1,000 words. Within this text you will finds hints or connections that will give you a clear context for your answer. In return, examiners will expect that your answers are relevant to the specific detail of the case study. It isn't enough to repeat the theory you have learnt in class on a particular topic. In the June 2003 exam, for example, there was a question on the usefulness of decision trees. Many candidates made the theoretically correct point that a decision tree needs to be based on market research findings. They failed to notice that the case study clearly stated that the marketing manager had 'undertaken a market research programme, from which he constructed a decision tree'.

- Do:
    — make use of the hints given in the case study;
    — write about this specific firm in its specific situation.
- Don't:
    — rely on textbook theory alone.

All of the questions on paper 6 are structured to allow you to develop a two-sided answer. This is intended to give you the opportunity to show your full appreciation of the topic being discussed. However, it does require you to be selective. The questions will be quite broad to allow you to develop your answer as you wish. You will need, though, to limit the quantity of points you try to cover. As with all exams there is a limit to the time available and if you try to cover everything that comes to your mind when reading a question then you will find yourself short of time later in the exam. One approach to take, then, is to take two contrasting points – one for and one against, or an advantage and a disadvantage – so that you know you have given a balanced answer. Also, by limiting yourself to just two key issues, you will have the opportunity to develop your ideas fully. Instead of just stating something, you can follow it through to a sensible conclusion.

- Do:
    — try to present a balanced, two-sided argument.
    — follow your ideas through.
- Don't:
    — try to cover too many different points.

Of the 80 marks available on this paper, 32 are awarded for evaluation – 40% of the total. It is also the area that tends to let most candidates down. All the questions will invite you to come to a conclusion. However, it isn't sufficient to just state an opinion. Your conclusion needs to follow directly from the rest of your answer and to be justified by you.

Evaluation can be shown in other ways as well. Within your answer you could weight the relevant arguments by showing which points are really critical for this firm in this situation, and which are unlikely to have little effect on this firm. Similarly you could introduce the idea of timescales into your answer, perhaps considering the implications for the firm in both the short and long term. There are several ways in which you can demonstrate your perceptiveness to the examiner. Whichever you choose, you are trying to show the examiner that you are able to make logical and justifiable judgements on the basis of both your textbook knowledge and on the specific situation of the business featured in the case.

- Do:
  — make your judgements follow on from the rest of your answer;
  — give an overall answer to the question asked.
- Don't:
  — just make an assertion without supporting arguments.

A2 REVISION CHECKLISTS

Revision checklist for Marketing, Finance, People and Operations. Can you?

	Very well	OK	No
Understand a simple profit and loss account and balance sheet, recognising the meaning of working capital, shareholders' funds and assets employed			
Identify relevant ratios for tackling different financial issues, e.g. financial health, efficiency, profitability and working capital management			
Calculate and comment on ROC, acid test, gearing, debtor days and asset turnover			
Set the analysis of a firm's accounts into a wider context of its objectives, ethics (e.g. window dressing) and market conditions			
Calculate and comment on payback, ARR and NPV results. Assess qualitative issues relevant to the firm's situation			
Show, interpret and analyse the effects on a firm's break-even position of changes in variables such as price, costs or capacity			
Calculate the impact on short-term profit of a special order, and assess its overall value bearing in mind qualitative factors			
Write at some length on the strategic value of asset-led marketing rather than market-led or product-led			
Remember, illustrate and see both the value and the limitations of the marketing model (versus a more subjective approach, i.e. hunch)			
Draw or interpret extrapolated data based upon a sales trend (for forecasting) or correlated data (to help make marketing decisions)			
Build up or interpret a marketing plan, showing a full understanding of setting and spending a marketing budget			
Understand workforce planning as the way in which an HR strategy is put into practice (especially following a key decision)			
Understand the important role of trade unions within a business world split between individual and collective bargaining			
See the risks within business of poor communications, both internally and externally (and the relationship with motivation)			
Calculate and interpret data on personnel effectiveness, with the ability to build a detailed argument, e.g. on absenteeism or productivity			
Draw up a network, showing a good understanding of the value and limits of CPA, as applied to different business contexts			
Make and assess strategic location decisions, both UK and international, using quantitative and qualitative factors			
Recognise the value and limitations of the use of IT in business across a wide range of business functions			
Recognise that risky decision making is a key aspect of business, yet often made with imperfect knowledge in irrational ways			
Acknowledge that risk and reward usually go together; in business – as in exams – if you don't shoot you don't score. Learn to love risk!			

Revision checklist for A2 External influences, Objectives and Strategy. Can you?

	Very well	OK	No
Explain causes and effects of economic growth upon businesses directly and indirectly (e.g. pressure group activity due to concerns about environment)			
Understand the importance of international competitiveness for UK firms (and the need for an integrated approach through people, operations and marketing)			
See the opportunities and threats from emerging markets, especially the new 2004 EU members, plus the growth prospects in China and India			
Show understanding of the EU as a free trade area that operates behind protected walls; knowledge of the business importance of the euro			
Explain the implications for business strategy of economic variables such as interest rates and the exchange rate			
Understand the role and the scope of government activity, regarding economic policy, the framework of the law, and deregulation vs intervention			
Understand, and be able to distinguish between, social responsibilities and the shareholder vs stakeholder debate			
Show awareness of the difference between ethics and ethical policies; be clear that public relations/image may get in the way of ethical behaviour			
Be clear about the pressures firms face re environmental campaigners, pressure groups and individuals – and the costs and opportunities involved			
Understand how and why social and environmental audits are undertaken, be aware of controversy about which firms use them, and whether they should be a legal requirement			
Recognise the nature of Board level (strategic) decisions and how they are made in relation to the whole firm, not just a department			
Recognise the need to accept, measure and evaluate risk in relation to potential reward – hence the need to understand decision trees			
Express a good understanding of strategic models such as the Boston Matrix, Ansoff's Matrix and Porter's strategic matrix and recognise when each one is helpful			
Understand relevant terminology, the purpose and the possible effects of takeovers and mergers (and management buy-outs) on stakeholders			
Understand the pressure to grow (perhaps rapidly) and the pressures rapid growth places on finances, management structure and organisation			
Understand the process, purposes and problems of specific changes to company size when floating, when retrenching or when first growing overseas			
Grasp the importance of business culture in determining the ethos, the behaviour and success of a business; realise the difficulty of culture change			
Draw clear distinctions between aims and objectives, objectives and strategy and strategy and tactics; know the debate re mission statements			
Make strategic decisions and justify reasoning, faced with significant business opportunities or crises; see the importance and difficulty of this			
See how and why contingency plans are made, and assess their value in specific business contexts			

ANSWERS

BUSINESS STUDIES FOR A2 REVISION GUIDE

Section 1: Marketing

UNIT 1.1

1. Sales can be achieved by attracting customers new to the market – without the need to steal customers from existing firms. However, growing markets attract new entrants so levels of competition are likely to be high. 2. Our sales/total sales in the market × 100.
3. Volume, value. 4. Segmentation allows different products to be tailored to suit the differing needs of each market segment. This allows firms to charge higher prices. 5. a) Quantitative research investigates what people do, using mainly closed questions in order to provide quantifiable data on a large enough sample to give statistically valid results. Qualitative research investigates why customers do the things they do and the motives behind customer behaviour. It is conducted on far smaller samples and is not expected to give statistically reliable data; b) i) Quantitative, ii) qualitative. 6. Sample size too small, poorly constructed sample, poorly worded questionnaire, interviewer bias. 7. Strategy is a medium to long-term plan to achieve objectives; tactics are short-term responses to external changes. Tactical measures may actually counter the ongoing strategy, but be deemed necessary in order to cope with the immediate threat.
8. Sales, market share, customer awareness, distribution levels. 9. A niche can provide a safe haven from larger competitors. Niche marketing allows customer needs to be met more exactly, thus allowing the charging of a premium price. 10. Far higher potential sales levels than in a niche market. Promotion can use mass media that reduces the cost per head being reached. 11. Product features, product design, branding, advertising, PR. 12. By making a product seem different from its rivals in the minds of consumers, a firm can effectively reduce the amount of products that consumers will willingly substitute for its own if price rises. This reduces the sensitivity of demand to changes in price. 13. % change in demand/% change in price. 14. % change in demand/% change in real income. 15. Introduction – negative, still reeling from development costs; growth – starting to move towards the positive, but promotional spending may be high; maturity – should see positive net cash flow; decline – may retain a positive cash flow if costs are slashed sufficiently, but eventually cash flows will become negative. 16. A

pricing strategy is the overall plan for the way a product is priced, the method is the way the actual price is arrived at, while tactics are short-term price changes designed to deal with an external change.
17. The number or proportion of possible retail outlets that a firm persuades to stock its products. 18. Market share and market growth.

UNIT 1.2

Student howler

1. The term 'assets' is being used in a non-financial sense. Do not assume that all assets are shown on a firm's balance sheet.

Test yourself

1. It may encourage the firm to think innovatively, rather than sticking with what they know; it may reveal where consumer tastes will be heading in future. 2. Close links with existing retail outlets can enable a firm to gain distribution for new products with relative ease. It is also possible that retailers can provide useful feedback or insight as to consumer reaction to the firm's new products. With loyal retailers on board, the new products will stand a far better chance of success as consumers should be able to access them easily, increasing the likelihood of product trial – a vital aspect of new product launches. 3. The suggestion is that as market research fails to generate many significant innovations, most market-orientated firms will be forced to produce 'me-too' products reflecting the latest developments in the market. Without the ability to innovate, adding value can be hard; however, this is not impossible if the firm has a strong enough brand. It is quite valid to argue that market-orientated firms can gain first mover advantage through their close monitoring of shifting market trends. Even if new products are not hugely innovative, they may be able to tie up emerging niches before competitors can launch a product suited to their needs. The statement is probably a little strong – although it has some validity, many market-orientated firms can pursue strategies that are not low cost based. 4. The asset-led approach is fundamentally based on the identification and use of a company's key strengths or competencies. However, asset-led marketing pays close attention to the market and is based on matching opportunities identified in the market to the company's strengths. Opportunities will only be

pursued if the firm is able to use its strengths to exploit those opportunities.

UNIT 1.3

Student howler

1. There are few areas of subject knowledge that are ignored so often. This response is typical of the student who enters the exam with absolutely no knowledge of the marketing model.

Test yourself

1. Decisions based upon strong knowledge of the market; decisions based upon choosing between two or more possible strategies. 2. May not know about the technique; may consider it too slow or expensive; may not need it, if the proprietor is really close to the market and its needs. 3. The scientific approach can allow firms to enhance their chances of staying in touch with customer tastes. In a fashion market this is important. However, the great concern for a fashion retailer will be how to ensure that decision making is not slowed by the use of the model. If too many research data are required before a strategy is developed, or if the firm is unwilling to roll out its full strategy until the results of test marketing are in, there is a great danger that tastes will already have changed before decisions are made. 4. Innovations such as the Walkman and the VCR have performed very poorly in market research. The problem is that innovations of this type offer customers benefits that they have never considered before. They can therefore fail to understand the benefits that these innovations can bring. In some cases, however, real innovations are easy for customers to understand, meaning that these products will produce the positive market research results required to succeed even with a reliance on scientific marketing decision making. A scientific approach to decision making probably does reduce the chance of technological breakthroughs, but by no means does it eliminate such successes. 5. With no market research it is hard to keep track of what is happening over time to customer needs and wants, and firms may lose touch with their market. This is likely to happen more quickly in markets where tastes can change rapidly as a result of fashion or fast-moving technology. The result may be products that appeal to few people being sold in the wrong way.

UNIT 1.4

Student howler

1. The student has identified the wrong causality. It is far more likely that more advertising boosted sales, though it might be accepted that higher sales in a previous period allowed a higher advertising spend in this period. Causalities can be tricky.

Test yourself

1. Extrapolation means predicting future events based upon past trends. 2. A positive correlation occurs when two variables rise in step with each other (and fall in step), e.g. advertising and sales. The correlation is strong when the relationship is very consistent, e.g. advertising up 10%, sales up 5%; and advertising up 30%, sales up 15%. 3. The graph shows a fairly strong negative correlation, meaning that as temperatures fall, sales rise. The product could be any cold weather product from car windscreen de-icer, to woolly hats or toboggans. 4. The graph in Figure 1.4D below shows that two years (1992 and 1996) saw particularly strong sales and 2000 saw a significantly disappointing sales level. 5. Extrapolation is based on the assumption that past trends will continue into the future. This is only likely to occur if there are no significant changes in factors affecting the variable being extrapolated. If sales are being extrapolated the long-term trend may change significantly if a new competitor enters the market or if the product being sold becomes obsolete. Decisions based on extrapolated data must be treated with caution unless the extrapolation has found a way to account for expected changes in external and internal factors (see Unit 1.5 on sales forecasting).

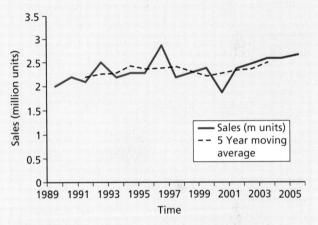

Fig. 1.4D: Actual sales compared with trend

UNIT 1.5

Test yourself

1. Market research is based on interviewing a sample of consumers; test marketing means trying out a product in real shops with real customers, but just in one (perhaps small) part of the country. 2. Can order stock quantities more accurately; may reduce the amount of stock surplus that needs to be sold off cheaply in the Sales. 3. There is little doubt that an extra, unpredictable external factor affecting sales will make forecasting very tricky in a fashion market. Although it may be relatively straightforward to assess how often fashions will change, where they will go is much harder to figure out. It is then practically impossible to decide whether or not the new fashions offered by a firm will actually be successful. However, firms do manage to make forecasts in these markets, yet these will often be based on experts' estimates rather than any hard research data – given the time that would be required to conduct thorough market research. 4. Marketing planning involves setting a firm's marketing objectives and strategy. Objectives will

need to be realistic and therefore an appropriate sales forecast will allow the firm to set realistic objectives relating to sales levels. Practical details within the marketing plan will also need sales forecasts, such as setting distribution targets, or as an aid to pricing decision making. **5.** The table below shows how the moving average trend could have been extrapolated, based upon the change in sales trend between the second quarter 2 years ago and the first quarter this year. The forecast figures have been based upon a sales increase of 2.32 (000s). This figure is rounded to two decimal places. Note that the sales estimate of 138,920 for the third quarter next year is not seasonally adjusted.

Year	Quarter	Sales (000s)	Centred moving average
3 years ago	4	120	
2 years ago	1	100	
	2	100	108.75
	3	110	111.25
	4	130	112.5
Last year	1	110	112.5
	2	100	113.75
	3	110	116.25
	4	140	120
This year	1	120	125
	2	120	*127.32*
	3	130	*129.64*
	4		*131.96*
Next year	1		*134.28*
	2		*136.60*
	3		*138.92*

Centred moving average figures in italics have been extrapolated.

UNIT 1.6

Student howlers

1. The marketing budget must cover all marketing expenses, not just advertising – the advertising budget will just be a part of the overall marketing budget. **2.** The budget also contains sales targets – it is not simply a statement of how much can be spent.

Test yourself

1. a) Low–high (it depends, really); **b)** high; **c)** low; **d)** zero. **2.** Being the number 2 to such a massive number 1 means that Pepsi managers have to think of their actions in relation to their dominant rival. If they cannot afford to match Coke's expenditure, they might have to focus on matching it in certain sectors (such as 10–20-year-olds, perhaps). **3.** Advantages – should ensure that little money is wasted since only actions identified in the marketing plan will be funded. This may help to ensure that marketing activity is carefully targeted at potential customers, possibly reducing

money wasted communicating with consumers who are not likely to buy the product. However, task-based costing requires a lot of management time to assess the cost of each activity. **4.** Since sales growth can be achieved by attracting customers new to the market rather than stealing customers from their current suppliers the argument suggests that an ad hoc approach to marketing activity should work perfectly well in attracting these customers. However, without a carefully thought through strategic approach to marketing there is a danger that different marketing actions may produce conflicting messages about the brand. Careful marketing planning should be carried out, although planners need to constantly assess whether the planning process is slowing up marketing actions to the extent that the firm is missing out on new opportunities due to slow reactions. **5.** The marketing budget may be cut, as the firm's overall finances may be strained as a result of last year's flop. Furthermore, faith in the ability of the marketing department may be damaged causing the firm to push funding elsewhere to try to gain a competitive edge – perhaps into R&D spending. However, there is an argument that suggests that more money should be allocated to marketing next year in order to try to repair any damage to reputation and possibly because the advertising flop may be explained by the budget made available being too small.

UNIT 1.7

Test yourself

1. An asset-led approach means basing the marketing strategy on a businesses key strengths, such as distribution networks or brand image. **2.** A market-led approach places consumer needs at the heart of marketing activity – all of which will stem from the identification of consumer needs and attempts to satisfy those needs. **3.** The general direction in which a time series of data is moving. **4.** Projecting a long-term trend into the future. **5.** Involves identifying any possible relationship between two variables. **6.** Marketing budget and brand awareness. **7.** Price and sales. **8.** Identifying the relationship between budget and sales levels from previous years will allow a firm to select an appropriately sized budget to meet its sales targets. **9.** Set marketing objectives, gather data, form hypothesis, test hypothesis, control and review. **10.** Carefully tested marketing plans should have identified possible problems before they occur. A formal system of continual monitoring and review of marketing activities allows adjustments to be made to marketing strategies to cope with external changes. **11.** Hunches may be more likely to produce genuinely innovative marketing actions, given the tendency of new ideas to perform fairly poorly in market research. **12.** A marketing plan presents marketing strategy for all to see. It includes the logic behind the plan (objectives) along with the actual practical details of the marketing activities that will be undertaken. It therefore provides vital information for all departments within the organisation. It should also ensure a

coordinated approach to marketing activity.
13. a) Planning production levels in line with marketing activities, planning stock levels and ordering of materials and components; **b)** workforce planning will need to see the plan, to ensure staffing levels are right at times of key activity in the marketing plan; **c)** budgets will be informed by the sales targets set in the marketing plan. Meanwhile the finance department will need to actually find and supply the money needed by the marketing department. **14.** A marketing budget sets out sales targets to be achieved and the amounts of money that can be spent by the various sections of the marketing department to achieve their objectives. **15.** By ensuring that a firm is spending as much as its rivals, there should be enough money available to ensure that their marketing message is not drowned out by other, higher spending rivals. However, this method is tough on any firm which is not the market leader since they will be spending proportionately more of their turnover on marketing.

Questions (When hunches go wrong)

1. Jerry clearly relies on his instincts when making marketing decisions. These had been good until the launch of the Vitalize. At least an objective seemed to be clearly set – to reach the sales target of £30m in the first year. However, given Jerry's track record and the information in the case it seems likely that few data had been gathered to assist with the planning of the launch. Jerry's strategic approach was untested and so once the product had been launched targets were missed. If the model had been used it is likely that information gathered would have produced a better informed strategy, while the testing of the strategy would have indicated a poor reaction from consumers. This would have allowed a reassessment of the launch strategy before the full-scale launch took place, saving the company the expense of a flop and Jerry his job.
2. Jerry appeared to be aiming his product at a well-defined niche within the market; by setting a high price, distributing through specialist retailers and providing a product with a particular USP he should have been able to carve out a good share of this niche. The decision to avoid distributing through mass-market retailers may have caused problems though – since that is where the vast majority of customers would expect to buy chilled desserts. With the need to take them home to the fridge fairly quickly, unless they were being bought on impulse for immediate purchase, Jerry's distribution strategy probably fell down. Weekly shops are now almost exclusively done in 'one stop' at major supermarkets – precisely where Jerry's product was not stocked. It is highly unlikely that customers would be willing to make a special trip to a health food shop to buy yoghurts. Combined with a forecast that appears to be based on a mass-market approach the results were poor. However, the fundamental reason for the failure of Jerry's strategy

could well be the lack of research involved in his non-scientific decision-making process. **3.** Forecasting sales for new products traditionally relies on quantitative research or test marketing. However, with only minimal research conducted in this case, the forecast may have come from other sources. Perhaps an estimate based on the correlation of launch budget and first year sales may be the key, or the forecast may even have been an estimate based on Zoe's experience of the market. **4.** An insufficient marketing budget may mean that the firm is unable to promote its product effectively or unable to secure sufficient distribution. Shortage of funds may even lead to poorly constructed market research. However, this case illustrates that poor decisions can lead to new product flops – even if the marketing budget was large. Jerry made some strange choices in constructing his marketing strategy and then failed to properly assess customers' reactions to the product and mix before launch. This was not the result of the budget being too small, rather a failure to take marketing decisions in a scientific manner. This case study therefore does little to confirm the statement in the question, although there is no doubt that the cause of failure of a significant number of new product launches is insufficient marketing spending. **5.** Ensuring that marketing budgets keep up with competitors should ensure that the firm is able to broadcast sufficient messages to avoid being drowned out by rivals – ensuring that a high share of 'advertising voice' is maintained. However, smaller firms will be unable to afford to use this method, while at times the method could be criticised for failing to ensure the most efficient use of marketing spending, by ensuring that a firm should be able to compete on the basis of the quantity of its marketing expenditure rather than the quality of its marketing. **6.** There does appear to be a positive correlation. Indeed the picture is even clearer if the launch of Miller Mini Pots is ignored as being an extraordinary success. The best fit line, illustrated in Figure 1.7B, shows the relationship more clearly, though if the Mini Pots launch was ignored, the best fit line would shift downwards and fit the remaining four points much more closely – giving a far stronger correlation.

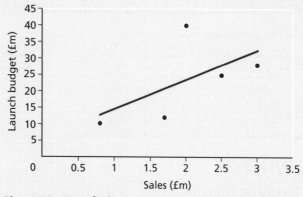

Fig. 1.7B: Best fit line

Section 2: Finance

UNIT 2.1

Test yourself

1. Costs which do not vary in proportion to output, e.g. managers' salaries. **2.** Direct costs can be related directly to a cost centre; indirect costs are general overheads. **3.** Fixed costs divided by contribution per unit (selling price minus variable cost per unit). **4.** Total revenue, fixed costs and total costs. **5.** Margin of safety is the difference between a firm's current level of sales and its break-even point; on a break-even chart it can be drawn as a horizontal line between demand/sales and the break-even point. **6.** Can spot problems in advance, allows solutions to be planned, encourages forward planning in other areas. **7.** Cash in minus cash out. **8.** Overtrading occurs when a firm expands too rapidly for its capital base to cope with. The result is that the firm runs short of cash as inflows are not given time to catch up with the ever increasing outflows. **9.** It is very flexible – you only pay for what you use, but overdrafts carry very high interest rates. **10.** A venture capitalist is an individual or firm that provides financial backing for relatively risky business ventures. This finance is often provided as a mix of loan and share capital. **11.** Profit is the difference between revenue and costs. However, a cost need not incur a cash flow (e.g. depreciation on machinery) while revenue does not necessarily mean that cash has been received (e.g. items sold on credit are recorded as revenue when they are delivered, even if cash is not received for another 2 months). **12.** Adding a little to last year's budget to allow for inflation, or zero budgeting which sets each budget to zero each year and expects the budget holder to justify every pound they bid for. **13.** If managers are given full control over how they allocate their budgets, they will be given the responsibility for keeping within that budget. According to Herzberg this responsibility is a key motivator and may thus help to motivate the managers in question. **14. a)** 2000 units × contribution of £8 per unit = total contribution of £16,000. Deduct fixed costs of £10,000 to leave profit per month of £6,000; **b)** £10,000/£8 = 1250 units; **c)** 2,000 − 1,250 = 750 units.
15.

	January	February	March	April
Cash in	45	40	44	40
Cash out	40	43	36	42
Net cash flow	5	(3)	8	(2)
Opening balance	15	20	17	25
Closing balance	20	17	25	23

UNIT 2.2

Student howler

1. Selling more units does not affect the break-even point. It simply means that the firm's position on their break-even point has moved to the right.

Test yourself

1. a) Break-even moves up; **b)** break-even falls; **c)** no change to break-even point; **d)** break-even falls.
2. Break-even analysis is most useful to single product firms selling in relatively stable external environments. This company is likely to produce a range of different products and will operate in a market where tastes change rapidly. Therefore, although break-even analysis could be used, perhaps product by product if fixed costs can be split between the different products, it will have limited value. Meanwhile, in a changing environment, changes to the graph are likely to occur so regularly as to limit the usefulness of the technique.
3.
a) BE: FC/contribution p.u. = £36,000/£0.5 = 72,000 units; safety margin is therefore 80,000 − 72,000 = 8,000 units;
b) BE = £40,000/£0.5 = 80,000 units;
c) BE = £36,000/£0.6 = 60,000 units: safety margin = 80,000 − 60,000 = 20,000 units;
d) BE = £36,000/£0.7 = 51,429 units;
e) to calculate new demand: Elasticity (0.5) = % change in demand/% change in price (20%), so the demand will fall by 10%, from 80,000 to 72,000. As BE is now at 51,429, the new safety margin will be: 72,000 − 51,429 = 20,571 units.

UNIT 2.3

Student howler

1. As explained in the exam insight section of this unit, extra output means that average cost per unit will be lower because the fixed element will fall.

Test yourself

1. The answer lies in what happens to the amount of fixed costs that each unit has to cover. If more units are produced, fixed costs are spread more thinly over more units and therefore the total cost of each unit is lower.
2. Extra profit – if the order generates a positive contribution; keeping an existing customer happy; attracting a new regular customer. **3.** If they do not have sufficient spare capacity; may not want other customers to find out; order is unlikely to lead to future business. **4.** Working at full capacity may involve increased costs, such as overtime or night shift payments. Meanwhile, full capacity implies no time for routine maintenance which may lead to less reliable machinery.
5. *Current profit*:

£8 (contribution p.u.) × 1000 (sales) = £8,000 (total contribution)
£8,000 − £5,000 (fixed costs) = profit of £3,000
Special order brings:
£2 (contribution p.u.) × 800 units = £1,600 which is all extra profit.
Therefore the order will increase that month's profit by just over 50%.

UNIT 2.4

Student howler

Working capital can viewed as a necessary evil – it is not a profitable use of money and should therefore be kept to a minimum.

Test yourself

1. The firm's financial debt to the shareholders: share capital plus reserves. 2. Assets employed balance with capital employed. 3. a) the balance sheet is like a photo taken at a moment in time and therefore stock, debtors, cash and creditors are frozen at that moment; b) firms should aim to have sufficient working capital to operate effectively, to pay the bills and to take advantage of any business opportunities that may arise. 4. The firm has expanded – as shown by the increase in capital employed. More external finance has entered the firm – from issuing another £50,000 of shares and borrowing an extra £100,000. Meanwhile, £50,000 of last year's profit has been retained and the firm appears to have squeezed an extra £50,000 from its working capital – hence the reduction in current assets. The extra £250,000 has gone into boosting fixed assets.
5. The balance sheet certainly reveals much about a firm's finances. It will show where it has received its money from and how it has been used at any moment in time. Of course, applying financial ratios to the balance sheet can tell us a lot more (see Unit 2.7) so on its own a balance sheet has limited relevance. As with financial ratios, being able to compare a balance sheet with that of a rival, or with previous years, can tell us a lot more about a firm's health.

UNIT 2.5

Student howler

1. This is understandable, but overgeneralised and therefore over the top. Window dressing creates no magic. If you dress up this year's accounts it makes it harder to do better next year. So the only firms tempted to window dress are those with difficult short-term positions. Firms such as Cadbury–Schweppes, Unilever or Next have no wish (or need) to use financial data deceptively.

Test yourself

1. Profit quality measures the proportion of the annual profit that is from one-off instead of ongoing operations. 2. To keep the share price from falling, making the firm vulnerable to hostile takeovers.
3. Profit and loss account for Whittakers PLC for year ended 31/12/04:

	£000s
Sales	1,200
Cost of sales	650
Gross profit	550
Overheads	390
Operating profit	160
One-off expense	140
Profit before tax	20
Tax	15
Profit after tax	5
Dividends	15
Retained profit	(10)

4. a)

	Year ended 31/03/05 (£000s)	Year ended 31/03/04 (£000s)
Sales	240	250
Cost of sales	140	150
Gross profit	100	100
Overheads	75	65
Operating profit	25	35
Extraordinary item	–	(15)
Profit before tax	25	20
Tax	10	7
Profit after tax	15	13
Dividends	10	8
Retained profit	5	5

b) The firm's sales fell from 2004 to 2005. Gross profit remained unchanged because the firm's cost of sales fell, as it should following a fall in sales. However, the Directors must be worried that, despite the fall in sales, overheads increased significantly. 2004 showed a far healthier operating profit and so this seems to have been a far better year's trading for the company than 2005 in terms of profitability. The one-off item in 2004 reduced profit before and after tax figures, but increased dividend payments in 2005, probably designed to keep shareholders happy despite a worsened operating performance, led to identical retained profits for the 2 years.

UNIT 2.6

Student howler

1. Depreciation does not involve any cash moving – all the cash went when the asset was purchased.

Test yourself

1. To spread the cost over the lifetime of the asset, making it less of a burden on short-term profit.
2. They deduct the accumulated depreciation from the original purchase cost. 3. a) £100,000 – £20,000 = £80,000/5 = £16,000; b) new depreciation charge = £100,000 – £30,000/10 = £7,000 per year, boosting annual profit by £9,000. 4. The FD may wish to avoid underestimating the asset's value – a practice that

could cause sudden financial shocks. It may also be a technique to allow the firm to declare a smaller profit this year in order to reduce its tax liability. **5.** The calculation of depreciation requires three pieces of information, only one of which is factual – the original or historic cost. Residual value and useful life will more often than not be estimates. Since balance sheets show the value of fixed assets as being the original cost less accumulated depreciation, balance sheet valuations of fixed assets have been based on two estimates. This potential inaccuracy will also affect the profit and loss account as the depreciation charge for the year will be included in the expenses – thus affecting the figure for operating profit. All of this will undermine the reliability and accuracy of the information provided by these accounts. However, independent auditors should have checked the firm's depreciation assumptions to ensure they are realistic. However, recent high profile accounting scandals suggest that auditors may not always pick up on dubious accounting practices.

UNIT 2.7
Student howler

1. Don't leap to extreme conclusions. As seen from the Tesco example some firms can operate on very low acid test ratios. Meanwhile 0.98 is as close to 1 as can reasonably be expected.

Test yourself

Ratios

	2005	2004
a) Acid test	13/10 = 1.30	9/12 = 0.75
b) Gearing	40/120 × 100 = 33%	80/140 × 100 = 57%
c) Gross profit margin	60/240 × 100 = 25%	70/220 × 100 = 32%
d) Operating profit margin	15/240 × 100 = 6.25%	15/220 × 100 = 6.8%
e) Return on capital	15/120 × 100 = 12.5%	15/140 × 100 = 10.7%
f) Asset turnover	240/120 = 2 times	220/140 = 1.57 times
g) Debtor days	9/(240/365) = 13.7 days	6/(220/365) = 9.95 days
h) Stock turnover	180/12 = 15 times	150/15 = 10 times
i) Dividend yield	(7/47)/2.10 = 7.09%	(5/32)/2.90 = 5.39%

2. a) Profitability – ratios to consider – gross margin, operating margin, return on capital: Both profit margins have dropped since last year. This indicates that the firm is generating less profit for each pound of sale. ROC has increased because there is now less money invested in the business. **b)** Financial health – ratios to consider – acid test, gearing: Acid test has improved – it is now comfortably above 1, although its starting point of 0.75 did not look worryingly low. Even more encouraging is that the firm has cut their gearing level from above the dangerous 50% to well below at 33%. This has in turn reduced the firm's interest payments significantly. **c)** Efficiency – ratios to consider – asset turnover, debtor days, stock turnover: The firm is now generating more sales from its reduced asset base. This, along with an increased stock turnover, indicates a greater level of financial efficiency. The increase in debtor days suggests that financial efficiency may have dropped, but this may have been due to offering slightly more generous credit terms to customers to encourage the increased sales. **d)** Ability to please shareholders – ratios to consider – earnings per share, price earnings, dividend yield: Earnings per share have fallen, yet the increased price earnings ratio suggests the market is now more confident about the firm's future earnings. The market will also have been pleased by the increased dividend yield – caused by a greater dividend payout this year than last.

Overall the ratios present a mixed set of results. The figures were designed to suggest that this was a firm that had tried to adjust its strategy to focus on a lower price section of the market, so the reduced profitability is perhaps not surprising. They maintained a relatively healthy set of accounts by reducing their expenses and reducing their debt burden. The stock market appears to have been fairly happy with this new strategy.

UNIT 2.8
Student howlers

1. For every Enron there are hundreds of accurate financial statements. Be sure not to jump to conclusions on the basis of one or two isolated examples. **2.** Just because they are numbers doesn't mean they are accurate. See the answer to the first question below.

Test yourself

1. Depreciation calculations involve three variables, only one of which is a matter of historical fact. The historic cost of the asset cannot be questioned, but any attempts to estimate a residual value and useful life may allow an element of subjectivity to enter the accounting process. **2.** The profit and loss account will show a one-off profit on the sale of the asset – thus boosting profits before and after tax (though not operating profit). The balance sheet will see a lower value for fixed assets, with the amount for which the asset was sold being added to the current assets section, quite possibly as cash – thus improving the firm's liquidity position. **3.** Historic scandals, along with a sense of mistrust about the genuine independence of some auditors, have led to a reduction in the level of trust in published accounts. However, accounting regulations are continually being tightened up to deal with each loophole that is discovered to try to improve the transparency of financial reporting in general. Though fraud such as that uncovered at Parmalat may never be entirely eradicated, the vast majority of companies' annual reports contain accurate, independently verified information on which investors can confidently make decisions.

4.

Project A				Project B			
Year	NCF	Discount factor	DCF	Year	NCF	Discount factor	DCF
0	(5)	1	(5)	0	(5)	1	(5)
1	4	0.94	3.76	1	0	0.94	0
2	2	0.89	1.78	2	1	0.89	0.89
3	1	0.84	0.84	3	2	0.84	1.68
4	1	0.79	0.79	4	6	0.79	4.74
NPV for A: £2.17m; NPV for B: £2.31m.							

UNIT 2.9
Student howler
1. Quick payback may not mean highest profit and a project may also have a number of qualitative problems that mean it's not the firm's best option.

Test yourself
1. Payback = 2 years and 10 months; ARR = 6.25%. **2.** The payback period may be too long for the firm, while the project may not fit in with the firm's overall direction. There may be belief that the forecasts on which calculations are based are unreliable or the firm may not be able to afford the initial investment. **3.** Forecasting may have been done poorly, perhaps by someone who wanted the results to turn out in a particular way. Unexpected external (or internal) events may nullify the forecasts.

UNIT 2.10
Test yourself
1. Revenue expenditure is money spent on items that will be used once, current assets and expenses, whereas capital expenditure is money spent on fixed assets. **2.** Estimates for useful life and residual values. **3.** Profit that is generated by an activity that is not part of the normal, ongoing trading activities of the business and is therefore unlikely to be repeated. Selling a fixed asset for a profit is an example. **4.** Paying interest, tax, dividends, or retaining it within the business. **5.** Liquidity refers to a firm's ability to meet its short-term debts. **6.** Stocks are valued at the lower of cost or net realisable value. **7.** If profits are lower than expected, if gearing seems worryingly high or if liquidity looks poor. **8.** The firm does most of its selling for cash, and, linked with a very fast stock turnover, they are a cash-rich business that could generate a huge amount of cash from sales in a very short space of time. **9.** Taking less credit from suppliers, injecting new capital in the form of cash. **10.** Stock turnover = cost of sales/stock; debtor days = debtors/(sales/365); asset turnover = sales turnover/assets employed. **11.** If interest rates are low, and if the firm is growing rapidly but profitably, loan capital may well be considered a relatively cheap and safe source of finance. **12.** Cutting price will mean direct costs will account for a greater proportion of revenue – reducing gross margins. However, if the price cut generates more sales, the expenses, which are mainly fixed costs, may well be spread over more units, thus generating a higher net margin. **13.** Previous years, budgeted figures for this year, other similar firms. **14.** Current customers may find out and leave, they may not have sufficient spare capacity, the order may not fit in with the strategic direction the firm wishes to take. **15.** The total revenue line would rise more steeply, meaning that the break-even point falls. **16.** Cash flow forecasts. **17.** Money is tied up in the project for a short time. While money is tied up and not recovered (paid back) by the investment, there is the danger that it could be lost. This may be the result of external factors, so a shorter payback means less time when external factors can affect the success of the investment project. **18.** To allow for the time value of money – i.e. cash received in 5 years' time is not worth the same as it is today. Therefore future cash flows are discounted to allow for the money that could have been earned if that money was available now. **19.** Does the investment tie in with the firm's objectives? How reliable are the data being used?

Questions (Bone china crunchtime)

1. Break-even = FC/contribution p.u.
      = £5,000/£1 = 5,000 units
   Safety margin = current output − BE = 10,000 − 5,000 = 5,000 units
   Monthly profit = safety margin × contribution p.u. = 5,000 × £1 = £5,000

2. Financial effect of accepting the order:
   Extra contribution generated = £0.25 × 5,000 units × 8 months = £10,000
   Extra fixed cost − printing machine = £1,000 per month × 8 months = £8,000
   So extra profit over 8 months = £2,000
   In favour of accepting the order:
      Extra profit, route to expanding overseas, helps to use spare capacity
   Against accepting the order:
      Extra profit is minimal − just a 5% increase. This seems unlikely to lead to other orders. The danger of receiving press coverage could mean current customers find out about the special price and switch supplier.
      Overall, the order is unlikely to be accepted. The overseas expansion mentioned related to the European market − Cuba is unlikely to be a key export market for Cohen's.

3. a)

	Shop	Machine
Payback	2 years, 7.2 months	2 years, 10 months
ARR	13.5%	17.5%
NPV (assumes 6% discount factors)	£402,500	£102,250

   b)
   In favour of shop:
      Higher NPV (but on larger investment).
      Shorter payback (but not hugely).
   Against shop:
      Offers limited prospect for growth, especially internationally − therefore may fail to meet objectives.
   In favour of machine:
      Ties in with objective of growth − should open up new market segment − bringing added value due to design capability.
   Against machine:
      Figures worked out by main supporter of the idea − may be unreliable data.
      Overall, both clearly have pros and cons − neither seems a miracle strategic solution to the issue of growth, but the machine may well provide the greater potential for growth, even if it may be a riskier proposition, especially given possible question mark over data.

4. Payback shows least risk investment, may be an issue for smallish firm looking to borrow a major sum. It doesn't show profit however. ARR provides measure of profitability but in this case fails to show the delay in cash flows from machinery purchase. This is shown by NPV, with those further distant cash flows discounted heavily. The NPV can seem misleading; however, since different initial investments are involved the machinery would be expected to give a lower result.

Section 3: People

UNIT 3.1

Test yourself

1. Physiological, security, social, esteem, self-actualisation. 2. a) Responsibility, achievement, recognition, advancement; b) Salary, working conditions, relations with boss, relations with co-workers, company policies. 3. The beneficial impact on staff morale of managers taking a personal interest in their staff. 4. While still rewarding individuals, bonuses will only be large if everyone has pulled together in order to achieve the company's aim of greater profit, thus encouraging a sense of teamwork. 5. A voluntary group of workers who meet together to discuss possible improvements in their area of the firm. 6. Staff may become demotivated, while managers may not fully understand the situation about which they are making decisions. 7. Involving people in decision making can help to satisfy their esteem needs, while also giving them a sense of responsibility. If their ideas are put into practice they are likely to feel a sense of achievement. 8. The number of subordinates for whom a manager is directly responsible. 9. Delayering means removing layers of structure so therefore the vertical chains of command will shorten. 10. A structure with both traditional, function-based vertical lines of authority but also diagonal lines of authority representing cross-functional project teams. 11. Workforce planning, recruitment and selection, training and remuneration. 12. Herzberg felt that the more an employee could do the more you could motivate them. Since Herzberg's motivators revolve around growing and advancing at work, training to develop new skills will help to offer staff the chance to meet the motivator needs. 13. History, leadership style of senior management, structure. 14. Recruiting the right, properly skilled staff can improve productivity. This should be the result of careful workforce planning that has identified the skill needs of the organisation. Meanwhile training staff is likely to enhance productivity levels further in the long term as their skills improve. 15. Proper HRM does cost money − employing HR staff, careful recruitment procedures and substantial induction and training programmes will cost the firm. However, the resulting increases in productivity (see previous question) should counterbalance this effect. 16. Culture is by definition the way in which people are used to behaving. It takes time to shift patterns of behaviour and is very difficult to achieve. Since there is often a prevailing attitude of 'we've always done it this way', staff may become entrenched in the ways of the old culture.

UNIT 3.2

Student howlers

1. Generalisations do not work since different methods are better for different jobs. While oral methods may give greater scope for discussion, written methods would be more appropriate if communicating highly complex technical data. 2. Growth makes effective communication harder but a smart management team will have managed their communications systems effectively and put in place steps to try to ensure that the effectiveness of communication is not adversely affected by growth.

Test yourself

1. a) ii; b) iii; c) i. 2. Extra branches means growth, so the problems that stem from growth as outlined in the unit are all likely to be applicable. However, the extra difficulties presented will relate to travel and language. If UK managers want to discuss issues with branch managers in Europe but are unwilling to do so by telephone, they will need to travel a greater distance than they would within the UK. Meanwhile language barriers will emerge and although shop managers may be expected to speak English, local shop floor staff may find it difficult to understand corporate information, such as policies and objectives. This would necessitate extra cost in translation. 3. The main advances in communication that may be attributed to IT are email, the internet, corporate intranets and arguably mobile phones. The common feature of each of these advancements has been to generate more communication. People are easier to reach with a mobile phone, and emails can easily be copied to many different staff. Intranets can become clogged up with information if regular 'housekeeping' does not take place. Meanwhile the internet, although a valuable source of information, is at times a quagmire of irrelevant information that takes a very long time to sift through before relevant information can be gathered. On the whole, firms that have carefully thought about how the new technology can be used to increase the *effectiveness* of their communication will have benefited from these advancements whereas those who take a piecemeal approach to communication will simply find staff buried under a mass of information that may be of limited use.

UNIT 3.3

Test yourself

1. Recruitment decisions may be rushed, leading to poor appointments and inefficient staff. Staff shortages may damage levels of customer service, or delay the opening of new pubs. Delays to openings mean delays in receiving cash inflows and therefore extended payback periods on investments. Such problems may impact on the image of the whole chain, casting the potential success of their growth plans into some doubt. 2. Careful planning of HR issues ought to allow a firm to ensure that its staffing needs are met.

However, the success of the corporate strategy depends on the other aspects of the plan equally – marketing, finance and operations must all be implemented effectively to enhance the chances of success. External influences may also cause problems in the most carefully planned strategies. 3. The marketing strategy will contain details of forecast sales and will therefore provide a clear indication of the likely staffing levels required. Specialist marketing activities may need to be dealt with through HR developments, such as the recruitment of more sales staff. Meanwhile, the operations plan, containing details of production levels and possibly technical research, will be a clear indicator of the types of skill that will be required to provide the product or service being offered by the firm.

UNIT 3.4

Student howler

1. A small amount of labour turnover can help to bring in new ideas but if a firm is losing nearly half its staff every year the costs of this level of labour turnover will undoubtedly outweigh the benefits.

Test yourself

1. • *Labour productivity* – has fallen over the 3-year period, but remained steady over the last year. This is likely to have been caused by a combination of the other problems shown in the table, but fundamentally people are clearly not being managed effectively. The effect is likely to be a decline in the firm's competitiveness since each unit of output is likely to carry a higher labour cost. • *Absenteeism* – has risen over the 3 years and this may well have been the result of poor management practice. Rising labour turnover levels may also have contributed. The effect will have been to disrupt production, as evidenced by the fall in productivity levels. • *Labour turnover* – again worsening (rising), probably due to management attitudes, along with a prevailing feeling amongst the staff that the place is going downhill. Leaving rates may be accentuated if there is little local unemployment since alternative jobs will be easier to find. The effect of higher labour turnover will be increased recruitment and possibly training costs – again hitting the firm's competitiveness due to the increase in fixed costs. • *Accident levels* – these are rising which is not good news. There is likely to be some link to the reduction in motivation, since more accidents are likely to occur if staff are not focused on doing their job to the best of their ability. However, it is also possible to link this worsening indicator to the worsening figures for labour turnover and absenteeism. The effects of the high accidents are likely to be felt in these other ways. 2. High labour turnover sounds like a reflection of the firm's poor management – either in terms of morale or pay/remuneration. Yet it may be largely due to natural causes such as retirements. Losing a number of experienced staff may be a problem, but the answers lie in preparation and

training, not in pay rises for all! As with everything in business, unless you know the causes of a problem, you are in no position to make decisions about solutions. **3.** The five indicators covered in this unit do give a decent idea of how effectively managers are managing. However, they do not provide clear answers since they can be influenced by factors other than HRM, such as the state of the local economy and job markets and the reliability and quality of suppliers. The trouble with trying to measure the effectiveness of people management is partly that purely objective measures such as these do not gather human opinions on management – yet this exercise is likely to become subjective if included in an assessment of managers' skills. Meanwhile expectations of what is 'good people management' may differ with some firms welcoming strong team spirit and innovation, whereas others would be looking for simple productivity increases. In short, the task is arguably impossible but indicators such as these can certainly give useful information on the effectiveness of management.

UNIT 3.5
Test yourself

1. Teamworking within a sales environment can present significant problems. Since commission is likely to form part of the payment system, staff who are rewarded for team performance may well feel that weaker members of the team are benefiting from their expertise. This can lead to resentment, lower motivation and possibly increased staff turnover. Other areas within the dealership may be more appropriate for teamworking, perhaps amongst mechanics, where a shift to teamworking may increase motivation. However, problems may still arise if management is unwilling to delegate sufficient authority to these staff to make decisions within the team. **2.** A works council is a consultative group. If staff views have not previously been heard, the council may help to overcome a feeling of having no say in business decisions. However, the council has no decision-making powers and therefore employees may feel that its creation is simply an attempt to make them feel involved without actually giving them any power. **3.** Employee shareholders will benefit financially from an increase in the company's profits and share price. Since these are largely determined by the effectiveness of staff performance, staff should understand the need to improve their own performance if they are to benefit financially from their shareholding. This logic works in theory, but in practice, in large PLCs, employees are likely to feel that there is little that their individual performance can do to affect the firm's overall profits.

UNIT 3.6
Test yourself

1. Unions may prove to be a valuable mechanism for listening to staff views on major issues; recognising a union can help to satisfy staff security needs since they will feel they have the protection of their union in the event of a dispute. **2.** Although collective bargaining with hardened trade union negotiators may lead to higher rates of pay than a firm would ideally want, and time spent dealing with union representatives may take up management time, the effects of a positive working relationship with trade unions should balance these out. If the union is able to explain to its members why the firm needs to change working practices or lay off some staff, industrial action could be avoided and this is extremely beneficial. Meanwhile workers may well be working more effectively if they do not feel the need to worry about how they are being treated by their managers – they have the reassurance of trade union backing to meet their security needs. **3.** A trade union would be signing away the right to use what may be considered its most powerful weapon. The reasons it might do this relate to the accompanying terms that would go with the agreement. Management would expect to offer assurances relating primarily to consultation and participation in decision making, while other assurances about future pay deals and changes to working conditions may be offered. For the management, not only does a no-strike deal represent a crucial indicator of the union's willingness to work in partnership, but it also allows the firm to plan for the longer term without the uncertainty caused by possible industrial action.

UNIT 3.7
Test yourself

1. Poor morale is likely to cause barriers to communication. Staff who are demotivated will be less willing to listen to messages from above, and less likely to engage in two-way communication. Suggestions from staff may also dry up. **2.** Poor communication may reduce morale since staff lose a sense of commitment to the organisation. If low level staff feel isolated from management a 'them and us' divide may arise, possibly leading to industrial relations problems. **3.** May be part-time staff – so hard to have whole staff meetings; lack of motivation and commitment from temporary staff at peak times; possible lack of communication skill from management at a small outlet. **4.** Many layers of hierarchy means many layers for messages to pass through; low level staff feeling a lack of commitment to the organisation; physical distance between branches/offices may cause problems; large firms often rely too heavily on email and written communication. **5.** Allows them to treat 'better' staff differently; means that staff have less power in any negotiations. **6.** Saves management time – since one agreement with the workforce's deputation covers all staff. **7.** A group of employee and employer representatives who meet regularly to discuss issues that affect the whole firm. **8.** Mayo suggested that human relations were important at work and teamworking allows staff to interact with their other team members. For Maslow, teamworking would be a clear method for trying to ensure that employees' social needs were met in their working lives. **9.** To preserve the jobs of their members; to protect the rights of their members in the workplace; to improve working conditions for all members. **10.** Negotiating on behalf of members with employers; legal advice and representation; publicly campaigning on issues such as the minimum wage. **11.** Arbitration means making a judgement between two sides; conciliation does not involve making a judgement but refers to attempts to bring the two sides closer together so that they can reach an agreement. **12.** Saves time dealing with several unions. May work more effectively as a channel of bottom-up communication since all views are channelled through one route. **13. a)** Output per period/average number of employees per period; **b)** number of staff who left work/average total staffing level × 100; **c)** number of days work missed/total possible days worked × 100. **14.** Lower productivity levels mean that labour costs per unit are higher. The result is that profit margins will fall unless price is increased. **15.** Low recruitment costs. Increased effectiveness of teamworking as teams can settle down. Reduced training costs – less induction training needed. **16.** Accidents may halt production, leading to lower output levels and therefore higher costs per unit. Accidents caused by breaches of health and safety legislation may lead to fines. **17.** High unemployment locally; excellent pay and working conditions; interesting work.

Questions (Room for growth?)

1. Causes of the problems could include the three directors not meeting regularly, which surely could have been avoided. Opening a second branch means that face-to-face communication between branches becomes harder, but, again, this problem could have been minimised. Extra layers would have been added within the hierarchy and – although necessary – would have lengthened chains of command. However, the effect does not seem to have been great in this case – although this problem would appear to have been unavoidable. A lack of suggestions, especially from staff at Room 1, could have been avoided if appropriate systems of employee involvement had been set up – perhaps helping to avoid the reduced motivation of these staff which seems to be the heart of the problem. Most of the problems could have been avoided or at least minimised. **2. a)** Higher staff turnover would increase recruitment and training costs. Meanwhile service levels may have fallen, while the sense of a team falling apart may have damaged the motivation of original staff. This may be felt in the raised level of absenteeism, which in itself would be disruptive, possibly meaning more overtime work, poorer service if short-staffed or the need for senior staff to fill in, thus reducing the time they have available for addressing strategic issues. Increased waste levels would mean an increase in costs and thus a reduction in profitability. **b)** If the fundamental problem is poor motivation, the firm may need to go back to the basics of motivation theory – examining

the extent to which the jobs being done allow staff to meet their needs at work. To specifically reduce staff turnover, more careful recruitment may be necessary. Absenteeism may be reduced if some financial incentive were made available but much research evidence suggests that firms that use this method to reduce absenteeism find little success, since absenteeism is more often an indicator of deeper rooted problems. Waste levels should be reduced if staff perform more efficiently, perhaps the result of higher levels of motivation which could be linked with proper staff training. **3.** Key methods of encouraging employee participation include works councils, worker directors, quality circles or employee shareholdings. In this context, since many of the problems appear to be operational, quality circles may be the answer. Separate groups for kitchen and front of house staff will allow each group to identify ways to improve their area of the restaurant and are likely to be small enough to enable each member to make meaningful contributions. It may however be tricky getting all staff to feel involved if the restaurant relies on staff working early and late shifts – though this problem is unlikely to be insurmountable. **4.** A strategic or a planned approach to HR would certainly have helped greatly. The expansion plans appear to have paid little attention to the HR issues involved. Other than ensuring that one of the founders was running each restaurant, there seems to have been little effective workforce planning. The results are seen in staff shortages, poor recruitment decisions and worsening personnel performance indicators. If HR had been planned carefully as an integral part of the expansion planning the firm would be likely to have avoided many of these problems.

Section 4: Operations

UNIT 4.1

Student howlers

1. Just in time may be appropriate in some circumstances, but cannot be guaranteed to bring an improvement in every case. Beware of generalising. **2.** Lean production aims to reduce the waste of resources, but will use as many resources as are required to meet a desired level of output.

Test yourself

1. An economy of scale looks at reductions in average costs due to operating on a larger scale, while a diseconomy of scale considers the increases in average cost caused by the larger size of the firm. **2. a)** 67%; **b)** It could increase output, perhaps after following a policy of market penetration, or could cut capacity, perhaps by subletting part of its productive capacity. **3. a)** Job, because the one-off speciality will require the process to be devised, used once and then amended for the next task. **b)** Flow, because there will need to be a large, continuous level of production. **c)** Batch, because each order will stand alone in its make-up and quantity. 4. Both are equally important – the art is in getting the balance between the two right every time. 5. Better information on current stock levels, automatic communication with suppliers. 6. A collection of measures designed to reduce waste in many forms throughout the business. 7. The firm could become the first to launch a new product or be the first to develop ideas to meet changing customer needs and wants. By reacting quickest the firm may be able to stay ahead of competitors and develop a brand loyalty based on their always being up-to-date. The novelty of products could become the firm's USP.

UNIT 4.2

Student howlers

1. Although cost will be important, it will never be the only issue considered in a location decision. 2. Being footloose means that a firm has the ability to choose its location. However, where it is located will still be important for business success.

Test yourself

1. Cost, suppliers, workforce, transport links, environment, quality of life. 2. Break-even analysis, investment appraisal. 3. Costs, such as land, labour, transport. 4. Environment, quality of life, room for future expansion. 5. Might allow a greater distance between the business and customer or different parts of the business. 6. As part of its economic management, as part of its social development. 7. Grants, tax incentives, cheap premises, planning permission. 8. Likely to consider different issues, such as the ability of workers to move and the effect of the move on relationships with customers and suppliers. 9. A poor location may stop a business from being successful, but by itself a good location cannot ensure success. The right location must be supported by all the other aspects of the business being right as well.

UNIT 4.3

Student howlers

1. Paying wages at a lower level in developing countries than in developed countries may not be a means of exploitation. It may well be that the wages paid are in line with, or even above, the normal wages in that country, even if these are well below those paid elsewhere. 2. An international location may reduce production costs, but it may not always do so. Korean firms investing in a UK car plant may well find its costs rising, but these costs may be outweighed by other benefits, such as the avoidance of EU trade barriers. 3. While UK firms may face more direct competition, many firms will benefit as they supply or service the new factories. The techniques and work practices introduced may well become common practice, improving the efficiency of all UK firms.

Test yourself

1. Globalisation is the trend for businesses to be operating on a world-wide basis. 2. Cheaper labour, cheaper raw materials, more skilled workforce. 3. Entry to the large EU market, government grants towards the start-up costs. 4. For: protects European industry; protects jobs and economic health. Against: provokes a similar reaction which hinders EU firms trading with the rest of the world; unfair on less developed nations who may be struggling to establish their economies. 5. Must study quantitative factors (costs, revenues) and qualitative (reaction of customers, reaction of suppliers). 6. More internet access may give a firm like Amazon, who only sell online, almost complete freedom in their location decision. But, since most retailers have stores that people visit, the fact that a growing proportion of their sales are online will not affect their location decision at all. 7. It is important as it has a direct bearing on things like costs, quality and the relationship with suppliers. However, many other factors will also be important in determining a firm's success. 8. It can offer grants, influence exchange rates and impose trade barriers to influence location decisions, but a firm would also consider many other issues, so the government will never have full control over such firms.

UNIT 4.4

Student howlers

1. There are some situations where a CPA would not be the best course of action, and may actually slow down progress on a task. 2. Like all business plans, there has to be an element of flexibility so that the firm can react to changing circumstances. 3. All activities are important – even those not on the critical path must be planned for and must be monitored.

Test yourself

1. Critical path analysis is a tool for the planning and monitoring of complex projects. 2. The number of the node in sequence; the earliest start time of the following activity; the latest finishing time of the preceding activity. 3. The activities will have an earliest start time and latest finish time in both the preceding and following nodes that equal each other. 4. a) Critical path = A,B,D; the shortest possible duration is 10 days. b) Critical path = A,C,D,F,G; the shortest possible duration is 15 weeks. 5. (from 4a) Activity C: 7 – 2 – 3 = 2 days' float; (from 4b) Activity B: 6 – 4 – 0 = 2 weeks' float, Activity E: 15 – 3 – 8 = 4 weeks' float. 6. Can help minimise the time taken for a project; can allow the use of just in time stock control. 7. The results of R&D are unpredictable and can't be programmed in advance. 8. This is correct to the extent that these activities must be managed exactly if the whole project isn't to be delayed; however, all activities must be carefully monitored not only for reasons of timing (if they are delayed too long, they will become critical) but also to ensure efficiency and quality are maintained.

UNIT 4.5

Student howlers

1. This statement refers to market research, which is too often confused with R&D in exam answers. 2. Not all firms would benefit from R&D – small firms may not be able to afford it, and others may be in a traditional, unchanging market. 3. R&D may be important to firms, but it will never be the sole determinant of the firm's level of competitiveness.

Test yourself:

1. Invention means coming up with new ideas, innovation is giving these ideas a practical use. 2. New products and new production techniques. 3. R&D is finding new products or production processes, whereas market research involves finding out about customer tastes and preferences. 4. Short term, UK firms may record higher profits as less is being spent on R&D; however, in the long term, the new products and increased efficiency that foreign firms are likely to enjoy may cause UK firms' profitability to fall. 5. Financial cost, the opportunity cost of the resources used, the de-motivational effect of a lack of success, the time devoted to the unsuccessful programme. 6. It should do, so that it can keep making progress and maintain its market position. Stopping now may give it higher short-term profits, but rivals may then overtake them. 7. By itself, product innovation is useful but only as a starting point for success. Many other factors will help determine whether or not a business is successful. 8. There may be short-term disruption, but if the innovation is of a high enough quality the long-term benefits ought to outweigh any short-term disruption.

UNIT 4.6

Student howlers

1. It may do, if implemented correctly and if the competitors don't possess the same technology. In some cases, using IT may keep the firm in line with competitors or, if things go wrong, could turn out to be a disaster for the firm. 2. They may have certain advantages, such as accuracy and the ability to endlessly perform repetitive tasks, but they still tend not to be as flexible as humans and would not be able to make suggestions under a continuous improvement programme. The best is a balance of humans and robotics. 3. Although it may do so, a lot depends on how flexible the firm's production was before the technology was introduced. How long does it take a worker to put down a hammer and pick up a screwdriver?

Test yourself

1. Robotics, precision, repetition, flexibility, persistence. 2. Accurate records, contacting patients and sending reminders by text, etc., better level of treatment, better balanced pain relief. 3. Positive – better quality output and training can lead to improved motivation. Negative – fear of change and the new, redundancies, feelings of alienation. 4. Improvements in efficiency, quality, response time, new product development and after-sales service. 5. Competitors may already be ahead of the firm, the new IT may not be used efficiently; other factors, such as the attitude of the workforce, may act against the potential benefits. 6. Short term – expensive to purchase, liquidity issues if the money is borrowed. Long term – if used correctly the technology should pay for itself and generate additional profit. If used incorrectly the firm could be left with an expensive, long-term debt and falling revenues as it loses out to competitors. 7. Costs – financial, relationship with the workforce. Benefits – improvements in productivity and quality.

UNIT 4.7

Test yourself

1. Developing new or existing products through scientific research and technological research. 2. Any, but could include MP3 players, iPod, Dyson cleaners, etc. 3. As soon as possible to ensure that replacement products are ready when needed. 4. Planning ahead by splitting a project into individual activities and sequencing them as effectively as possible. 5. The amount of spare time available to complete an activity within a project. 6. Allows the whole project to be completed as quickly as possible; allows the use of just in time stock control. 7. EST shows the soonest point at which the following activity can be started, LFT shows the latest time by which a preceding activity must be finished. 8. Customer records, financial records, personnel details. 9. More up to date, more accurate. 10. Reduces costs (e.g. office space); makes communication less direct. 11. Increased quantity of communication, less opportunity for feedback. 12. Break-even analysis, investment appraisal. 13. Solve local unemployment issues, encourage local investment. 14. Reduce direct production costs, easier entry to overseas trading blocs. 15. Increasing UK unemployment brings the firm a poor public image and it could cause communication problems. 16. Output, waste, productivity.

Questions (Virgin's tilting trains)

1. i) The application of machinery to business operations; ii) investigations into solving business problems or issues. 2. Customers are demanding faster travel (air, etc.) so railways are developing faster trains, of which tilting is one example. 3. Research, development, modelling, prototype production, trials, production. 4. For: only by R&D will new ideas be found and developed. Against: there are no guarantees. 5. For: meeting customer needs, improving competitive position. Against: no guarantee of success; easier, cheaper options exist.

Questions (The First 'Walkman'?)

1. i) A sample, experimental product; ii) the right to be the sole user of an invention. 2. Research and

development; other firms. **3.** For: mass production techniques, bulk buying; Against: lack of responsiveness, diseconomies of scale. **4.** For: ability to apply techniques like TQM. Against: standardisation may cause a lack of responsiveness. **5.** Depends if with or without permission and/or payment, but could still ensure a 'major' product reaches the marketplace – it is likely that the Walkman would not have been produced if Sony had not developed the original idea.

Section 5: External influences

UNIT 5.1

Student howlers

1. In a boom some businesses will lose out, if they produce inferior goods, where demand falls as people become better off, or if there are other firms in the same market who take more advantage of the opportunities available. **2.** It would help a firm that sells abroad, but firms that import find their costs rising. **3.** Acting ethically may increase costs, but will often lead to increased demand and ultimately more profit.

Test yourself

1. Figure 5.1A illustrates a typical business cycle. **2.** If a pound can now buy more euros, goods in the Euro zone priced in euros will take fewer pounds to buy. UK firms will be able to afford to bring in more, or better quality, goods. **3.** As unemployment rises, firms will face a falling demand. In an effort to maintain sales, firms are unlikely to increase their prices. However, if unemployment is falling, more people in jobs will lead to an increase in demand, so there is greater scope for prices to rise. **4.** Rising interest rates would make it harder for buyers to afford mortgage repayments, leading to a fall in demand for houses. This, in turn, would push house prices down. So the builder's revenues would be hit twice over – falling volume and falling price. In addition the rising interest rates would increase the overhead cost of borrowed money. The builder would struggle with revenue down and costs up. **5.** This refers to the idea of fairness. In competition law, for example, the law attempts to make sure that no one firm has an unfair advantage

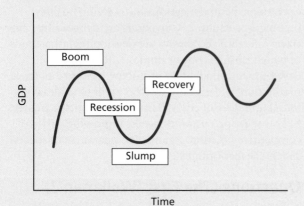

Fig. 5.1A: Example of a typical business cycle

over its competitors. **6.** Managers, employees, shareholders. **7.** Customers, suppliers, local community. **8.** The moral principles that may underpin business decisions. **9.** Improved production processes, new product development. **10.** Employee resistance.

UNIT 5.2

Student howlers

1. Not *all* firms will suffer – many firms prosper when an economy is in a recession. **2.** A firm may be following a perfectly good strategy already, and who is to say when a recession will start or its effects be felt?

Test yourself

1. Recession, slump, recovery, boom. **2.** Its market position, the income elasticity of its product or service, the severity of the recession. **3.** How much demand changes as a response to a change in income. **4.** It may already have a strategy it feels can survive a recession, or it may not believe the forecast. **5.** A small firm is more likely because it cannot benefit from economies of scale and is less likely to trade abroad in more buoyant markets. But this does not mean that this will always be the case. **6.** If some products suffer, others may hold their own or even prosper, especially if the products are spread across different markets. **7.** For market development to be effective, the current market usually needs to be expanding to allow the firm to pick up new customers. A recovery is likely to be the most appropriate time. **8.** More. New products will usually benefit a firm, whether this is in a recovery or a recession. Since it is a long-term investment, it ought to be an ongoing commitment for most firms in most industries.

UNIT 5.3

Student howlers

1. It may do, but the firm may still think the investment is worthwhile and will continue its investment. **2.** If an investment has been made it will be very difficult, if not impossible, for a firm to change its plans. **3.** There will be no direct effect. If anything, the increase in interest rates will cause a firm to cut back on its investment and so eventually reduce the level of gearing.

Test yourself

1. Payback, average rate of return, net present value. **2.** A monthly meeting of the Bank of England's Monetary Policy Committee looks at the available economic data and decides how it can best meet its targets for the level of inflation and growth. **3.** Future – the firm will want to know what the costs of the investment will be over its whole life, rather than what the current cost may be. **4.** Directly through costs and indirectly through consumer demand. **5.** Competitive position, objectives. **6.** Most consumers will have a lower level of disposable income, and so in general spend less. 7. They may help provide a feel-good factor in what could be hard economic times. 8. In the short term, little or no effect. In the long term, as long as interest rates continue rising, firms may borrow less and so reduce their gearing ratio.

UNIT 5.4

Student howlers

1. It may be, but this doesn't take into account the location of the unemployed and whether or not they have the right skills for one particular firm. 2. This may help to increase demand, but while some firms prosper others will be losing their competitive advantage and losing out to better quality products. 3. Apart from being impractical, the aim should be to anticipate changes and select appropriate strategies. The time lag also gives firms more scope for a considered response.

Test yourself

1. Decrease in demand, increase in costs. 2. Decrease in demand, increase in available labour. 3. Rising, but at a lower rate. The second figure says that prices are going up by 2.0%, although this is a lower rate than last year when prices went up by 2.5%. 4. Unemployment is likely to be falling, since inflation and unemployment normally have an inverse correlation but this effect may not be immediate. 5. Rising – more unemployment means fewer people have jobs so there will be less disposable income, so less demand. 6. Rising – as more is demanded, businesses will be less able to match demand so will effectively ration output by increasing their prices. 7. Both will be affected, but in different ways. The local firm could be hit hard if the changes damage the local economic situation, while the multinational will suffer if the trading conditions between the UK and other countries decline.

UNIT 5.5

Student howlers

1. There are some benefits for some firms, but an increase would also give firms problems. 2. It may be possible to take a successful product abroad, but there is not likely to be any immediate certainty of success.

Test yourself

1. The ability of a firm to establish itself in more than one market place. 2. The price of UK goods abroad will fall in terms of another currency, so there may be an increase in demand for the goods abroad. 3. A rise in the value of the pound would mean that producing abroad becomes relatively cheaper and products from the UK become more expensive to sell abroad. It would benefit them to move production abroad. 4. Quality, image, USP, after-sales service. 5. They will benefit as all countries become more accepting of foreign

products, but the power of these global brands may make it more difficult for other products to become established. 6. Selling its products in a foreign market, not buying raw materials or components from abroad.

UNIT 5.6

Student howlers

1. All companies are affected because the government affects the economic environment in which they operate. 2. The government still controls many aspects of economic policy, and sets targets for the Bank of England to achieve.

Test yourself

1. The way an economy is controlled through the manipulation of the governments spending and revenue. 2. The way an economy is controlled through the manipulation of interest rates. 3. Nationalisation is the process of the government taking control of an industry through direct management; privatisation is the return of such industries to private ownership. 4. Too much demand and economic activity, which may lead to inflation rising. 5. Low levels of demand and economic activity, which may lead to unemployment rising. 6. An increase in costs, perhaps affecting profit margins or a decrease in the firm's ability to compete. 7. A fall in interest rate will cause a general increase in the level of demand. A large income elasticity of demand suggests that this firm will be proportionately better off.

UNIT 5.7

Student howler

1. UK firms can deal with European firms freely under the rules of the single market (but they do need to convert their currency).

Test yourself

1. A market where there are no barriers to prevent trade and business between member states. 2. Free movement of capital, free movement of people, limited barriers to trade, common technical standards, harmonisation of taxes. 3. Trade may be easier and cheaper, financial forecasting may be more accurate. 4. More potential customers, the opportunity to produce in a lower cost area. 5. A business strategy that treats all of Europe as a single, homogeneous market. 6. Differentiate between different market segments or engage in some form of joint venture with foreign firms. 7. It is likely to provide a more even playing field, but may benefit countries whose laws are already similar, since they will have to undergo fewer changes.

UNIT 5.8

Student howlers

1. If this is the only reason for taking a decision, it can't be considered ethical. 2. This may well be one

reason for accepting social responsibilities, but it is not the only reason – some firms will be genuinely concerned with doing the right thing.

Test yourself

1. Social responsibilities are a firm's duties to its employees, customers, society and the environment. **2.** Ethics refers to the degree to which a firm considers 'right' and 'wrong' in its decisions. **3.** To see how well a firm is fulfilling its social responsibilities, and to lay the foundation for improvements in this area. **4.** The need for defence, the potential jobs lost, the potential loss of investment. **5.** More external pressures, greater competition. **6.** A firm may lose immediate profits by looking after social issues, but may gain from its standing in the community and its reputation, giving it a long-term benefit. **7.** Its objectives, personalities and market position.

UNIT 5.9

Student howlers

1. Even large firms can be affected by pressure groups – it is the power of the pressure group that is important. **2.** Firms can reduce waste by using techniques such as TQM.

Test yourself

1. A group that attempts to change decision makers' opinions. **2.** To influence decisions in their favour. **3.** Their resources, access to the media, degree of public sympathy. **4.** Waste and waste disposal, recycling, the use and source of energy, emissions into the atmosphere. **5.** Long-term cost reductions, better public image, attracting investors. **6.** The cost of new machinery/processes/training. **7.** Not all will benefit. The opportunities exist, but not all firms will necessarily benefit from these opportunities. Like all industries different firms have different competitive abilities. **8.** To provide an independent view of how a business affects the environment.

UNIT 5.10

Test yourself

1. A regular cycle of peaks and troughs in the level of economic activity. **2.** Recession, slump, recovery, boom. **3.** Percentage change in quantity demanded/percentage change in income × 100. **4.** Its market position, how reliant it is on the home market, the level of differentiation, the type of product. **5.** Market development, product development, market penetration, differentiation. **6.** The cost of borrowing money. **7.** The Bank of England's Monetary Policy Committee. **8.** Need, gearing, investment appraisal, future expectations. **9.** As one increases, the other will usually decrease. **10.** Product quality, product image, USP, price. **11.** The way a government changes its tax and spending plans to manipulate the economy. **12.** Cheaper and easier to trade, financial forecasting

easier. **13.** Social responsibilities are a firm's duties to its employees, customers, society and the environment. **14.** Waste and waste disposal, recycling, the use and source of energy, emissions into the atmosphere. **15.** A group that attempts to change decision makers' opinions. **16.** Competitors, legislation, pressure groups, technological change.

Questions (An ethical dilemma)

1. i) Doing what's right; **ii)** the world-wide link of computers. **2.** It was attempting to change decisions to suit its view. **3.** Newspaper – protecting the vulnerable in society; Amazon – protecting the right to free speech. **4.** For: to reflect current standards in society. Against: to do what it believes is right. **5.** Agree: long-term benefits, better standards. Against: initial costs, not the role of a business to regulate society.

Questions (EasyJet profits rocket)

1. i) The costs of running a business; ii) the competitive situation in which the business finds itself. **2.** Quality, convenience, ease. **3.** Shortages, political pressure from producing states. **4.** Matches – cutting costs to reduce impact of increased fuel prices. Doesn't match – dropping destinations in a growing market. **5.** For: unless they happen to match, the firm needs to decide how far to change its aims to match market conditions. Against: for a firm to be successful the two need to match.

Section 6: Objectives and strategy

UNIT 6.1

Student howlers

1. At best, a SWOT analysis makes it more likely that a firm will be successful, but it does not guarantee success. **2.** Although many do, others will start life as one of the other forms of business such as partnerships and limited companies.

Test yourself

1. Plans for the marketing, personnel, operations and financial functions of the business, as well as an assessment of the marketplace. **2.** The owners of the business are only liable for the amount they have invested in the business and cannot be required to pay more. **3.** The shares in a public limited company can be sold on the open market, while private limited company's shares can't. Public companies are usually larger. **4.** The ability of a firm to meet its short-term debts. **5.** Shareholders, staff, customers, suppliers, residents, the state. **6.** Research into the strengths, weaknesses, opportunities and threats facing a firm, leading to a plan or strategy to improve the position of the firm. **7.** The right to be the sole user of a new invention.

UNIT 6.2

Student howlers

1. Although expensive, it is more important that a balance be struck between sources of finances, rather than ruling one out completely. 2. They may be, but they could equally suffer from diseconomies of scale and become less efficient.

Test yourself

1. Financing growth, reorganising management, the speed of growth, the changing nature of the business. 2. Sale of assets, cash flow management, retained profit. 3. Trade credit, bank overdraft, leasing, factoring, loans, shares, debentures, venture capital. 4. Sale of assets, cash flow management, trade credit, bank overdraft, leasing, factoring. 5. Retained profit, loans, shares. 6. This is when a firm expands without the long-term finance it needs. 7. The factors that cause the cost per unit of the firm to rise as the firm grows. 8. Communication, control, coordination.

UNIT 6.3

Student howlers

1. They may benefit from economies of scale, but may also suffer from diseconomies. 2. Although risks may be spread, there can be additional risks from this form as well.

Test yourself

1. Mergers are generally voluntary, takeovers usually forced. 2. Horizontal, forward vertical, backward vertical, conglomerate. 3. i) backward vertical; ii) forward vertical; iii) conglomerate; iv) horizontal. 4. Control a majority of shares. 5. The availability of capital and the ability to correct the mistakes that may have caused the business to be sold off.

UNIT 6.4

Student howlers

1. Although there should be some consistency, firms operate in a dynamic market and should be prepared to change direction when necessary. 2. Although difficult to do, it is possible to manage the change of a corporate culture

Test yourself

1. A qualitative statement of the firm's aim. 2. No, it is a general statement of intent rather than a specified set of targets. 3. Corporate aims ought to give a clear direction to a business in the long term. 4. It may build team spirit, and encourage commitment to the organisation and cooperation within it. 5. A culture is the often implied norms of behaviour that affect the way things are done in a business. 6. Attitude to risk and blame, resistance to change, willingness to accept the needs of stakeholders. 7. The organisational structure and the power structure, the formal rules laid down by the firm, the way everyday decisions and tasks are carried out, communication within the firm. 8. Culture, since this shows how people actually behave in a firm.

UNIT 6.5

Student howlers

1. It gives general guidance and direction, but doesn't dictate all actions. 2. All business involves risk, but market penetration may be a lower risk strategy.

Test yourself

1. An objective is what the firm wants to achieve – the strategy is the way it can be achieved. 2. Maximising profit, maximising shareholder wealth, growth in the size of the firm, diversification, improving the market position. 3. The objectives, the resources available to the firm, the results of an analysis of their market. 4. The threat of new competitors entering the market, the level of rivalry between established companies, the power of the purchaser, the power of the supplier, the threat from substitute products. 5. The degree to which the firm is staying in its existing market or entering a new market, and the degree to which it is using a new product or staying with its existing one. 6. Market penetration, market development, product development, diversification. 7. It involves a firm in areas of which it has no firsthand knowledge. 8. As a firm operates in a changing market, it needs to be prepared to change as well.

UNIT 6.6

Test yourself

1. An ad hoc decision is one made without reference to plans or research data. 2. On the basis of routine and experience. 3. May be biased, the decision may not be appropriate to changing circumstances. 4. Scientific decision making is the use of a formal, set process to make sure that decisions are arrived at in an objective manner. 5. Set objectives, gather data, make decision, implement decision, review decision. 6. A decision tree is a diagram that sets out the options available to a firm together with the possible outcomes and the likelihood of them occurring. 7. The problem is clearly set out, managers can use the tree as a starting point, probabilities may make the data more realistic. 8. Bias, data may not be accurate.

UNIT 6.7

Student howlers

1. Since a strategy is based in part on the external environment, which will change, the firm needs to be adaptable to change it. 2. It gives a framework for assessing options, it doesn't tell them what they should do.

Test yourself

1. Political, economic, social and technological factors.
2. Market size, market growth, market trends and market share. 3. A benchmark is a measure based on the standards of the most efficient businesses in a firm's market. 4. Benchmarks are used to set targets to allow a firm to undertake continual improvement.
5. Strengths, weaknesses, opportunities and threats.
6. To become the lowest cost supplier within a mass market, to have highly differentiated products within a mass market, to become the lowest cost supplier within a focused market segment, to have highly differentiated products within a market segment.

UNIT 6.8

Student howlers

1. Even though the precise time or nature of a crisis is unpredictable, general precautions can be taken.
2. The crisis could still happen, but the contingency plan means the response to it should be better.

Test yourself

1. A crisis can be any event that threatens to damage a firm, either directly or through one of its brands.
2. Physical damage, environmental disasters, faulty or dangerous products, hostile takeover bids, major customers withdrawing their order, prolonged strikes by the workforce. 3. Preparing for a potential crisis.
4. Public relations. 5. Cash flow management.
6. Change the style of management used. 7. Avoid over-committing to plans such as just in time. 8. To stop rumours and to keep the firm coordinated.

UNIT 6.9

Test yourself

1. Financing growth, reorganising management, the speed of growth, the changing nature of the business.
2. Sale of assets, cash flow management, retained profit, trade credit, bank overdraft, leasing, factoring, loans, shares, debentures, venture capital. 3. This is when a firm expands without the long-term finance it needs. 4. The factors that cause the cost per unit of the firm to rise as the firm grows. 5. Mergers are generally voluntary, take-overs usually forced. 6. Horizontal, forward vertical, backward vertical, conglomerate.
7. A culture is the often implied norms of behaviour

that affect the way things are done in a business.
8. Attitude to risk and blame, resistance to change, willingness to accept the needs of stakeholders. 9. An objective is what the firm wants to achieve – the strategy is the way it can be achieved. 10. Maximising profit, maximising shareholder wealth, growth in the size of the firm, diversification, improving the market position. 11. The objectives, the resources available to the firm, the results of an analysis of their market.
12. The threat of new competitors entering the market, the level of rivalry between established companies, the power of the purchaser, the power of the supplier, the threat from substitute products.
13. The degree to which the firm is staying in its existing market or entering a new market, and the degree to which it is using a new product or staying with its existing one. 14. Scientific decision making is the use of a formal, set process to make sure that decisions are arrived at in an objective manner. 15. A benchmark is a measure based on the standards of the most efficient businesses in a firm's market.

Questions (Where good food costs less)

1. i) The firm with the largest proportion of sales; ii) a medium- to long-term plan for achieving objectives.
2. Competitors, economic environment, location.
3. Porter would suggest that the statement was contradictory, and should either go for differentiation (good food) or price (costs less), not both.
4. Important as it is a direct means of communication with the consumer, and because it is the focal point of the strategy, it should also determine the day-to-day decisions of the firm.

Questions (A tale of two strategies)

1. i) When two firms set up a business division that will be operated jointly; ii) the accepted behaviour and attitudes within a business. 2. They need a large financial base to continue a strategy of acquisition; they may find the growing business suffers from diseconomies of scale. 3. Pros: cheaper, doesn't extend the business too far. Cons: dilutes the firm's control of the business, may lock the firm into agreements it later can't get out of. 4. It does because different strategies clearly work in a single market – however, both strategies only work because they are appropriate for each individual firm.

INDEX